The West Georgia Mills and Their People

The Williams Sisters, Pauline and Oree

Photo courtesy of Charles and Ann Broom

The West Georgia Mills and Their People
The Sons and Daughters of Fullerville and Villa Rica

By Perry "Bill" Bailey

Also by Perry Bill Bailey

West Georgia Cooking

Copyright 2010

ISBN 1452829519

EAN-13 9781452829517

LCCN 2010905909

createspace

To the working class people of West Georgia
and to those in danger of losing hope.

"Never give up on yourself in spite of the disregard of others.
You are a child of God and are worthy in his eyes."
Author unknown

In memory of:

My dad: James Olin Bailey Sr.

My mother: Ruth M. Bailey

My oldest brother: James Olin Bailey Jr. (Jimmy)

My younger brother: George Douglas Bailey (Douglas)

My friend: Mrs. Charles Williams

My friend: Dick "Bruiser" Barber

My friend: Larry Butler

My friend: Olin Ivy

Cheyenne Sauls, granddaughter of John Wayne and Elaine Sauls

The music lives on. It will never die.

I came to life as all have done who be,

Alone and small and made in God's own image.

Placed in the keeping of those who made me

And laid in village arms for pilgrimage.

The path was steep; the way not clearly shown.

Life's hurts and struggles barred my way above.

The pain most dreadful, to be daily known,

Was that of a young child who longed for love.

But life will stir then leap as pure as flame.

The goals of dreams long sought refine to plan

And proclaim with thanks God's love and holy name

For the gift of the soul He gave to man.

    Time of pain will come. I do not fear it,

    For it has forged my soul and fired my spirit.

Dedicated to Perry "Bill" Bailey on the authorship of this book.

-Catherine Burns

Table of Contents

The West Georgia Mills and Their People by Perry "Bill" Bailey

About the Author

My Husband by Rhonda Hovater Bailey

Rhonda and Bill   Photo courtesy of Ann Broom

I met my husband, Bill Bailey, in April of 1981. I was listening to the radio on that Saturday night, hoping to hear a hot new song that was just hitting the air waves. Bill Bailey was on the air and announced that he had an LP to give away to the fourth caller. Now, I was never one to try to win radio contests, but something compelled me to pick up that phone and dial the station's number. As fate would have it, I was the fourth caller. As I gave the necessary winner's information such as my name, address, phone number, etc., we became involved in a conversation.

I felt an attraction to this powerful voice on the airwaves, along with the sarcastic humor that went along with it. He asked if I would meet him the next day. Bill said that since we didn't know each other, we should meet in a public place. This took me by surprise since I was the one always worrying about being safe. But this was Bill's typical humor. I never knew what he would say next. But it got my attention, and he kept me laughing the whole time we were on the phone.

We did meet that Sunday afternoon at a local mall. We walked around for a while, laughing and talking. I knew I couldn't stay too long because of church that night. Then he blew my mind by asking if he could go to church with me. He followed me home, met my parents, and we all attended church that Sunday evening. Afterwards, he came back to my house and ate supper; leftovers from a good home cooked Sunday dinner. That's when he fell in love with my mom's squash casserole. He ate like I've never seen anyone eat before. He looked rather undernourished so I thought he must be starving. But as he quickly pointed out, living on his own, he hadn't had a good home cooked meal for a long time; and the food was just delicious.

I could write a book on my husband but not now; maybe one day I will. I must say that Bill has overcome many challenges since we met. He's a man with a lot of confidence in himself. Perry was overwhelmed in his childhood days that were filled with so many negatives. I can say that Bill definitely searches for positives to battle the obstacles that stand in his way.

After dating for a while, I tried to get Bill to talk about his past; and I even asked to meet his parents. He would always tell me "one day" and change the subject. There were no pictures in his apartment of his family. All that was on display were various certificates and awards from the radio stations where he had worked over his years in broadcasting. He had pictures of himself at press conferences or interviews with such celebrities as the Osmond Brothers, Boyce and Hart, and other media notables. When he first showed me this wall of pictures and awards, he said, "Rhonda, let me introduce you to my ego wall." But deep down, I could tell Bill was proud of his accomplishments even though he would laugh it off as his ego wall. I knew right then that if I married this man that my husband's career would be in broadcasting. I wasn't so sure at the time if I liked that idea because I knew it would mean traveling a lot, and I had already learned that you had to keep your rating up to keep your job. I felt a little insecure about that situation.

We married in December of 1981, and I can truthfully say I have no regrets. As I stated earlier, Bill's powerful voice was an attraction, but as I got to know him, there were many more important attractions to follow. I realized quickly that Bill was a very good person, a God fearing man, and a hard worker dedicated to his profession. He always tried to help someone in need and was willing to put others first. He always gave a listening ear to anyone's troubles and was willing to offer advice and encouragement to them. Rather than being selfish, Bill was always proud to see others accomplish things, especially those who were less fortunate. He's never been one to drink or use drugs. He believes in meeting obligations before indulging in pleasures, an example that he instilled into our daughter at a young age. A firm believer in education, he encouraged me to finish my RN degree and has given constant encouragement to our daughter throughout her schooling. He believes that if you want something badly enough, you can find a way to reach your dream. When I have viewed something as impossible, I have seen him go beyond the boundaries and achieve his dream many times. The simple things in life make him the happiest, such as talking to a good friend, working in the yard, watching a good clean movie, or simply spending time with family.

Bill stepped out of the Perry Bailey shell and claimed his life. I've heard him say many times that the people in Villa Rica never knew him, not even his family. I can say that is so, and it is their loss. Perhaps the reason they didn't take time to know him was because all he had to offer was Perry. He has burned some bridges in his lifetime because he tells people what he truly thinks. If you don't want to know the truth, then don't ask Bill. I don't know of too many people who haven't burned a bridge or two as well. He's constantly working on new bridges and ironically one of his favorite gospel hymns is "I'm Building a Bridge".

My Dad by Kassey Bailey Green

Kassey and Perry "Bill" Bailey"
Photo courtesy of Rhonda Bailey

My dad is a good, hard working man who continues to live the American dream. He has always been a great inspiration to me and has shown me that anything is possible when I set my heart and mind to it. Without him, I would have settled for less in life.

When I was in preschool, he taught me how to spell hard words, do the multiplication tables, and even read higher level books. He would quiz me on some of the things I had learned on a chalk board I had gotten for Christmas one year. My teachers bragged to my parents about my good grades. Some even said I could've gone on to the next grade.

He wanted me to be the best I could in school. I tried my hardest, and finally I was able to return the favor. I graduated from high school with an Advanced Diploma. Now I'm currently in college working on my Associate's in Graphic Design, and I retain an A average.

I can also say he's helped make me into the responsible person I am today. He taught me about limits and restrictions from the time I was a child. I knew that I couldn't always have want I wanted.

He taught me to drive. When I was older and had a job, he gave me the responsibility of making my own car payments. At the time, I didn't understand why I had to pay for my own car when other kids at my school were bragging about their parents giving them BMW's with no strings attached. It was only after a few of them wrecked their expensive cars that I realized why my dad had wanted me to pay for my own car. If you buy something yourself, you are more likely to take great care of it.

I share a lot of common interests with my dad as well as a few traits. Number one is the love of music. Dad has a history in radio as a broadcaster. He's worked at several number one radio stations in his life time. He has met with well-known music artists. I guess that's where my artistic abilities come from. We both enjoy music, movies, books, and anything else in the art and entertainment business.

We both love history, and we love to watch historical movies and documentaries. We also enjoy photographing historic landmarks.

We both share in having motivation and determination. If we have a great idea and are told that it'll never work, we become determined to prove this wrong. When my dad was little, he told friends and family that he wanted to be a radio announcer. They told him to quit dreaming because it would never happen, but he fulfilled his dream. He has even had people tell him that he would never write this book; and the fact that I am writing now is proof he has made this dream come true as well.

My dad means so much to me, and he has helped make me the person I am today. I consider myself lucky and blessed that I still have my dad and that he is so great. He has always been there for me. So many others are denied this. I just want to thank my dad for showing me dreams do come true. I love you dad! Kassey.

The Challenges and the Events
By Perry "Bill" Bailey

I never thought that I would actually see my dreams come true before my very eyes. I had dreams for many years before announcing the book to the Villa Rican newspaper. I remember the nervous energy that I felt as Spencer Crawford, editor of the Villa Rican newspaper, interviewed me about the book I was writing. I knew I had to come through and produce a book. After reading the book announcements in both the Villa Rican and the Times Georgian newspapers, reality kicked in; and I thought to myself, "Oh my, what have I done?" Actually, I had been avoiding the idea of this book for many years, and I had tried to run from it. The reason I ran from the idea was because I felt that I was no one special. I had always been told that I "couldn't do nothing." My family didn't believe in me nor did my friends and classmates. Their doubts made me have self doubts. I knew I had the tools, the knowledge, and the ability; but I also knew that I was going to need support from contributors to make this book possible.

Weeks passed by after the book announcement, and I had not received one e-mail or phone call from anyone interested in contributing. When I finally did start receiving e-mails, they were very negative, not positive. I even got a few dirty e-mails. One person even went so far as to post stuff on a Villa Rica forum changing his name and pretending to be me. This person posted sarcastic remarks to discredit me and stir up trouble on the forum. He then changed his name and replied to his own phony posting. It was said that I would only sell five books, and that those would be sold to my family. I got phone calls from unknown numbers threatening me not to write anything negative. This was very discouraging. It doesn't really matter who these people are. It's just that it was hard to believe that people would go to this extent to try to hurt or discredit someone.

I have always been a thinker and a doer, and I knew that I had to go through with this book. There was no turning back. I was going to have to win the confidence of my contributors, and I knew it was going to be hard because they had not seen or heard from me in a long time. What I had going for me was the support of my family, Rhonda, Kassey, and my son-in-law Steve. I also had support from one very good friend, Cathy Burns. I had no idea that she would become the editor of my book. Cathy and I talked about my dreams; my book; the challenges; and the obstacles that I faced. She had many suggestions to offer, and I knew that I needed an editor unacquainted with the area. I asked her to be the editor of my book, and she has encouraged and motivated me throughout my writing process. I have been blessed to have her.

Not yet receiving any correspondence of interest for my book, I decided to sit down at the computer and write about the events that I had recorded in my journal—a record which I had kept from childhood on. I knew that this book had to be written with or without contributors, and I began to search for as much information as possible. My wish has been to produce a fine, responsible book that honors the people of Fullerville.

When I first started this book, I had no idea that I would form a fund-raising committee in an effort to save the historical jail that still stands in Fullerville just begging for attention to be saved along with its history. When my friend Jimmy Causey and I were just kids in Fullerville, we would often ask each other why the city did not take an interest in saving the old jail. I wrote letters for years to the mayor and city council asking them to consider preserving the old Fullerville jail, but I never received any response. Shortly after I announced my book, I formed a volunteer committee of five people to help raise money to save the historical jail. I started making frequent trips to Villa Rica to help and to work with the volunteers for the jail preservation. That's when I noticed contributors for my book began to surface. It dawned on me that the attention created by the effort to preserve the jail was bringing me into contact with people who wished to contribute their stories to my book. After a rather bumpy start, I met an old friend, Joyce Massey Fain, whom I had not seen in forty years. She became the Director and Vice President of the organization to restore the old Fullerville jail. This all came about at the May 2010 First Fullerville Reunion that I had organized. There I met Joyce Massey Fain and her husband Mel. We talked for several weeks about my book and the old jail as our old friendship was rekindled. Not only was Joyce made Director and Vice President of what is now called the Fullerville/Villa Rica Preservation Committee, she has also served as a personal assistant of mine for the Villa Rica area, handling appointments for interviews and information for the book. Her husband Mel, also serves on the preservation committee and has been most helpful and supportive He has done some beautiful photography for both books. These two people have been a blessing to me.

As far back as the early eighties, I would travel to Villa Rica and walk in the old Fullerville ball park reminiscing about the old days. I visualized the ballpark with the lights on, the ball players on the field, and the grand stands filled with people. It brought back memories of the now older Fullervillians, like Cecil Sauls, John Wayne Sauls, Footsie Blair, Sarah Sauls, and Paul Free. I thought then that this ball park should be called Sarah Sauls Field or at least have some type of street sign honoring her for her contributions to little league baseball.

Every time I visited Villa Rica, seeking information for the book, my thoughts would come back to me that I needed to get Sarah Sauls name connected to the ball field. When I mentioned it, I was faced with negative remarks saying that such would never happen. I did receive the support from some, but no one wanted to be the one to present it. So I had an idea while organizing the May 2010 First Fullerville Reunion. I purchased two plaques honoring Mrs. Sarah Sauls. I invited the mayor and two city councilmen, Rusty Dean and Woody Holland, to the reunion. Word had already gotten out that I was going to honor Sarah at the reunion but no one had any idea of the surprise announcement that I was going to make. After honoring Sarah Sauls with the two plaques and thanking her for all her contributions to the ball park, I made a motion in front of a standing room only crowd that the ball park road sign that leads into what now is the soccer field in Fullerville be changed to Sarah Sauls Drive. I wasn't prepared for the reaction, but people immediately began clapping their hands and shouting, "Go Sarah". I knew right then that we would get our sign. Rusty Dean and Woody Holland saw the reaction from the people supporting the Sarah Sauls Drive sign. At the next city council meeting, Rusty Dean introduced the suggestion, and the mayor gave his approval. I knew then that this mayor and city council would be a positive for Villa Rica and for Fullerville.

I have also awarded a plaque to Mr. Wayne Shelton of the Fullerville Mission honoring him for his outstanding service to the community. I felt that it was only right to focus attention on two individuals who richly deserved recognition. It was my way of saying, "Thank you." Mayor Collins followed up by presenting each with a key to the city. He was the first mayor in Villa Rica history to issue keys to members of the Fullerville community. Certainly his actions are to be greatly appreciated.

I made a video over a year ago, and for several months it circulated on YouTube. The video gave a tour of Villa Rica and the Fullerville community, in which I mentioned in the video that Fullerville had no sidewalks. I wrote letters to the editor of the Villa Rican regarding sidewalks. Wayne Shelton of the Mission went to a city council meeting and, as far as I know, he was the only one from Fullerville to attend and make his voice heard regarding sidewalks. Evidently, the mayor and the city council heard Wayne's voice. The mayor and city council have seen that beautiful sidewalks have been put into Fullerville.

The negative comments I had received about the current mayor and city council have been erased from my mind. These are hard working men who have listened to the people of Villa Rica and to the Fullerville community. Credit must be given to Mayor J. Collins, the city councilmen who back him, and his city managers, Larry Wood and Jeff Reese, who got the work done. They should all be honored because it can truthfully be said that they are the first ever to give the recognition and improvements to a community that was so ignored in the past. I know deep in my heart that if we had had Mayor J. Collins, Larry Wood, Jeff Reese, Rusty Dean, and the other city councilmen who helped bring these projects into being for Fullerville back when I was young, it wouldn't have taken a news story to get sewage in Fullerville. Many older people may now enjoy walking on the sidewalks in Fullerville, and the children may play safely away from the street. This is why I have documented this in my book--so that it will never be forgotten. I praise these fine men who are looking after their citizens in Villa Rica.

It took the combination of supportive people and the volunteers who have helped with the jail and book projects to make things happen. Power of the people does exist if you allow it. There comes a time when we should turn off our TVs, radios, and computers, and pay attention to our community. We must first do our part as citizens and express our needs. When one voice speaks and gets attention, imagine what a chorus of voices can do.

Acknowledgements

My deepest appreciation goes out to all the wonderful people who contributed their encouragement, their stories, photographs, and time to the making of The *West Georgia Mills and Their People*. You will meet them all in this book.

I also thank my editor who designed the book cover and worked so hard to bring this book to publication. Her rather unique sense of humor made the task an enjoyable one—most of the time.

My Special Thanks To:

Rhonda Hovater Bailey
Ann Broom
Bob Broom
Charles Broom
Catherine Bryan
Susan Burns
Jimmy Causey
Mayor Jay Collins
Spenser Crawford
Joyce Massey Fain
Gerald Fields
Kenneth Fields
Kassey Nicole Bailey Green
Kenneth Lemons
Doug Mabry
Daniel Phagan
Jeff Reese
Elaine Sauls
Sarah Sauls
Wayne Shelton
Danny Skinner
The Villa Rica Police Department
The Washington sisters
The Reverend Charles Williams
Vicki Mattox Williams

The past should never be forgotten.

Introduction

The Legacy of the Mill Workers

Shamefully unrecognized for the most part, those who labored in the mills of America left behind a special cultural heritage. Fortunately today, this legacy is being preserved in the drama, music, poetry, and prose of America.

The Drama

"All the world's a stage, and all the men and women merely players." -William Shakespeare

Mill Stories, by playwright Robert Riddle Baker, is set in the 1930s. It portrays the lives of the Lincoln Mill workers of Huntsville, Alabama. Repeat performances are given, because of popular demand, by Renaissance Theatre in Huntsville, Alabama.

The poems of *Piece Work*, a book by Barbara Presnell of Asheboro, North Carolina, have now become a play by the same title. It is part of the repertoire of the Touring Theatre Ensemble of North Carolina.

The Music

From past to present, laborers have lifted their voices in song. A wealth of music exists, done both by and about these people, recounting their tribulations.

Robert Burke Warren, a music historian and contributor to FIQL, has compiled the Playlist, *Textile Mill Songs*, with comments. (Partial list; reprinted by permission of Mike Wu, FIQL.com 03/03/10) (For the complete list. See Appendix A Textile Mill Songs.)

Textile Mills have a long and varied history in America. Some of that history is not pleasant....

1. Si Kahn– "The Aragon Mill" from the album *New Wood*

"The Aragon Mill" was written by Si Kahn in 1979 and refers to the closing one of the main employers in Aragon, Georgia; The Aragon Textile Mill.

2. Pete Seeger– "Winnsboro Cotton Mill Blues" from the *Smithsonian Folkways* compilation *American Industrial Ballads*

 Winnsboro, SC is about 75 miles south of Gastonia, NC. This track comes from the *Smithsonian Folkways* compilation *American Industrial Ballads*, which documents the unprecedented industrialization of the 19th century. The album contains songs of struggle, which emerged from the coalmines, textile mills and farmlands of America.

The Poetry

"For what, we ask, is life without a touch of Poetry in it?" - Sir W. S. **Gilbert**

Ron Rash writes in both poetic and prose formats. In 1998, he published *Eureka Mill*, a poetry collection. The title is taken from the name of the South Carolina textile mill where both his parents worked. Rash deals with the hard labor, the physical hazards, and the loss of personal and family connections due to relocation.

Barbara Presnell (see above)

Linda Ferguson's *Bird Missing from One Shoulder* is about her parents, who were textile mill workers. People came to the small mill towns where they began families and worked loyally until the jobs were no more.

Michael Chitwood writes in, *The Weave Room,* about the textile region of his home area, Southern Appalachia. Many poets explore spoken language, love, and family in their poems; but Chitwood's poetry is also about work.

The Prose

Today the abundant writings of authors, inspired by the stories of the mill workers of the eastern United States, are being appreciated. Many communities, from North to South across the East, now have their own special literature. These writings relate the events of the bygone days in the mill villages to the overall history of an era. The West Georgia area is especially fortunate because those with the interests and talents are succeeding in preserving the memories of former times.

Mary Talley Anderson: *The History of Villa Rica (The City of Gold)* is the initial work on Villa Rica history. 1976

Burell W. Holder: The *History of Temple Georgia* covers the 1883 time period when Temple was chartered. VI, 1976; V2, 1982 via Ruth Holder

Elaine Bailey: *Explosion in Villa Rica* recounts the tragedy of a devastating mishap in the center of Villa Rica, Georgia. 2009

Edmond "Hoot" Sauls: *The Linthead* is an autobiography which tells about growing up in Fullerville, Georgia. 2010

Perry "Bill" Bailey: *The West Georgia Mills and Their People* describes the mill people, their lives, and their work. 2010

Perry "Bill" Bailey and Catherine Burns: *West Georgia Cooking is a collection of old family recipes. 2010*

-Catherine Burns, editor 2010

Part I

Fullerville, 1916 – 1956

The Children of Fullerville
Photo courtesy of Ann Broom

The Town

Judson Thomas Fuller

Photo courtesy Darlene Allenthrop

The mill village of Fullerville was incorporated in 1916 and constructed adjacent to the town of Villa Rica to house those who came to work in the mills.

The north Villa Rica district is also referred to as Hixtown, which was the original name of Villa Rica. However, this can cause confusion since this is not where Hixtown was originally located.

Hixtown was first settled about a mile and a half up Hwy 61 near where the Tanner Medical Center in Villa Rica currently sits.

When the railroad at last came through Villa Rica in 1892, it brought the potential for growth and development to the area. Many of the buildings from Hixtown were moved to what is now the North Villa Rica Commercial Historic District. Local lore states the last of these moved buildings was demolished for a parking lot in the 1990s beside the Lofts. (Ref. Wikipedia)

Fullerville Established

By Mrs. M. F. Word

This story was found in a book called Memoirs of Georgia

Before there was a Fullerville, GA, there were mills.

Judson Thomas Fuller, farmer, Villa Rica, Carroll Co., GA, son of Alfred and Amanda (Evans) Fuller, was born in Meriwether County, GA in 1851. His paternal grandparent, William Fuller, was a native of South Carolina, and came to Georgia in 1828 and settled in the woods in Meriwether County. He was one of the pioneers, started on labor and pluck, and became one of the county's leading and wealthy citizens. Mr. Fuller's father was born in South Carolina, came to Georgia with his father, and helped to clear and then work the farm. His maternal grandparents, Elijah and Mary (Reed) Evans, were also natives of South Carolina, who came to Georgia about the time Meriwether County was laid out, and were among the early settlers in its woods. He was a tanner by trade and became rich. Mr. Fuller was reared on the farm, and as he passed through youth during the war enjoyed quite limited educational advantages. In 1866 he came to Carroll County and began life by hiring out. By persistent, well-directed effort, economy and good management he has acquired a fine property - 1,400 acres of good land, including a large, well-improved farm within five miles of Villa Rica, and an elegant home in the little city, where he is living a contented life, happier than if he were a millionaire. Such men are the nations reliance in extreme emergencies. Mr. Fuller was married in 1872 to Miss Mary E. Johnston - born in Walton County, GA - daughter of William and Elizabeth (Malcom) Johnson. This marriage has been blessed with seven children, Beulah, Lela, Maggie, Hardy, Thomas, Maude and DeWitt. Mrs. Fuller is a consistent and devoted member of the Baptist church. It is almost needless to add that Mr. Fuller is one of the little city's most substantial and reliable citizens, and he and his interesting family rank with the best.

The Fullerville community has a proud and rich background made up of hard-working people who saw the mills as a step up from the sharecropping labor. Fullerville was granted a charter from the state of Georgia in 1916. Before Fullerville, Georgia was annexed into Villa Rica, Georgia in 1956, Fullerville existed as it's own town for 45 years with a bustling industry that included a cotton mill, a hosiery mill, a company store, local eateries, a lumber yard and a casket company. It could be argued that Fullerville had more industry than Villa Rica at the time. Fullerville had it's own city hall and a wooden jail, which later burned as a prisoner set fire to it as he tried to escape. A new jail was built of cement later which still stands today.

Speaking of the company store, from my interviews with various people who at one time lived and worked in Fullerville, there was no company store in Fullerville. That was not to say there wasn't a company store. The nearest thing to a company store was located in the town of Villa Rica. According to these folks I interviewed, they always recognized E.T. Doyal and Sons as the company store.

Most of the people of Fullerville who worked in the mills considered E.T. Doyal and Sons to be the company store because of E.T. Doyal and Sons influence with the Villa Rica Mills, being President, Chairman, and Board of Directors and owners who owned the majority of the mill village that they rented and sold houses out to the employees of the mills. If you read your history on the company store you would know E.T. Doyal and Sons was nowhere near the company store. E.T. Doyal and Sons were good to the people who worked for them.

I managed to run across a gentleman who was an employee of E.T. Doyal and Sons Store. Kenneth Ellers told me that he was age 15 or 16 when he went to work for E.T. Doyal and Sons as a delivery boy. According to Kenneth Ellers, Joe Doyal would go to the mills and take grocery orders. When Joe got back with the orders, Kenneth and another employee of E.T. Doyal, Raymond Yates, would pull the orders and put them in round bushel baskets. Kenneth said he did the delivering so he would load up the baskets on an old truck and deliver them to the houses. Back then, nobody locked their doors so Kenneth just sat the groceries on the kitchen table and whatever needed to go in the refrigerator, he would put in there for them. People got their groceries on credit. When the people got their paychecks from the mills, they would pay for what they had ordered.

Kenneth went on to say he never expected any tips and no tips were ever left out for the delivery boy because the mill workers just couldn't afford tips at that time. But they always let him know how much they appreciated him. Kenneth was paid $30.00 a week. After he graduated from high school, he continued to work for the Doyals another year before leaving.

Justin Fuller started out with the Villa Rica Cotton Mill and then later established the Villa Rica Hosiery Mills along with his sons Hardy, Tom, and Dewitt in 1911. Another idea that the Fullers thought of was keeping their employee's closer to work. So they came up with the idea to build eight homes for their employee's. Fullerville was now established. The mill village continued to grow as more houses were added by E.T. Doyal and Sons.

According to *The History of Villa Rica (City of Gold)* written by Mary Talley Anderson, Emmett T. Doyal was born in Paulding County, Georgia in 1899. He married Ida Beulah McBrayer of Paulding County, Georgia. Mr. Doyal was a bookkeeper, was in the mercantile business in 1924, served as Director of Villa Rica Mills, Inc., President and Chairman of the Board of Villa Rica Mills, served on the Board of Directors and was Vice President of the Bank of Villa Rica, owned real estate, was a delegate to the 1960 Republican Convention in

Chicago, served as a city councilman, a deacon of Villa Rica Baptist Church, and served as Chairman of the 1936 Building Committee, served on the Board of Education; and he was a member of the Villa Rica Masonic Lodge No. 72.

Fullerville Incorporated (Charter)

The Fullerville, GA Charter 1916   707

Fullerville Town Incorporated

An Act to incorporate the town of Fullerville, in the County of Carroll, and to provide for a mayor and council for said town, and confer certain powers and privileges upon the mayor and council thereof, and for other purposes.

Section 1. Be it enacted by the General Assembly of Georgia, and it is hereby enacted by the authority of the same, That the town of Fullerville, in the County of Carroll, be and the same is hereby incorporated as a town, under the name of the Town of Fullerville. The corporate powers of said town shall be vested in a mayor and five councilmen, by the name of the mayor and council of the town of Fullerville, they may sue and be sued, plead and be impleaded, and exercise all the corporate powers that may be necessary in performing their duties.

Sec. 2. Be it further enacted, That the corporate limits of said town shall extend one-fourth mile in all directions from J. H. Hogue's store in the Cement Block building, in said town of Fullerville.

Sec. 3. Be it further enacted, That J. H. Hogue be and he is hereby appointed mayor, and W. A. Ball, J. H. Kimbrel, W. F. Fuller, C. M. Floyd, and Henry Cole are hereby appointed councilmen of said town of Fullerville, and R. J. Voss is hereby appointed clerk of said town, to hold their offices until the first annual election, as hereinafter provided.

Sec. 4. Be it further enacted, That on the first Tuesday in January, 1917, and every year thereafter on the same day, an election shall be held in the council chamber in said town for a mayor, five councilmen and a clerk, who shall hold their offices for one year, and until their successors are elected and qualified; but no one shall vote or be eligible to the office of mayor, councilman or clerk of said town who does not reside within the corporate limits of said town, and who is not qualified to vote for members of the General Assembly of this State. Said election shall be held and conducted in the same manner as elections for county officers in this State; provided, that any two councilmen shall be competent and qualified to hold said election, and the certificate of the managers shall be sufficient authority to the persons elected to enter on the discharge of the duties of the office to which they have been elected., In the event that the office of mayor, any member of council or clerk shall become vacant by death, resignation or otherwise, said vacancy shall be filled by the mayor or mayor pro tem. And the council, from among the citizens of the town qualified to fill said offices.

Sec. 5. Be it further enacted, That before entering on the discharge of their duties, the mayor, councilmen or clerk, and all other officers, shall subscribe the following oath, which may be taken before any officer authorized by the laws of this State to administer oaths: I do solemnly swear that I will faithfully discharge all the duties devolving on me as mayor, councilman, clerk or other officer, as the case may be, of the town of Fullerville, Carroll County, according to the best of my ability and understanding, so help me, God.

Sec. 6. Be it further enacted, That said mayor and councilmen shall have power and authority to levy and collect a tax, not exceeding three-tenths of one per cent., upon all property, both real and personal, within the corporate limits of said town, and the same may be enforced by execution issued by the clerk in the name of the mayor, and levy and sale of property as in case of sales of property liable to State and county taxes. All levies of tax executions to be made by the marshal or deputy, and to be conducted as sales of the sheriffs in this State in cases of tax executions. They shall also have power to require all persons within said corporate limits, who are subject to road duty under the laws of this State, to work on the streets of said town, or they may prescribe a commutation tax, which may be paid in lieu of work on the streets.

Sec. 7. Be it further enacted, That said mayor and councilmen shall have power and authority to pass all laws and ordinances that they may deem necessary for the government of said town of Fullerville, or the protection of property from loss by fire or damage therein, provided they be not repugnant to the constitution and laws of this State, and the United States.

Sec. 8. Be it further enacted, That the mayor of said town, and in his absence the mayor pro tem., who shall be elected by the councilmen from their own number, shall be chide executive officer of said town. He shall see that the ordinances, by-laws, rules and orders of the council are faithfully executed; he shall have control of the police of said town, and it shall be his duty especially to see that the peace and good order of said town are preserved and that persons and property therein are protected, and to this end he may cause the arrest and detention of all rioters and disorderly persons in said town; he shall have power to issue executions for all fines, penalties and costs imposed by him, and to issue warrants for the arrest of disorderly persons in said town, and in default of immediate payment of all fines, penalties and costs imposed by said mayor, he may imprison the offender in the common jail of Carroll County, not to exceed twenty days, and punish by fine and imprisonment in the guard house of said town, the fine not to exceed twenty-five dollars, and the imprisonment not to exceed twenty days, or work on the streets of said town twenty days in the discretion of the mayor. It shall be the duty of the mayor, or acting mayor, to hold mayor's court as often as may be necessary for the examination of any offense that may be reported to him, or the trial of such persons as may be brought before him: he shall be ex-officio, a justice of the peace, so far as to empower him to commit to jail or admit to bail persons charged with violating the criminal laws of this State in the same manner and under the same rules and regulations prescribed by law for justices of the peace.

Sec. 9. Be it further enacted, That said mayor and councilmen, at their first meeting, or some subsequent meeting, shall elect a treasurer of their own number or any citizens of said town, and also elect a marshal and deputy if necessary. These officers shall be required to take and subscribe an oath before said mayor that each of them will well and faithfully discharge their several duties as treasurer and marshal, as the case may be, to the best of their skill and knowledge.

Sec. 10. Be it further enacted, That the clerk and marshal receive such salaries as the council may deem just and proper.

Sec. 11. Be it further enacted, That said mayor and council have power to tax all shows to which an admission fee is charged, and all enterprises as they may deem to the best interest of said town.

Sec. 12. Be it further enacted, That the mayor and council of the town of Fullerville shall have the power to pave, lay off, vacate, close, open, alter, cut and keep in good order and repair roads, streets, alleys, sidewalks, cross-walks, drains, gutters and ditches for the use of the public or any citizen thereof, and to keep them free from obstructions, and to abate or cause to be abated what, in the opinion of a majority of the whole council, shall be declared a nuisance, and to provide for the building of houses or other structures, and for the making of division fences by the owners of adjacent properties, and the drainage of lots by proper drains or ditches; to build or remove fences, palings or any and all obstructions that said mayor and council may deem best for the said town, to enact all necessary rules and regulations to protect the health of the town, and for general sanitation.

Sec. 13. Be it further enacted, That all laws and parts of laws in conflict with this Act are hereby repealed.

Approved August 8, 1916.

The Mills and Industries

The Mills and Their People

The people of Fullerville not only supplied the work force for their community's mills, but they also supplied workers for the mills of the general area. Although they lived in Fullerville, they traveled to nearby communities for employment opportunities.

The mills also gave rise to local cottage industries.

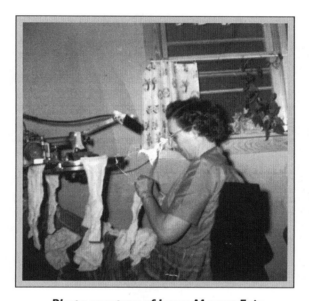

Photo courtesy of Joyce Massey Fain

Christine Smith, hard at work in her Fullerville home looping socks for the Villa Rica Hosiery Mill in Fullerville. Making production meant more money. Production meant working hard and fast.

Fortunately for those interested the coming of the mills to West Georgia has been well researched.

This book deals with the lives of the people of Fullerville, Villa Rica and the surrounding area and how they were touched by the mills that employed them.

Their memories are found in their stories and photographs.

Banning Yarn Mill Workers in Front Cotton storage building

Photo courtesy of John Wayne Sauls

The Mills

On October 13, 1902, Villa Rica Mills Inc. was chartered as the Villa Rica Cotton Oil Company. Over time, they expanded into lines of manufacturing and processing. The company owned and operated several gins, a yarn mill, hosiery mill and garment plant. They took pride in the fact that they were the only manufacturing company in Carroll County that were able to take raw cotton and process it completely for human use. First the cotton would go to the gin. Then it was spun into yarn and lastly knitted it into hosiery. As time came to pass, cotton production eventually dwindled, and the company discontinued the operation of its gins and mills. Banning Yarn Mills bought the company's yarn mill, and continued to produce hosiery. It remained one of the largest companies of its kind. (Ref: The Carroll Historical Quarterly, Spring and Summer issue, Vol. 1, no 2 1968)

Banning Mill, a textile mill, is believed to have been built between 1855 and 1861.

The first textile mill in the Carroll County area was built in the 1840's. It was owned and operated by Thomas T. Smith and William Humphreys, also known as the Bowen brothers. The mill was called Bowen's mill. It later burned causing the business to go bankrupt. The site was then sold to a Mr. William

Amis who owned Amis Manufacturing. During the era of the Civil War he saw to the construction of a brick mill, a dam to increase water power, and also a church known as Antioch Primitive Church. The Church still stands today.

To this day it is believed the mill was spared from destruction because of its secluded location. Sherman's Army simply had not found it. Many rumors circulated about how the mill survived. One being that the workers had hidden the machinery in the cotton fields. Another story related that the machinery was taken to a remote area by train until it was safe to return it to its rightful place. Mr. Amis renamed the mill Carroll Manufacturing after the war.

Tragically, the New Manchester mill located 20 miles away at Sweetwater wasn't so lucky. There was evidence that Union Troops had in fact camped on the mill's grounds. Mr. Amis later sued the Union Army for property damages.

Arthur Hutcheson, along with Robert McBride, Joseph Hayden and Thomas Bramlett, bought the mill in 1882 and named it Hutcheson Manufacturing. Mr. Hutcheson had houses built around the mill for his many workers. He made improvements to the mill as well. He increased the size from 17,500 to 36,000 square feet, added a sprinkling system for fire control, upgraded the machinery, and added many other safety improvements. He even built a school building which today is the home of the Corinth Baptist Church on Banning Road.

The mills got electricity between 1885 and 1889. This made Georgia one of the first states to have an electrified business. People would travel from far and wide in their horse-drawn carriages to view the spectacular lights at night.

Mr. Hutcheson also owned a sawmill, two pulp mills, a paper mill, a sock mill and a grist mill all about a mile from Snake Creek. He is buried in the graveyard at Chapel Methodist Church.

Poncet Davis and David Stokes bought the mill in the 1920s. They later added a rubber plant and named the whole operation Banning Cotton Mills. It was forced to close during the Depression years. It was later bought by a Mr. Upchurch in 1940, and it was then sold to A.L. Fuller.

The rubber plant facility along with over 100 bales of cotton was later destroyed by a flood in 1944. The flood caused the dam to break, and it has never been repaired.

Mr. Fuller sold the mill to Charles Brown and Annie Fickett Senn in 1948. They called it Fickett-Brown Manufacturing.

The mill was purchased again in 1953 by Douglas Matthews, G.F. Freeman, H.G. Houseworth, Harry and Martha Allen.

In 1958, the mill was bought by C.E. Goodrow and was named C.E. Goodrow, Inc. When Goodrow partnered with R.L. Kimsey Cotton Mill of Floyd

County, the mill was given the name Banning Yarn Mill. The second mill located in Villa Rica, Georgia was called Banning Yarn Mill #2.

The Banning Mill in Banning, Georgia closed its doors in 1971 and was sold to Mike McGukin of Carroll County, Georgia. Mr. McGukin opened a restaurant and a dinner theatre in the old mill and later added eight apartments for students and artists, until the year 2000.

The poker scenes, bridge scenes, and creek-side scenes in the hit movie *Fried Green Tomatoes* were filmed on the grounds of the Banning Yarn Mill in Banning, Georgia.

The Villa Rica Mills Incorporated

In 1911 the Villa Rica Hosiery Mills was established by three brothers: Hardy Fuller, Tom Fuller, and Dewitt Fuller. The mill started with ten machines and produced men's hose. Those owners built eight houses for their employees; hence the town of Fullerville began. The mill later increased in size, requiring more machines and more employees. The mill was sold in 1919 but continued to operate until 1926 when it became the possession of the Villa Rica Mills, Inc.

Golden City Hosiery Mill was established in 1929 under the ownership of C. M. Griffin. A fire destroyed the mill in the 1950's but it was quickly rebuilt. For many years thereafter, the Golden City Hosiery Mill made socks for military service men. Mr. Griffin died in 1960 and the mill was sold to Grady Brown who also operated Jean's Hosiery Mill. (Ref: *The History of Villa Rica (City of Gold)* by Mary Anderson.)

H. G. (Grady) Brown was the former owner and operator of Golden City Hosiery Mill, Jean Hosiery Mill and Custom Built Cabinet Company in Villa Rica, Georgia. He began school shortly after his family moved to Douglasville at the age of five. He stated that he had to quit school at the age of fifteen in order to go to work. He began working at the Duncan Hosiery Mill east of downtown Douglasville. This mill no longer exists. He stated that he worked there between one to two years before it went out of business.

He stayed with a brother in Carrollton, Georgia during the Depression days and worked at Lawler Hosiery Mill. It was during this employment that he received his Social Security card when they first became available in 1936. He stated that he didn't have one of the early numbers but he did have it issued to him the first year that people who worked began to get theirs. It was during this time that he met his future wife, Ruth Fuller. She was a native of Villa Rica, Georgia. They were married on March 18, 1939.

They moved to Nashville, Tennessee for a couple of years and worked at Belle Meade Hosiery Mill. He spent the majority of his life in the Villa Rica community after the mid-1940. His brother had started a mill in Fullerville, Georgia and asked if he would help run it. Later on Brown started his own mill business.

He recalled that he began his business in a little metal building next to Petty's Store in Fullerville. He borrowed $12,000 from the bank, went to the other side of McDonough, and bought 28 old knitting machines. His wife's grandmother owned an old metal building which they remodeled. It was around 30 X 40 feet. He employed six people at first, and the business grew within the next years.

He built Jean Hosiery Mill on Old Town Road in 1947 because they needed more space. At first it measured about 40 X 68 feet. Later additions were made of 20 feet at a time with acquisition of more machines. The equipment was kept up to date with all the latest designs.

Charlie Griffin, a former mayor of Villa Rica and his widow played a huge part in Brown's development of Golden City Hosiery Mill. Griffin and Brown were good friends and when Griffin died, his wife sold the business to Brown about 1965. It paid for itself within two to three years.

He recalled that later they purchased the Glamour Girl and Fowler warehouse because they were running out of room. Afterward, they were able to average around 60,000 dozen socks weekly. Frank Pope's warehouse was bought for storage.

Many Georgia cotton mills built company towns, like Fullerville, Banning, Shannon, and Lindale to maximize their profits and manage their employee's. The mills rented the mill houses to their employees. Usually in these mill towns you would find a company store, a mill church, and a mill school.

The cotton and hosiery mills mostly employed white workers, adults as well as children. Jimmy Causey, a lifetime Fullervillian, relates that his mother started working in the mills at age nine. My mom and dad were also quite young when they began working in the mills. Other Fullervillians also have commented about their parents working in the mills as children.

By nineteen hundred, ninety percent of mill workers in the south lived in company owned mill villages. The highest paying jobs for men in the mills were supervisory and machine mechanic positions. The mill employees referred to the machine mechanics as "fixers".

Oliver Curtis Sauls (2/25/16 - 12/23/98) was born to Blanche Oliver Sauls and Bammie Lodessa Simmons Sauls on Feb. 25, 1916 in Pelham, GA. He was the eldest of six children.

The Sauls family moved to Fullerville, GA when Curt was a young boy. When his father died in 1936 Curt, who was already working at the cotton mill, began training for a position as a fixer. He later became a supervisor. He also worked at Banning Mills in Fullerville GA, Banning, GA and Dalton GA. He then went to work at Villa Rica Knitters, owned by Gene Doyal. He was still working there when he celebrated his 80th birthday. Almost all of his working years were spent in Fullerville.

He married Esma Lee Cole on Feb. 24, 1939, and they had three children. As with most families, the household included extended family. This was common in the village. Families took care of each other, and the grandmothers cared for the grandchildren while the parents worked in the mills.

Curt loved playing baseball on the mill team. When his baseball days were over, he played softball--until he was 76 yrs old.

In the early 1940's Curt served as the first mayor of the Fullerville village. One year later his brother Cecil was mayor for the next four years, and Curt was the clerk for

Curt, Esma, and Richard Sauls
Photo courtesy John Wayne
and Elaine Sauls

Cecil's term. He was always proud of his home town and considered it the only place to call home.

During the 1950's and 60's times were hard for mill workers. Most like Curt lived from week to week, buying groceries on credit and paying the grocer when the employee received his wages. As times improved, Curt would loan certain neighbors and employees money to help them thru the week. These people he trusted to honor their debt. Neighbors knew who was trustworthy and who was not! Sometimes he trusted the wrong person, but not often.

They were never happy away from home and family, and home was Fullerville. -John Wayne and Elaine Sauls

In 1938, the Fair Labor Standards Act changed many of the cotton mill and hosiery mills' work standards. It created the minimum wage, a work week of a maximum of 40 hours, and overtime pay. The companies could no longer employ children. And by the twentieth century, companies began to compete for good employees, thus offering better and improved company benefits.

In the south, black Americans worked for lower pay and had fewer opportunities. Black American mill workers worked as janitors and grounds keepers. Their wives worked in the homes of the white families watching after the children, doing house duties, and so forth.

Previously, in the nineteenth century, hosiery mills were more prevalent in the northern states. These began to migrate to the southern states following the cotton mills during the 1920's in hopes of avoiding labor unions. In the 1960's, labor unions did attempt to organize but were unsuccessful. The mills were able to discourage union organization by offering company benefits and improvements in the mill facilities, such as air conditioning, and better treatment of their employees. This did not take place in the mills in Fullerville in the 1960's. As far as benefits, they did offer a health insurance policy that was expensive and had poor benefits. Most Fullerville mill workers who had to go to the hospital usually wound up in debt to the hospital and the doctor's office that would take quite some time to pay. If any improvements were made in the cotton mill and hosiery mill in Fullerville, such as air conditioning, better health benefits or working conditions, it came later, after 1969. After talking to some Fullervillians, the conditions didn't get any better from 1969, until closing.

The mills no longer built mill villages or company towns like Fullerville for their employee's. By the 1960's more and more employees were able to purchase automobiles allowing them to drive from their homes elsewhere for their jobs.

More changes also took place in the 1960's. With the employment of mostly white men and women in the mills, United States integration laws forced the mills to hire people of all races. The Civil Rights movement offered African American men and women employment opportunities and better pay.

The cotton mill and hosiery mill in Fullerville provided thousands of local families with employment for over a century. For many families, the mills provided a way to leave share cropping to provide a better life for themselves and their families. The mills also provided employment for women both in house or at home who needed an income for themselves or to help their families. (Ref: The Public History Center, Textile History, "Carroll County's Textile and Apparel Industries", West Georgia College)

Ray Matthews had a small hosiery mill on Walker Street in Villa Rica for a short time. His son Bobby Matthews took over the little mill and later built Vince Hosiery Mill in Fullerville on the site where the lumber yard had been. Vince Hosiery Mill was the last hosiery mill to close down in Villa Rica. Loyd Easterwood owned a hosiery mill in town right next to the Police Station. The building has been torn down, and the new amphitheatre resides in its place. Easterwood's Son-in-law, Tommy Hooten, had a small hosiery mill on Old Stone Road in the tin building for a short it while. The mill was destroyed by fire. The hosiery mill on Walker Street was taken over by Bobby Matthews. Unfortunately, the gin was struck by lightening and burned to the ground.

The Cotton Gin Industry

The Villa Rica Cotton Gin
Photo courtesy of Ernie Blevins, historian

As conceived by the textile barons of the northeastern United States, a plan for more efficient textile production was put into place. Rather than ship the many loads cotton produced in the South to the North for processing, a system was set up to carry out the entire process in the areas where the cotton was grown. The distance between the field and the finished product was shortened thereby saving many dollars in transportation expenses. Thus began the textile industry which brought such great change to the South.

The plan successfully reduced the cost of producing textile products. The new concept brought major development to previously undeveloped areas of the South as the mills and their support industries multiplied.

The West Georgia workers came to the mills because they provided a better way of life for themselves and their families.

The Cannon Casket Company

Cannon Company Workers
Photo courtesy of the author

The Brumfield family of North Carolina pioneered the development of the casket manufacturing business. Mr. B.V. Brumfield was associated with the Charlotte Casket Co., and later organized the Atlanta Metallic Casket Co. at Atlanta, Ga. (REF: By Allen T. Boger, Jr. Charlotte, N.C., Taken from September 1951 Grit and Steel)

The uniforms furnished to the workers by Cannon Caskets were dark green with the person's name on the shirt. The uniforms lasted no time at all because the chemicals used in the metal casket making process would eat right through the fabric. The workers in the metal casket department had to change out of their work clothes on the back porch because their uniforms were so contaminated that they would ruin just about anything they came in contact with in the house. People put card board on their car seats to protect the upholstery. It is not known why Cannon Caskets didn't allow their employees to shower and change on site before going home. Perhaps the workers just didn't want to take the time to clean up and change at the plant. At least Cannon, as many plants whose processes rely on the use of hazardous chemicals, laundered their workers uniforms, although not as often as at the end of shift as is required today. This enabled the company to keep track of replacement needs and spared them from any complaints that might have been made by the home laundry crowd. I have no idea how or where Cannon disposed of the processing waste. The inevitable comment in this enlightened day and age is, "I just can't believe this!" Thank the Lord for OSHA! For an extended and personal history (See Part 2 The Cannon Casket, Story by Katie Spinks Elliott via Ann Broom.)

The Lumber Business

The Fullerville Lumber Yard   Photo Courtesy of Paul Free

While World War II was under way, the area children watched the German prisoners being transported to and from their work at the mill.

The importance of lumber to any developing area has long been recognized. It provides the frame work which sustains the present and assures the future.

The Sulphur Mine, the Switch Track, and the People

Fullerville was a mill town, but it was divided into two sections which were separated by the switch track which ran across Rockmart Road. On one side of the switch track was the Banning Cotton Mill, Plant No. 2, and on the other side was the Villa Rica Hosiery Mill. The two mills were rivals. It is not known what started it all. Perhaps it was all because of baseball. The employees of the two mills played against each other.

According to the old timers of Fullerville, the residents who lived on the hosiery mill side of the road developed the attitude that they were *uptown* Fullerville and were better than those living on the cotton mill side. Those who have lived on both sides of the switch tracks realize that the only way that one could possibly be *uptown* Fullervillian was to purchase one of those elegant, classy Fullerville homes and add all the amenities required for a more comfortable life. All this was something a homeowner could add, and some did.

There were people who wanted to do better and who can blame them for that. However, for some reason, the people who wanted to do better convinced themselves that they were better than their own kind living in the same small mill village.

The train, loaded with empty railcars, would leave the main railroad line going through Fullerville and proceeding on the switch track all the way to the Sulphur Mine.

At the mine, it would drop off empty railcars and pick up the ones which had been loaded by the workers.

On its way back through Fullerville, the train would make stops at the lumber yard, the Villa Rica Cotton Mill, the Villa Rica Hosiery Mill, and Cannon Caskets picking up the cars loaded with finished goods and leaving empty ones behind to be filled.

Villa Rica Sulphur Mine.
Photo from Villa Rican newspaper courtesy of Ernie Blevins, historian

(For further information on the Villa Rica deep mining industry, see *The History of Villa Rica, City of Gold,* by Mary Talley Anderson.)

The Housing and the Switch Track

Justin Fuller started out with the Villa Rica Cotton Mill and then later established the Villa Rica Hosiery Mills along with his sons Hardy, Tom, and Dewitt in 1911. Another idea that the Fullers thought of was keeping their employee's closer to work. So they came up with the idea to build eight homes for their employee's. Fullerville was now established. The mill village continued to grow as more houses were added by E.T. Doyal and Sons. (See above, Mrs. M. F. taken from the book Memoirs of Georgia)

Typical Fullerville House
Photo courtesy of Charles and Ann Broom

The first eight houses built were on the cotton mill side of the area. Houses continued to be added with the hosiery mill also building homes on their side of Fullerville. When the house construction was completed, Fullerville was a mill community consisting of 67 houses in all. One thing that can be said about Fullerville is that no one has ever seen old junk cars rusting away in the yards, or old washing machines, refrigerators, or other junk piled up on the front porches. The yards were always cut neatly, and the women of the mills kept beautiful flowers and shrubs in their yards. Fullerville always had a sense of pride.

Perhaps some felt superior because their houses were newer, but the houses on the hosiery mill side were smaller. Indeed, the cotton mill side was prettier because of its large oak trees. There was simply no such thing as first class or second class citizens in Fullerville. Everyone in Fullerville made the same amount of money, except for the fixers and supervisors; and their wages were not significantly higher than the others. The housing was constructed for the mill people.

Unfortunately, none of the Fullerville houses were insulated and had no underpinning or indoor plumbing; not even the newer ones. Except for the indoor plumbing, some of the houses still lack these features even today. The result was that the occupants burn up in the summer and freeze to death in the winter. Under the circumstances, the only means of cooling was raising the windows and opening the doors. If affordable, a window fan was a tremendous plus. The winter heating bills were terribly outrageous, and frozen pipes were the norm.

Many who were fortunate enough to buy their own homes added the improvements they could afford.

The Fullerville homes were sold over and over again by the owners of the mills. Those who purchased housing and were later caught in a layoff were foreclosed. It did not matter how long the person had been a faithful worker and how probable the return to the work force would be.

Businesses, Services, and Events

The people of Fullerville were served by many well remembered businesses and services located both in town and in the surrounding area. Most important, these local business people worked closely with the people of the community. Credit was accepted and was a way of everyday life.

The Hickory Level Store.

Permission to use by Ruth Holder

The store was located in the Hickory Level community of Villa Rica, Georgia.

In 1927, the second story of the store housed Dr. S.F. Scales' Hospital.

The Coca Cola Wagon. Permission to print courtesy of Mrs. Burell W. Holder from the book, The History of Temple, Georgia, by Burell W. Holder.

In the hometown of Asa Chandler and throughout the area, *Coca Cola* and ice were distributed by the Villa Rica Electric Light and Power Company, which bottled the soft drink between 1903 and 1923. Delivery was made to the surrounding food service businesses.

Waldrop's Café. Preacher Waldrop's Café was also on Dogwood Street. There he served up some of the best hamburgers in town. (See West Georgia Cooking 2010)

Dan the Barbeque Man. Dan Spinks was known more for his barbeque than his hamburgers. Everyone around Fullerville called him "Dan the Barbeque Man." I worked for him a little while carrying lunches to the Banning Cotton Mill. I was just a kid carrying the lunches; and my pay was 25 cents, two hamburgers; and a coke per day. My father made me quit after my first paycheck.

Bitsey Hamrick's Grocery. Bitsey Hamrick's grocery store and another small café known as Dan Spinks Café were located on Rockmart Road across from Dogwood Street.

Petty's Store. Another well known landmark that was 'located across from the old McGuire House. Neither building exists today.

The Rolling Stores. These innovative stores brought needed items to those living in outlying areas and supplied the city dwellers with fresh produce.

They were a valuable service to all. The fresh produce raised on the adjacent farms was purchased or traded and sold in town.

They maintained a regular and dependable service to the entire area.

The Rolling Store   Photo courtesy Dorothy Seals

The Rolling Store. Max and Dorothy Seals operated the Rolling Store from their main grocery store on the corner of Old Town Road and Highway 101.

The Rolling Store was a converted school bus that was filled with groceries and supplies and driven out to the rural areas in order to accommodate the needs of the rural people. Later a second vehicle was added to their enterprise.

Mr. Seals would draw out the route that he would service with the rolling store filling the rolling store each day with fresh supplies. The route went as far out as the New Georgia area.

The stores were always spic and span, and one could smell the sweet smell of the fruit and vegetables. The rolling stores not only carried food and supplies to the rural areas, but they also carried feed for the cattle and farm animals.

The rolling stores operated on a cash or trade basis. The farmers had chickens, eggs, butter, sweet milk, and butter milk; and these would be exchanged for items that the farm families needed. Some cash was used to purchase supplies, but not always.

The Rolling Stores always arrived on the same day every week. The people in the rural areas around Villa Rica looked forward to those days and depended on the service. Their existence was invaluable to those living away from town.

The C. E. Allen Rolling Store with Dennis Allen.

Photo courtesy of Marykate Allen

The Redding Grocery. **Ed Redding owned the grocery store directly across from the hosiery mill in the 1940s. His father, Ray H. Matthews, was superintendent of the knitting department at the hosiery mill in the 1940's and early 1950's. He later established his own mill in Fullerville.**

Butler's Grocery. **Butler's Grocery Store was also located on Rockmart Highway in Fullerville. It was a small, tin roofed building having one big room, a small kitchen, bedroom, and an inside bathroom. They were able to have indoor plumbing because they were located near Dogwood Street and were able to connect to the sewage system. The Butlers used the one big room as the store, but it was also served as a small living room containing their television set, radio, chairs and rocking chairs. In the spring and summer, Mrs. Butler would have the porch full of her pretty flowers. They didn't have a whole lot of stock, but main items were usually available: a few canned goods, soft drinks, candy, and loaf bread. The three name brands of bread they carried were Sunbeam, Colonial, and Marietta, along with a few pastries from the bread companies. They were open seven days a week.. Most of the stores in Fullerville would close their doors on Sunday, but Butler's Grocery Store usually stayed open. People could get their groceries on credit at Butler's Grocery Store. The store never had gas pumps, but kerosene was sold because so many people used kerosene to start their coal heaters. Mr. Butler kept his own place warm with a coal heater. In about 1961 or 1962, Mr. Butler closed the store. The couple continued to live there for many years.**

The Leathers Grocery. In 1956 Mr. F. M. Leathers built his grocery store, a very impressive piece of construction for Fullerville. Mr. and Mrs. Leathers, along with their two daughters, Fran and Diane, worked in the store. (See Part 2)

Pearson's Barber Shop. Mr. Pearson ran Pearson's Barber Shop during the early nineteen fifties until the early sixties. Hair cuts were 25 cents, and a shower was 75 cents.

The Johns Jitney. In 1916, John W. Johns relocated his family to Fullerville after realizing that his profession as a blacksmith held no future. By 1919 the family was running a "jitney" (taxi) service for the community. The city license cost five dollars. (See the Johns Family History in Part 2.)

Note: The John's Jitney was the forerunner of the taxi service for Fullerville. In later years, the town was served by the **Chance Taxi Company** fleet.

Photo courtesy of Joyce Massey Fain

Butler's Used Cars. Behind the barber shop was Butler's Used Cars. The car lot was located on a field that had been used in earlier days to host traveling carnivals and circuses and to serve as a fair ground.

The Old Fullerville Jail   Photo courtesy Ernie Blevins, historian

Fullerville Law Enforcement. The Fullerville Jail served the city from 1916 to 1956. According to Fullervillians, the city's first jail was made of wood and burned to the ground. According to former Fullervillians, Buckeye Tolbert and Kate Elliott, who witnessed the burning of the first jail, a prisoner arrested for public drunkenness set the wooden jail on fire and tried to escape. The prisoner escaped the fire and was not seriously hurt. Based on Kate Elliott's present age and the time she witnessed the fire, the jail burned some time between 1938 and 1940.

The Fullerville jail is made of cement, not concrete block. No one remembers when the "new" jail was constructed, but they do remember many people serving time there, mostly for minor misdemeanors. Those guilty of major crimes were escorted to Carroll County Jail. The children played in the old jail when it was no longer in use calling it "The Calliboose."

Mr. Ben Rast and Mr. Ben Fuller served as Fullerville policemen for many years. (See Part 2)

Mr. Bryce Cole served as the Chief of Police for the City of Villa Rica for a number of years in the early sixties. Later he ran a store in Fullerville. His store was located in the same building which housed the Petty and Spinks businesses. There is now a flower shop located on the site of the former Petty Building.

He also served as a Villa Rica city council member . Later he purchased the old Redding Store, previously operated by the Redding's, Bitsey Hamrick, and later by Richard Hamrick. The building is now home to the Fullerville Mission.

Tiny Cole, the Villa Rica Voice, courtesy of the author

City Recreation. Bryce Cole's son, Danny was known as Tiny throughout his school and later years. Danny was loved by everyone who knew him. He had a love for sports and his community serving as Villa Rica's Recreation Director until his death.

Fullerville, Primitive Sanitation in a Modern World

The Fullervillians who owned their homes may not have cared whether the town got sewage lines or not. If so, it was possible that this would have put them in a whole new bracket as homeowners. It meant they would have become taxpayers; and nobody likes taxes it seems. They may have feared that bringing sewage lines into Fullerville would raise their property tax. However, it was not understood that the lack of proper sewage disposal was a negative for the whole community. Dozens of closely spaced neighborhood outhouses decreased all the home values of the area.

Some people from both sides of Fullerville got tired of waiting, *got smart,* and decided not to wait for decent waste disposal. They ran their own easements through yards of others and hooked into the sewage lines on Old Town Road and Dogwood Street. It is not known if these people ever had to pay a sewage bill. Only the city knows the answer.

Behind most homes was the outhouse. Liquid waste from the outhouses seeped into the surrounding ground, and the solid wastes were removed manually. The residents didn't pay any fee to have the outhouses shoveled out monthly. This expense was met by the tax payers. Initially, the collected wastes were disposed of in the Slickums; a wooded area.

Eventually, this practice was halted; and the solid wastes were deposited in the Villa Rica garbage dump. Yes, an old wagon and mule pulled the waste

Jimmy Causey Photo courtesy Sandra Matthews Smith

right through downtown Villa Rica once a month. The local residents called the old wagon the *honey wagon*. As the story goes, a father driving his kids along the road was held up in the long line of traffic behind the slow paced wagon. One child asked him about the cloud of flies accompanying the vehicle. Not wanting to get into the unsavory details of waste disposal, he replied that the wagon was carrying honey and that it was covered by a swarm of bees. Thus the name *honey wagon* came about.

It was a blessing to the city that bored kids would go to the dump and shoot rats for entertainment. The garbage was not buried; instead it was burned every Thursday. Once a month the outhouse wastes were added to the mix. All well remember the noxious, black cloud which rose from the dump often enveloping, due to wind direction, either Villa Rica or Fullerville.

A large open ditch which was always filled with water ran near the outhouses. It was thought that it was just an ordinary stream, but some parents warned their children to never play there because the ditch was where Fullerville dumped the waste from kitchen sinks and inside bathrooms. There were no septic tanks available for the houses in Fullerville at the time. The majority of houses had outhouses, but those with inside facilities used the open ditch for the disposal for their bathroom wastes. Unfortunately, little children did play in the ditch thinking it was just a creek. The waste traveled down the long, open ditch emptying into a large cesspool at the Villa Rica Cotton Mill. I do not know what sort of sanitary measures were taken with the cesspool. These were the same conditions that we now decry as hazardous to populations, especially to children, in the third world. There is no way to know the toll that was taken on the people of Fullerville due to the lack of proper sanitation. Nor do we know the same about Villa Rica which was located in such close proximity to the Fullerville community. Today, it is well known that what affects one portion of an area can infect the rest of it.

Mr. Harvey George Photo from the Villa Rican 1978
Courtesy Joyce Massey Fain and the George family

The Unsung Heroes Who Drove the Honey Wagon

When the mills and the city needed someone to drive the honey wagon, they first had to find an owner of a mule so they could rent the mule to pull the wagon. The rent for a mule was four dollars a day.

The next step was to find someone experienced in handling and steering a mule drawn wagon. Over the years, three qualified gentlemen were found to do the job. Each driver served for several years, but this was only a part time job. The one of the drivers was retired, and the other two had full time jobs as well. The three men were Henry Carter—the first driver, Ernest Gattis—the second driver--, and Henry George—the third driver. These three men were well respected in the Fullerville community. Even the children of Fullerville never hesitated to go out and visit with them when they came. They were hard workers, and they took good care of their families. Mr. Ernest Gattis was retired and took on the job for the extra money.

Mr. Harvey George had done various jobs ranging from working in the pulp wood business well digging and dump truck driving. He also worked in the cotton, hosiery, and the lumber mills of Fullerville. Later, he became a sanitation driver for the city of Villa Rica supervising the men working under him. Harvey George served in the Villa Rica Volunteer Fire Department for several years.

These men did a service that most would have refused to do. Others would have had too much pride to do such work even if their families were starving. However, these three knew that someone had to do the disagreeable job. They swallowed their pride and looked at it as extra income using their pay to put a little more bread and butter on the table and to buy items needed by the family. If these men were still alive, they should be recognized as true heroes of Fullerville. They did their community a valuable and needed service.

They have earned their place as a part of the Fullerville history.

Their families never went lacking for food or clothing because these men knew what work was and were not afraid to do it.

Mr. Harvey George
Courtesy of the George family

Health Care

Dr. Hogue. Perhaps the best remembered and most loved member of the medical community was Dr. William Love Hogue who was born in Paulding County and lived from 1880 to 1954.

Dr. Hogue began his early schooling in a rural grammar school and finished his lower education in Villa Rica. He attended the Atlanta Medical College which is now a part of Emory University.

He practiced medicine for 46 years beginning as a "horse and buggy" doctor in the rural area. This was a formidable endeavor considering the long distances, the condition of the roads, the merciless weather, and the 24 hour a day need for medical assistance. He moved to Villa Rica in 1920 and entered into private practice in connection with Malone Drug Store which later became the Villa Rica Pharmacy.

He is remembered as a kind, wonderful, Christian man by all. He treated everyone equally with respect and concern. He is said to have assisted in bringing 5,000 babies into the world.

Cash was not an issue with **Dr. Hogue.** He often took in such things as chickens, eggs, and other produce.

Perhaps there is one very outstanding thing remembered about **Dr. Hogue—HE MADE HOUSE CALLS!** (Ref: www.usgwarchives.org)

Children would often hear stories from grandparents, on both sides of the family, who had been sharecroppers, about how they took care of their sick and buried their dead. Sharecroppers had little help when it came to medical care. The oldsters would tell how the sick were cared for in the home and how doctors would come to the home when they could afford to have them. Neighbors would pitch in and help care for the sick. Mid-wives not only delivered babies, but they also provided care for the sick. The old folks would explain that they might be allowed to pay for medical help in eggs, milk, butter, fruits and vegetables.

Many families could not afford to have professional help when it came to burying their dead. They buried their own dead. That meant there would be no embalming, no fancy coffin, and no hearse. The neighbors would help clean and prepare the body, and the men would build a pine box to lay the corpse to rest in. The coffins were carried by six strong men unless there was a wagon and a mule available.

The mills offered a better life, yet that life was still hard in many ways. Health care, itself, was always a problem for those who worked in the mills. However, most families came from a background where little or no health care was available; and even minimal medical attention was an improvement. People just didn't go to the doctor or dentist for a six month or yearly check up. The cotton mills and hosiery mills didn't offer dental insurance, and the health insurance cost a great deal and paid very little. Parents always encouraged their children to brush their teeth and stay healthy because going to the dentist or the doctor was very expensive. An accident or illness would be financially devastating.

Additionally, the workers health was threatened by Brown Lung disease.

Brown lung disease (byssinosis, cotton bract disease, cotton worker's lung) is an occupational respiratory disease. The expression "brown lung" comes from the brown dust on the leaves surrounding the cotton bolls. It is caused by the long-term inhalation of cotton, flax, or hemp dust and characterized by shortness of breath, coughing, and wheezing. A protracted cough may develop. After approximately five years or more of constant exposure, the worker may develop chronic byssinosis, which may lead to permanent impairment of lung function. (http://healthmad.com/conditions-and-diseases/byssinosis-the-brown-lung-disease-on-textile-workers)

Today's generation has it easy compared to the older generations in respect to medical care. Could today's generation survive the hardships of past generations? There was no central air and heat and other comforts of life. There was no such thing as Medicare or Medicaid. Except for immunization, there was no free healthcare of any kind.

That Old Time Religion

Cecil Sauls Performing a Baptism   Photo courtesy of Shelia Sauls

The Fullerville Mission

The Fullerville Mission is currently run by Reverend Wayne Shelton. It serves the needs of the less fortunate by supplying food and clothing to all who come to its doors. The building itself has a long history in the Fullerville community.

In the early 1930's, it served as Mr. Goff's Grocery store. In the 1940's it was Mr. Redding's Grocery store, followed by Bitsey Hamrick, Bryce Cole and Richard Hannah. In the 1960's it was the location of a café run by Dan Spinks. Later it became a café and store belonging to Mr. Bryce Cole.

In 1956, Wayne Shelton was born to Harold and Joyce Elaine Shelton. He had 2 brothers, James and Grady. His grandparents were Shuford and Estoria Shelton. His grandparents, parents, and his siblings were all from Fullerville.

About that same time, two prominent preachers, Rev Ralph Tapley and Reverend Jessie Howell began having tent revivals under the big oak trees by the mills. God's presence could be felt there and people came from all around to hear the Word of God and to serve God. The Spirit of God has been in the community since then. In September, 1987, the Fullerville Mission was established to relight the fire that was begun in 1956.

Watching the tent revivals many nights as a child, Wayne knew God had a purpose for him, but he was unaware of what that was. It has always been amazing that God has allowed multiple denominations to work for the Lord's purpose. There has always been a presence of God in the Fullerville community and people helping each other thru hard times. Even now God has allowed Fullerville to be a help in the community.

The building itself was built in a recession by free labor. It has always had a purpose in the community.

One day as Wayne was on his way home from work, Mrs. Eva Hamrick was putting a "For Sale" sign on her building in Fullerville. Wayne stopped and talked to Mrs. Hamrick and purchased the building for $12,500.00. Mrs. Hamrick financed the building for Wayne and down came the "For Sale" sign. It was only up for 1 minute.

Wayne's mother and father were interested in arts and crafts so they opened an arts and craft store that gave out Bibles and tracts in order to pass on God's word.

At that time, Wayne was in business for himself so he bought the "Old Rock building" after he purchased it; someone told him that the person that he bought it from was a crook. Wayne missed one payment and went to the Old Rock Building and there was a lock on the door. Wayne contacted the man and was told that the building was never his to sell. Wayne was out $8,000.00 of his own money. As expected, Wayne was very upset and wondering what God was trying to tell him.

He put everything into storage then later opened up what has become the current Fullerville Mission. In the beginning, the Mission had only a front room that supplied clothing. There were many times when Wayne had to decide whether to pay his house bills or the Mission utilities. Wayne always chose to pay the Fullerville Mission bills. God always helped him with his house bills. The Fullerville Mission has grown since then, and Wayne has made several additions to the building.

Today, all are welcome; and they come from all around for help.

The town has always been separated into the "good side" and the "bad side." Many people feel unwelcome in the churches of today, but the Fullerville Mission takes in all people and tries to help them just as they are.

The community is truly blessed that God is working miracles through Wayne and the Fullerville Mission.

Brother Horace Wilson

Brother Horace Wilson was born in September, 1928, in Haralson County. The family moved to Carroll County when he was 11 years old. He graduated from the Carroll County Schools system, and went to work for the Plantation Pipeline Company. In 1950, the Korean War began, and Brother Horace's number was up for the draft. However, because of his experience with Plantation Pipeline, he was able to join an Engineering Outfit. They were soon activated and sent to Ft. Leonard Wood in Missouri. Because of his service in the military, he was later able to attend West Georgia College, where he graduated with a BS degree in Education. He taught school for a while in the Carroll County System.

Brother Horace had been raised in the Congregational Methodist Church and had been under conviction for 5 years before he was saved in August, 1953. Knowing what it was like to be miserable in a lost condition gave Brother Horace a great heart for seeing people saved. While in service, he had been reading a Gideon New Testament given to him by the military. He was saved after he came home from service at the Shady Grove Baptist Church between V. R. and Carrollton. He was called to preach 9 months later, and began pastoring 9 months after that. He has given his life to pastoring churches ever since.

1953 was a good year for Brother Horace. It was in 1953 that he met Willadene Barrow, also from Carroll County. She was working as an operator with Southern Bell (not BellSouth). They were married in 1954. Their son, Donald, was born in 1955. He has been a teacher in the Bremen School System for over 20 years. Their daughter, Denise, was born in 1958. She is married to Rick Bice, who has pastored East Hiram Baptist Church for the past 22 years. Their son, Mark, born in 1961, is in Real Estate Development in Hiram, and their daughter, Janet, born in 1962, is married to Pastor Kevin Kersey, who found Cornerstone Baptist Church sometime in the 1980's, and pastored it ever since.

Brother Horace's first pastorate was at Corinth in Haralson County in 1955. Then he pastored Fullerville Baptist Church from 1958 to 1962. During that time, he baptized a little girl who had been saved at a cottage prayer meeting named Sally Dobbins, who was later to become my wife. He also baptized a 12 year old boy named Kenneth Johns, although it is probable that this boy was not really saved until a few years later. After leaving Fullerville in 1962, he pastored Flat Rock and Second Baptist of Rockmart, then went back to Fullerville in 1966, and pastored there for 17 1/2 years. While at Fullerville, Brother Horace began a bus ministry that continues today, running as many as 5 buses with a high day on the buses of 300 persons. He also ran as many as 15 revivals per year.

Following the years at Fullerville, Brother Horace pastored at Kansas, and then at Calvary in Rockmart. Calvary had a Christian school, and he put his Education degree to work as the administrator. I had the privilege to work with him during the 1985-86 school years. We also flew to Dallas, TX together for Accelerated Christian Education administrators training. That week we both learned what it feels like to receive demerits for turning around in our seats.

After 4 1/2 years at Calvary, Brother Horace spent over 6 1/2 years at Happy Hill, 4 1/2 years back at Corinth, 1 1/2 years as Associate Pastor in charge of the Senior Ministry at West Carrollton. Brother Horace has now been back at Happy Hill for the past 3 1/2 years. Brother Horace's heartbeat through the years has been winning souls and discipling them for Christ. A man God has used greatly in this area, and a man who epitomizes what a preacher should be. He was God's Faithful Servant for many years. -Kenneth Johns

Reverend Ralph Tapley

Brother Ralph Tapley was born in August, 1918, in Douglasville. His family moved to Villa Rica when he was 8 years old. He grew up in the mill village in Fullerville. His Dad, Ollie Tapley, worked many years at the cotton mill. Brother Ralph also went to work at the mill at 18 years old, and worked there 5 or 6 years.

In 1939, he married Dorothy Williams, also of Villa Rica. They had 3 children, Max born in 1941, Sanford born in 1944, and Ricky in 1955. Dorothy died in April, 1992, following a long illness.

At age 21, Ralph came under conviction at Fullerville Baptist Church, but was not saved there. One day at work in the mill, he prayed all day long until finally a sweet spirit came over him. He went to tell Pearl Rainwater, that he had been saved. She threw her apron up and shouted. Brother Ralph joined Fullerville Baptist Church and was baptized in "cold water" in March at Willis Fish Pond on Highway 101 in Villa Rica. Brother Ralph was called to preach in 1942 at Fullerville Baptist. He said he would dream at night about preaching. During prayer meetings, he would stand up to testify and end up preaching!

Brother Ralph and Brother Jessie Howell soon strung up some lights in a grove of trees in the mill village, and held a revival. They also had a radio program together in Cedartown for 3 years. Brother Jessie would go on to pastor Fullerville, just before Brother Horace Wilson.

Brother Ralph was ordained in 1946, and began pastoring Callie Harbin Baptist Church. He pastored there for 3 years, then in New Brooklyn in Temple for 3 years, and Utopia in Villa Rica for 2 years. He also pastored Beulahland and Star of Bethlehem in Paulding County for short periods, and Macedonia near Ranburne, Alabama for 4 years. In the late 1950's, he was called to the 2nd Baptist Church in Douglasville, which he pastored for the next 32 years. 2nd Baptist was a remarkable ministry. Brother Ralph started with 17 people, and the church grew to fill the building. In the late 1980's, Brother Ralph resigned to take care of Dorothy. She died in April, 1992. In 1993, the Lord brought he and Reba Nell Bryant together. Her husband, Wallace, had died a number of years before. She had two daughters, Jean and Judy. God has blessed Brother Ralph and Sis. Reba Nell. They have been very happy together. Through the years, they have maintained his ties with 2nd Baptist. He has been back to preach Homecoming every year since he resigned

Brother Ralph is a good man...a faithful man... a man with a good sense of humor and a good spirit. God's faithful servant for many years, Brother Ralph Tapley. -Kenneth Johns

Dr. Charles Williams

Brother Charles Williams for many years has been one of the most highly respected pastor's in this area. He's one of those men who make you feel that Daddy's home and everything's all right. He has been a steadying, encouraging influence on generations of preachers. Brother Charles has always been a good man of vision, willing to step into a new area of ministry when he believes God is in it.

Brother Charles was born and raised in Fullerville, Georgia. He and his wife, Jean, are two of the many wonderful men and women of God who came from this little "mill village" town. Brother Charles was saved at his home, and then called to preach at the Fullerville Baptist Church. He had a favorite place to study his Bible and pray called Sugar Hill.

Brother Charles was ordained on November 21, 1954, and has pastored ten churches over the past 50 years. He has always had a vision, and been an encouragement to young preachers. In the 1960's, while pastoring at the White Oak Springs Baptist Church, a young layman named Jay Bice came to him with an idea for something that had never been done in this area He said that if he had a bus, he thought he could fill it with children to bring to church.

Brother Charles provided the bus, and then another, and then another. Eventually, they were running 12 buses and averaging 600-700 in church with a high day of 1,002.

After leaving White Oak, Brother Charles constituted the Calvary Baptist Church in Rockmart, in an old church building where the great Methodist preacher, "Old Sam Jones", had once pastored. During one revival at Calvary, 54 people were saved. Brother Charles' vision led him to begin a Christian School at Calvary also.

Twenty eight years ago, Brother Charles became the President of Windward Island Missions at the death of its founder, Brother Paul Johnson of Tennessee Temple University. Brother Charles was with him at the time of his death in the Windward Islands. This Mission Board serves thirteen national pastors.

Brother Charles and Sister Jean have been married for 58 years. They truly are a delightful couple. They sing together, attend revival meetings, and obviously enjoy serving the Lord. At age 78, and following open heart surgery, Brother Charles is now in his 15th year pastoring the Callie Harbin Baptist Church, which has grown from 13 to about 125 people. They continue to have a vision, and a desire to help young preachers. - Kenneth Johns

A Preacher in the Bailey Family

George S. Bailey and his wife Katie were very devout holiness believers. A favorite reminiscence has been about George S. and Pentley Clyo Bailey, who was better known as Preacher P. C. Bailey, and how he started the First Pentecostal Church in Villa Rica. Preacher P. C. Bailey worked at Goodyear Cotton Mill in Rockmart, Georgia before coming to Villa Rica.

The story passed down in the Bailey family was that Katie wanted a preacher in the family. She got a preacher lady, referred to as Sister Montgomery, to come from Rockmart. The three Bailey men tried out for preaching and Sister Montgomery picked the best one. The three Bailey men were Shelton, George S., Pentley Clyo. Shelton Bailey preached for one week, but he didn't do so well. George S. Bailey, preached the next week. Katie rather than Sister Montgomery decided that he was not qualified to preach because he couldn't read well enough. The third week P. C. Bailey preached. Both the ladies decided that P. C. was the best qualified.

Preacher P. C. Bailey made a good preacher. He built up a small church into one with a large membership which is still going strong. Some might say he was a self made preacher, and others say that he was called to preach by God working through Mrs. Bailey and Sister Montgomery. Only God and Preacher Bailey know for sure. All that matters is that he believed in preaching the word of God. He was a giving man and never preached for money. He worked in the mills as many did then.

When Preacher P. C. Bailey moved to Villa Rica, he needed a building in which to start his new church. A block building was found to be vacant in Fullerville. The building was one down from the Old Pearson's Barber Shop, which was then Taylor's Barber Shop. The owner of the building agreed to rent the building to Preacher Bailey. However, that all changed the next day. The owner of Taylor's Barber Shop and Mr. Cole did not think it would be a good idea to have another "holy roller" church that close to them, since the Congregational Holiness Church was located nearby. Preacher Bailey just said that God had a better place in store for his church and that they must follow his will. In a matter of weeks, a building became available and thus began the First Pentecostal in Villa Rica. -Perry Bill Bailey

The Bright Star Baptist Church

The Fullerville Baptist Church, which is located on Old Town Road in the Fullerville community of Villa Rica, Georgia, was organized in 1913 under the name Bright Star Baptist Church and was located on Rockmart Road which at one time was known as Jones Road. The Fullerville School also used the same building later. The Bright Star Baptist Church left the old school house on Rockmart Road in 1932, as they had purchased land on Old Town Road to build a new and larger building as it's members were increasing and needed more room. Bright Star Baptist Church members changed its name to Fullerville Baptist Church upon moving into the new building. (Ref: The History of Villa Rica (City of Gold) by Mary Anderson)

The Fullerville School

After the Bright Star Baptist Church left its original site on Rockmart Road in 1932, the building housed the Fullerville School.

According to Fullervillians, the old Fullerville school house closed its doors somewhere between 1938 and 1939. It has been said that a few World War II veterans used the old Fullerville school house as a night school where soldiers could complete their education on a GI Bill. Many young soldiers were drafted while in school, and wanted to get their diploma so they could get better employment.

The old Fullerville School building is still standing on Rockmart Road and is currently being used as a home. The Olin Bailey family lived in the old school house around 1961. (Ref: The late Olin Bailey 8/8/19 - 11/11/91)

Places and Events: Some Are Gone; Some Remain

The Fullerville Ballpark 1963.

Perhaps the memories most dear to the people of Fullerville and Villa Rica are those of the Fullerville Ballpark. Recollections of the soft summer evenings filled with fun are a still a tribute to those who made it possible.

It was a wholesome source of recreation and community for people of all ages who were drawn there either to play or watch.

The Fullerville sports programs gave rise to some very fine athletes including professional ones. Reflections on the importance of this facility are well documented throughout this book.

Despite an effort to rename it, the name Fullerville Ballpark has stuck fast.

The field remains today and is now a soccer field located on the newly renamed access road, Sarah Sauls Drive. Many thanks are owed to the people of Fullerville for their desire to recognize Sarah for her years of involvement with the ballpark and the activities there and to the Villa Rica officials who responded to their wishes.

Villa Rica, Georgia, Wednesday, July 24, 1968

BASEBALL TRAIN—This baseball train made up of a Ford tractor and four depot baggage carts carried Villa Rica Little Leaguers through town last Saturday advertising "Baseball Day."

The Villa Rica wagon train pulling the Little League ball players
Photo from Villa Rican news paper and Vicki Mattox Williams

In1963 that the Villa Rica Jaycees raised the funds to build a new grand stand, fence, and installed lights so that games could be played at night. They also added a concession stand. The Villa Rica Jaycees used the monies coming in from the concession stand to purchase needed items for the ballpark. The field is still there and is currently being used as a soccer field. The old water tank rises behind the field and is a reminder of the days past.

Rhonda Bailey at the Old Concession Stand   Photo courtesy of the author

According to an article in the Villa Rican Newspaper, May 15, 1963, No. 3 issue, the Fullerville Ballpark name was changed to the New Villa Rica Ball Field, but that name never actually caught on, and people even today refer to the ball field as the Fullerville Ballpark, which is now known as Fullerville Park, where soccer fields have taken the place of the ball field.

The Theatres

The Villa

It was an exciting day for Villa Rica and Fullerville when the Villa Theatre first opened its doors in the late 40's or early 50's. There had been no similar form of entertainment in the communities until that time.

The Villa Theatre hosted a variety of amusements. There were movies, live entertainment, and even wrestling matches. Even the great Freddie Blassie was known to wrestle at Villa.

The theatre offered a place for the hardworking people of the area to go for just a little while to relax and to forget their troubles.

It was certainly a wonderful addition to the community as far as the local teenagers were concerned. It was such a great place to meet friends, enjoy a movie, and consume large amounts of hot buttered popcorn.

Bennett and Lois Neal owned the building the Villa Theatre occupied, and Walter and Fannie Carter managed the Villa.

The Martin Theatre Company of Atlanta was the distributor for the movies that were shown in the Villa Theatre. Mr. Carter drove to Atlanta every week and picked up new reels for the next week.

According to Morris Brooks, black people were allowed to go to the movie even though there was segregation at the time. However, they had to sit in the balcony. Actually, the balcony had the best seats in the house. Of course, it was very special to the local teenagers.

Sadly, the theatre closed in 1964. Its closing was a great loss for the Villa Rica and Fullerville communities.

Located just four miles from the Fullerville/Villa Rica area, Temple, Georgia, was home to the Temple Theatre. It was owned and operated by the Hill family and was located on West Johnson Street.

It closed some time in the late forties.

The Villa

Photo courtesy of Paul Mararmol & Joe Garofalo

The Temple Theatre

Permission to print courtesy of Mrs. Burell W. Holder from the book, The History of Temple, Georgia, by Burell W. Holder.

The Celebration of Bygone Days

Author's note: Every year the people of Villa Rica and Fullerville looked forward to seeing the wagon train parade through town on its way from Douglasville Georgia to Villa Rica. This was followed by a street dance with several different bands playing rock and roll, country and western music. People would come from nearby towns to join the fun and to celebrate our pioneer history. Rest assured that a very wonderful time was had by all.

It is too bad that the celebration is no longer held. It was such good, wholesome fun for all.

The Founder of the Villa Rica Saddle Club

Source: The Villa Rican, Thursday issue, January 22, 1998.

We can thank the late Ray Tyson, who passed away in 1981, and who was the founder of the Villa Rica Saddle Club. Because of the founder's efforts to put the Saddle Club together, it became Georgia's oldest and largest continuous saddle club.

Jack Bell joined RayTyson as the first president of the Saddle Club. Jack Bell served as Carroll County sheriff for eleven years and was chairman of commissioners in 1998.

Because of these two gentlemen and their members, the Wagon Train rode for several years and I'm sure is missed by many today. The Villa Rica Jaycees also played an important part as well as other local people in making the Wagon Train and street dances possible. In 1998, the Villa Rica Saddle Club honored the late Ray Tyson's family, which was the 35th anniversary of the Villa Rica Saddle Club.

Announcement:

Douglasville-Villa Rica Wagon Train to Roll This Saturday

Jaycees to Sell Bar-Be-Que Plates, Give Away Riding Mower,

Street Dance Saturday Night

Wagons are being greased, harness repaired, and saddles and bridles readied as members of the Villa Rica and Douglasville Saddle Clubs get ready to make their annual trek from Lake Jane at Douglasville to Villa Rica and back to their starting point

This annual event, initiated to bring a little of the older and wilder America back to life for a day or so each year (and have a little fun, too), has been a combined project of the Villa Rica and Douglasville Saddle Clubs and the Villa Rica Jaycees for a number of years. It has not only provided local residents a look back into time but has helped enliven those dull July days.

The wagon train will leave Lake Jane at Douglasville, off Highway 78, at 8:00 a.m. on Saturday, July 27th arriving in Villa Rica at approximately 1:00 p.m. Upon reaching Villa Rica they will parade through the downtown section, tossing out half dollars along the way, and on to Elementary School grounds where they intend to camp overnight and where the activities of the day will be held. Somewhere along the trail Villa Rica Jaycees will meet the train and serve them refreshments.

Right in Style for the Festivities Photo from the Villa Rican Newspaper courtesy of Vicki Mattox Williams (background: the Villa Rica elementary and high school)

A full afternoon of activities has been planned for the participants and spectators at the school grounds. The events will include a horse show (open only to those horses making the trip from Douglasville), bar-be-que served by the Villa Rica Jaycees, a greased pig contest and other field events open to the general public. There will be no entrance charge on events other than the horse show which is open only to those participating in the trail ride or wagon train.

The barbeque plates to be sold by the Villa Rica Jaycees will consist of 1/2 barbequed chicken, potato salad, baked beans, potato chips, bread and tea. These will be sold at $1.25 per plate to the general public.

The Street Dance

A street dance will be enjoyed by all at the Food Town parking lot at Tri-County Plaza beginning at 8:00 p.m. Saturday night. Music for the dance will be furnished by the N.J. Defoor band.

At sometime during the dance the Villa Rica Jaycees will give away a Snapper Comet 6 h.p. 30 inch riding lawnmower to some lucky contributor to some of their civic projects.

Days to Remember: The Villa Rican   Courtesy Vicki Mattox Williams

Plans at present call for the return trip to Lake Jane at Douglasville to begin at 9:00 a.m. Sunday morning where the annual event will terminate until July of next year.

All area residents are invited by the three sponsoring clubs to be on hand next Saturday, July 27th, and to help make this one of the most enjoyable events of the year.

The Villa Rica Train Depot

At last a railroad line came to the area creating Villa Rica. The new city was formed by combining the towns of Hixtown and Cheevestown.

The first train came in June of 1882 opening the way for development and industry to both Villa Rica and later to Fullerville. (Ref. Wikipedia) For many years there was even passenger service available. Sadly, this is no longer true.

There is definitely nothing wrong with change and the improvement of the looks of Villa Rica or any other city for that matter. However, every town should have the old standing beside the new in order to create a true spirit of the present. Historical buildings like the train depot, the old Fullerville cement jail, and the old Villa Rica Theatre are worth saving.

Kate Elliott and Friends
Courtesy of Kate Elliott

The local people loved to watch the trains go by. It was fun to see the **US Mail** being picked up by a moving train whistling as it roared by and snatching the mail bag off its hook. It was good for all to see first hand how the mail system of the whole country worked and how the community was a part of it.

A huge Christmas tree was placed at the depot every year when **Villa Rica** decorated for Christmas. It was fascinating to see the **Georgia Power Company** pull the big tree off of a big flatbed truck and lift it into a standing position at the depot. It was decorated with the bright ball lights, and it was absolutely beautiful at night. The Villa Rica High School Wildcat Band would play Christmas music in front of the Christmas tree. It was so special and was enjoyed by all.

During the warm months, many Fullervillians and Villa Ricans would bring a hamburger and milkshake to the depot and sit watching the eastbound and westbound traffic pass by on Highway 78, the main road from Atlanta to Birmingham. It was definitely a place for folks to socialize. They would relax and talk for hours as they watched the traffic go by. It was an enjoyable pastime for those who needed to get out of their houses on hot summer days and nights.

Depot Demolition Photo courtesy of Katie Spinks Elliott

Many in Villa Rica and Fullerville citizens regret that the old depot is no longer there. It was an important part of everyday life.

It is missed. It is gone forever.

The Legendary Roger of Fullerville

No community is complete without a mystery. Fullerville has its very own Roger, a lurking menace, who may occasionally be spotted in a glance, but then is gone. Has Roger ever harmed anyone? Not that anyone *heered tell of;* but he has certainly frightened a lot of folks, especially children. Some say that Roger goes back to a time long before Fullerville came into being. Unfortunately, he remains an elusive shadow.

Some have speculated that Roger is Bigfoot or perhaps a wild human being. The more analytical think that he might be a bear. Then, of course, he might be just a plain, old fashioned *haint*.

Perhaps Roger, whoever or whatever he may be, is just as curious about us and what we are up to as we are about him.

(For more on Fullerville's famous Roger, see part 2)

Fullerville Incorporated with Villa Rica

Town of Fullerville incorporating with Villa Rica, Ga 5th day of January, 1956.

2278   LOCAL AND SPECIAL ACTS AND RESOLUTIONS, VOL. II
2279   VILLA RICA LIMITS EXTENDED
2280   No. 66 (House Bill No. 165).

An Act to amend the charter of the City of Villa Rica located in the counties of Carroll and Douglas approved March 24, 1941, and Acts amendatory, by extending the city limits of the City of Villa Rica as now defined so as to take in additional territory, including what is known as the limits of the Town of Fullerville in Carroll County, Georgia, adjacent and adjoining the city limits of the City of Villa Rica, Georgia, and for other purposes.

Be it enacted by the General Assembly of Georgia:

Section 1. Be it enacted by the General Assembly of the State of Georgia that the Act establishing a new charter for the City of Villa Rica of the counties of Carroll and Douglas approved March 24, 1941,... Acts amendatory thereof be, and the same are hereby amended as follows:

That the extension of the city limits of the City of Villa. "Rica shall include all of the limits of the corporate town heretofore known as the Town of Fullerville in Carroll County, Georgia, which said corporate limits of the said Town of Fullerville extend a radius of one-quarter (%) of a mile from the J. H. Hogue store located in the cement block building in the Town of Fullerville as defined by the Acts of 1916 incorporating the Town of Fullerville (Ga. L. 1916) approved August 8. 1916.

Section 2. Be it further enacted that the said city limits of the City of Villa Rica shall extend and include all of the territory heretofore known as the Town of Fullerville in Carroll County, Georgia, as shown by the Acts of the legislature incorporating the Town of Fullerville, and that the said territory to wit: radius of one- quarter (1/4) of a mile from J. H. Hogue's store.

GEORGIA LAWS 1956 SESSION   007Q

A cement block building, shall be and the same is hereby annexed to the city limits of the City of Villa Rica, and shall be included in the limits of the City of Villa Rica subject to the charter of the City of Villa Rica as approved on March 24, 1941, and all Acts amendatory thereof, and all ordinances and statutes of the City of Villa Rica and powers contained in the charter and Acts amendatory thereof and ordinances passed pursuant thereto by the governing authorities of the City of Villa Rica.

Section 3. Be it further enacted, that all laws or parts of laws in conflict with this Act be, and the same are hereby repealed.

Section 4. A copy of the notice of intention to apply for local legislation and affidavit of editor that said notice has been published as required by law, are attached hereto, and made a part of this Act as if fully set forth therein, and it is hereby declared by the authority aforesaid that all requirements of the Constitution relating to notice of intention to apply for local legislation has been complied with for the enactment of this law.

Georgia, Carroll County.

I, undersigned, do hereby certify that I am editor of the Carroll County Georgian, the newspaper in which sheriff's advertisements appear for Carroll County, and the attached advertisement was published in said newspaper on the following dates, to wit: December 22, 1955, December 29, 1955, January 5, 1958.

This 5th day of January, 1956.

/s/ Stanley Parkman,
Sworn to and subscribed before me, this the 5th day of January, 1956. /s/ Lillian T. Moore, Notary Public.

With this action Fullerville ended one era and moved into another.

Document courtesy of Doug Mabry, historian

Part 2

The Sons and Daughters of Fullerville and Villa Rica

The Looping Department Workers, Villa Rica Hosiery Mill, 1936
Photo courtesy of Jimmy Causey

The Stories of the Sons and Daughters

These are the stories of the people of Fullerville and Villa Rica as submitted by them recalling their memories of the past.

Praise the Lord for Hot Summer Days in North Georgia!

By Kenneth Johns

It has been a hot June, and July has started the same way! For some reason, all this early summer heat has made me nostalgic for lazy, hot summer days when I was a kid here in North Georgia. Bright sunshine, the warmth on my back, the heavy humidity relieved by an occasional breeze, all seem to take me back to a simpler time when Mother and Dad handled all the problems and I had all the fun.

I have fond memories of:

Walking home on the last day of school before summer vacation, pick-up baseball games, playing outside with the neighborhood kids until nightfall

Catching lightning bugs and putting them in a jar, catching June Bugs and tying a string around their leg to watch them fly, and fighting wasps with a piece of board.

Riding a bicycle to the pool for swimming lessons, to the library to check out books for the *Summer Reading Program*, to deliver newspapers on my paper route, and to my piano teacher for lessons.

Swinging as high as possible in the old tree swing while singing "We gotta sink the Bismarck to the bottom of the sea" at the top of my lungs.

Little League practice and wearing that wool uniform on game days.

Going barefoot and the feel of the hot, black earth between my toes while walking in the garden. Also, wearing black tennis shoes with the round white patch that said *U S Keds*.

Open windows and doors with a piece of cotton stuffed in the hole in the screen door. The noise of an electric fan. Running through the backyard water hose. Hanging an arm out the car window at 55 mph. The sound of the people singing at the Holiness Church about ¼ mile away.

Fried chicken every Sunday (It had been running around the chicken pen a few hours earlier). Fried hamburgers and canned chili every Friday night after Mother came home from the grocery store. Plums and blackberries picked and eaten on the spot. Cutting watermelons on the back porch. Homemade ice cream. Mother's "pineapple upside down" cake. Banana sandwiches and tomato sandwiches made early in the morning and eaten for lunch. Six ounce bottled Cokes for five cents, hotdogs for twenty cents, and hamburgers for a quarter.

Dusty red dirt roads. The sound of trains on the switch track, the crunch of tires on gravel roads, the sound of the wind in the trees before a thunderstorm, and the symphony concert put on by the "July Flies", cicadas and other insects all day long, but especially as night approached.

All day singings and dinner on the ground, Vacation Bible School, open windows to gaze out of during church, and funeral fans waving all over the auditorium.

These and many more memories come to my mind on hot summer days. Were we poor? Maybe, but, naw, I don't think so! We had lots of love, and many things our Heavenly Father gave us that were free!

Praise The Lord for Hot Summer Days in North Georgia!

Fullerville Ball Park   Photo from the Villa Rican newspaper courtesy Vicki Mattox Williams

The Sarah Sauls Story

By Sarah Sauls, interview with Perry "Bill" Bailey

Author's note on Sarah Sauls: I cannot write this book without giving one person the recognition she deserves. She is a person who is respected for her hard work and dedication to all of the sons and daughters of Fullerville.

She was the mother of four fine children whom she raised on her own after her husband Cecil passed away. She clothed them, fed them, housed them, and sent them through school. Other children adopted her as their second mom. All the kids of Fullerville knew they were welcome at the Sarah Sauls' home. I know this for a fact; I hung around there myself.

The kids of Fullerville didn't have to ask Sarah if they could have a Pepsi or a banana sandwich. They pretty much helped themselves as though Sarah's home were their own.

After Cecil passed away, Sarah became very active in community sports. She played softball on the women's softball league; she coached a Little League after a hard day's work at the hosiery mill. She would come home, get into her tennis shoes and her shorts and ball shirt, and head to the Fullerville ball park to coach the boy's Little League baseball team.

She worked hard with the ball field, putting the white line on the field, getting ready for a big game. She was one of the persons who made it possible to get the first ball lights and a fence for the Fullerville ball park. Boys from Villa Rica would be on the Little League team as well as Fullerville boys. Paul Free coached the women's softball team.

Personally, I want to thank you, Sarah Sauls.

The sons and daughters of Fullerville and Villa Rica love you.

A Chat with Sarah

Cecil and Sarah Sauls lived in the Cotton Mill section of Fullerville and shared a duplex with coal heaters with Olin and Ruth Bailey. They all got along very well. Ruth and Sarah were best friends. They never locked the doors between the walls of the house. Sarah's oldest daughter, Jean, would sing Ba Yo Ba Yo to the tune of Amazing Grace. The oldest Bailey boy, Jimmy, asked if she knew any other words to the song. They shared everything even food. What one didn't have, if the other did, they shared. People didn't mind sharing back then.

Roger Sauls was the first person to receive a scholarship from Fullerville or Villa Rica for playing sports. He got a scholarship to Auburn University for football as a quarterback. He played one year and then went to West Georgia College to play. He received his degree his from the University of Georgia and came home to become a football coach at Villa Rica High School. Roger is Cecil's youngest brother.

Cecil Sauls worked at the cotton mill later becoming a manager at Cannon Casket.

He served as mayor from 1947-1949

Cecil went on to play for the Atlanta Crackers, but he got home sick, decided to give up playing, and came back to Fullerville.

Sarah said several of her brothers had spent the night in Fullerville jail. The Police Officer of Fullerville was Mr Rast. They were put in jail from not having a shirt on when playing cards. The stores there at the time were run by Bitsey Hamrick, the Felix Leathers, and the Butlers. Customers could charge and pay weekly or monthly. Sarah would take her friends for RC cola and peanuts. Mr. and Mrs. Mault Waldrop owned a cafe on Dogwood St. They had great hamburgers with onions; the best hamburgers in town.

Sarah attended the Fullerville School until the 3rd grade and then went to Villa Rica. She belonged to the Bright Star Church. When the members built a new building on Oldtown Road in Fullerville, the new name, the Fullerville Baptist Church, was chosen.

She doesn't remember how much rent they paid up to the time they bought their house but she remembers she and Cecil bought the house she still lives in for $1200.00.

Sarah talked about how people in the cotton mills and hosiery mills paid their hospital and doctor bills. Basically, they paid on credit.

Sarah remembers Olin Bailey, Willie Williams and J.W. Keaton playing music on the front porch of the Bailey home.

All of Sarah's children grew up in Fullerville, and she is still living there. Of Sarah's children, who were involved in sports; Jean Sauls played softball and graduated 3rd in her class; Bob Sauls starred in football and basketball and was voted Villa Rica High School's most valuable player, Terry Sauls played basketball and baseball, and Sheila Sauls played basketball and was a cheerleader. Two of Sarah's grandchildren, Jessie Corn and Greg Harper, were drafted to play pro baseball. Jessie was on Boston Red Sox farm team and Greg was with the Braves team.

She has lived in Fullerville since she was three, and now she is ninety years old. What would the Sauls family like for this generation to learn from the book about Fullerville? "To learn the real history of it."

Jimmy Causey's Fullerville Story (including Roger)

By Jimmy Causey

Growing up in Fullerville was a lot of fun. Before we went to live on Pate Dr. in 1961, we lived on what people use to call Jones St. or Rockmart Rd. Across the road where Open Pantry Store is now. Then it was Leathers Grocery owned by Felix and Dorothy Leathers. I understand it was built in 1956. I remember it being built. We lived at this place when the gas explosion happened on Dec. 5, 1957. We heard a great noise. My mother Eva Dobbins Causey got me and one of my cousins and her children and set out in front of our house in our 1954 Belair CheVilla Ricaolet until my cousin and her children went to our aunt's house. My mother and her sister, Glady's owned the house, it burned. Jerry and Virginia Waldrop had bought the place. They had bad luck with the house burning, but later they built a nice ranch style home in its place.

We moved in 1961 to a house in Fullerville which was up above Bitsey Hamrick's store. We lived there a few months then moved in Oct. 1961 to Pate Dr. As I mentioned Fullerville was a great and fun place to grow up. Always there was someone to play with. Fullerville ballpark was just down the hill. The City of Villa Rica used the field for organized games, such as little and pony league baseball. They would also play men's baseball. They also played ladies and men's softball. Back then they didn't play slow pitch softball, at least the men didn't then, and instead they played fast pitch. Now I think the girls in high school played fast pitch ball. I remember thinking it strange you could throw a softball under handed faster than you could that a baseball under handed. I believe in later years they practiced and played midget football on the Fullerville field. I believe Mrs. Sarah Sauls had a lot to do with lights being put on the field; it was great not only for the people of Fullerville but for the people of Villa Rica.

I remember playing ball in Mrs. Sarah Saul's yard also in James and Ruth Sauls and Olin and Ruth Bailey's yard as well as my own yard. We would play football and baseball. But we played basketball in Mrs. Sarah's yard, sometimes full court. Bob, Terry, and maybe some of the others would put up a second goal. The ground was flat and made a good place to play. We played marbles. I learned how to gamble playing marbles, pitched horseshoes, shot one another with flips. We also played *rolly poley* with those big log roller marbles. I think children today wouldn't know what that game would be.

We could go to the mills, get boxes, cones, yarn came on barrels and we would have ourselves a time making huts, battling with those cones. Wet them, you could throw them a long ways and boy sometimes they hurt if hit just right. Go to the woods and play. We went to the big ditch and had a good time. We played all kind of games, some made up on the fly. When we got older we didn't play hide and seek, we played foxes and hounds which is hide n seek of steroids. It was a lot of fun. I know we had a lot more toys than our parents had if they even had any coming through the Great Depression Era. But even we didn't get the toys and gadgets that kids have today. I was just saying that because when I grew up, you didn't have to have a store bought toy to have a good time. Sometimes we would go down to Perry Bailey's house, sit in a old car his daddy had that didn't run. But we would go everywhere we could imagine and have a big time doing it and didn't even burn any gas. Perry would

57

come up to my house and play disc jockey on the radio, which he does now for a living.

I remember going to all the stores in our area, Leathers, Bitsey Hamrick's , Paul Spinks which was called Petty's store. Mr. and Mrs. Butler, their store in the front room of their house and also Preacher Waldrop's store and grill that had store good and the best hamburgers in town.

Do ya'll remember Duck and Cover in school? Cold war tactics, bet people that were kids when I was that lived in town remembers them letting us go home early one day if we had to be timed if you could get home in 15 minutes you could get blown up at home instead of school. Do you remember when Kennedy was killed in 1963? Going home and couldn't even watch TV for it. We didn't get to see Big Night Shocker or Tarzan and cartoons on Saturday. A lot of people saw Oswald shot on TV.

I remember working around the house and yard and earning an allowance money. I think daddy gave me .75 cents on Fridays. I know it doesn't sound like much but in the early to mid 1960"s you could do a lot or buy a lot, get with someone, walk to the show, go to the football games on Friday night's at the old field. Of course we got older, we cut grass, swept yards, washed cars to make extra money. Do ya'll remember .5 cent cokes, penny candy, five cent candy bars, banana popsicles, Eskimo pies or hunkeys, and many other treats. Hey, also lemon and lime sours, cherry cokes and all the treats that came from the soda fountain at the drugstores, Berry's and Doctor Candler's. Don't yall miss that, you can't get the personal touch just everywhere now. But I understand Berry's has a fountain.

Not to leave anything out, Roger he had many names. He lived in the woods behind the ballpark, what I understand, it was an old tale. He had been there many years, kept some of the children out of the woods, some would go anyway. Be brave and go hunting. I remember one time in particular, I was with Bob Sauls at the edge of the wood. Bob may have been shooting his gun and I was watching. I don't know, that's been many years ago. I guess Bob was about 14, I was 10, Bob had outgrown being afraid of old white Roger but I hadn't. Bob hollered "Here comes Roger, we had better run." I was already running at the word or name Roger. I was gone, didn't even look around until I heard Bob laughing, boy he got one on me. But it was fun to be scared; it was fun sometimes to hear ghost stories being told around the campfire when you are a boy. I thank the Lord for my childhood that I and a lot of kids had back then. I fear some of the children today don't have as rich childhood as people from era and before had. I think a lot of kids have missed out on a whole lot of fun.

I am Jimmy Causey, my father was Jamie Causey and my mother Eva Causey. I still live in Fullerville; go to church in Fullerville at Victor Tabernacle

Holiness Church. There I gave my heart to the Lord in Dec. 1978. God has really been good to me. Bless his name.

Malt Waldrop delivering lunches to the mill workers

Photo courtesy Helen Waldrop

Fullerville story

By Evelyn Y. Padgett

Growing up in Fullerville was a simple way of life. I was born on Third Street in the little 4-room house in the curve next to the fairgrounds. For our playground we had all the woods, and of course all the kudzu patches we could ever have hoped for. We wasn't scared of much of anything back then.

Our house stood far enough off the ground that we could play under it. We paved many a road under there, and built many a city.

Everywhere my brothers went, I tried to tag along, especially when they would take out the horse and cow to graze. Back then it didn't matter where you graze them, as long as you could find a big enough field, and didn't have to worry about them eating up someone's flower bed or garden. In the evening when we would start them to the barn my brothers would throw me up on the backs of the horse or cow, and I felt like I owned the world.

We raised most of the food we ate. Daddy would plant 2 and 3 gardens. We raised chickens, had milk cows to milk every morning and evening, along with growing pigs to fatten to eat in the winter time. My daddy wouldn't let the girls stay around when the hogs were being slaughtered, but we had our hands full when time came for putting up the meat.

I remember having to milk the cows every day and churn the milk and make butter every other day when I came home from school. And we had to get that butter salted just right, or we would catch it. Mama sold milk, butter and eggs for a little extra income and she didn't want anyone complaining about her butter. A few times she would give me a dozen eggs to sell, and I would walk around the village and sell them. Fifty cents was a lot of money to a little girl in those years.

There was a truck that came around every Saturday with fresh eggs and vegetables. It was called a rolling store, and was owned by Mr. Simmie Tidwell. I loved to climb up on the back of it and see all the goodies he had. But we always had to go to the grocery store for the essentials like sugar, lard, flour, etc. Many of our clothes were made from 25lb flour sacks that mama would save from her sacks of flour each week until she had enough to make us a dress. The owner of the store's name was Bitsey Hamrick. He knew all of us kids and once in a while he would slip us a sack full of candy in the grocery bag. My daddy always made us kids walk to the store to get his tobacco and smokes, and Mr. Bitsey told my daddy one time that if he hadn't known us, we wouldn't get any tobacco products from him.

My parents worked in the cotton mill, later called Banning Yarn Mills there in Fullerville. The mill is still there, but I think it is used mostly for storage now, I'm not sure. A lot of 18-wheelers sit there all the time. And off to the side is the old jail house.

Fullerville had an older black man who drove a horse and wagon around the village and cleaned out the outside toilets. I think his name was Carter, or Carver. I'm not sure. In fact, he bought one of his horses from my daddy. We enjoyed seeing him come. He always laughed and cut-up with the kids. And we enjoyed seeing the horse as well.

Back then we walked about everywhere we went, to church and school. I can remember my Daddy had a 2-horse wagon in my earliest years, but he later got an automobile.

Being close to the fairgrounds, we got to see the circus when they would come in to town with all the animals. They would let us watch at a distance the elephants, lions, etc. go through their routine as they would train them during the day. And every fall the fair would come to the same fairgrounds. So we saw a lot of excitement at the fairgrounds.

There was a grove of oak trees in the front of our house where we played and spent most of our days. My daddy along with other men would sit under the trees in the shade smoking and swapping stories while we played around them. Off to the side of the grove of trees was a house called a shotgun house, because you could see straight through it. If you stood in the front yard, you could look through and see the back yard.

We had to walk to school because there were no city school buses back then. Some mornings there would be several of us kids walking along enjoying the early mornings. As we neared the school, other kids would join us. Of course, if it was bad weather, momma would let us get a taxi to take us. Mr. Gene Lanning was the taxi driver. And we had to cross over a railroad track close to the school. There was no crossing, just a trail, so we really had to watch and listen. But we spent many an hour 'walking the rails'.

In the evenings when we started home, we would always stop and get a hamburger from Preacher Waldrop's cafe if we had a quarter. It was just a small cafe, but he sure did know how to make a hamburger. And they only cost 25 cents. They were the best hamburgers you could buy, and there's never been any like them.

Fullerville is not the same now. All the neighbors have changed and I don't know them anymore. There are still two or three families I knew when I was growing up. I miss walking and riding my bicycle all over Fullerville and everyone knowing you by your first name. I still ride around there every now and then and wonder where the ones I knew are today. I know many have passed on, but it makes me wonder about the paths the children that I played with chose.

Note: The cleaning of the outhouses was a one man job first done by Mr. Carter, followed by Mr. Ernest Gattis, until the late sixties. The job was then taken over by Mr. Harvey George until 1979 when sewage lines came to Fullerville.

The Gertrude Blair Story

By Gertrude Swafford Blair, interview with Joyce Massey Fain

My name is Gertrude Swafford Blair and I was born in Fullerville, Georgia, in 1921.

I was born at home to Essie James Swafford and Sidney Swafford. I was one of eleven (11) children. I have lived at the corner of Old Stone Road and Pate Drive all my life except for a short period when I was married.

We did not get married in the church or ask my father's permission. We just eloped one night. When my Father found out he was fit to be tied and threatened to shoot my husband but he came around after about two weeks. I then moved with my husband in the house right behind my parents on Pate Drive in Fullerville. My husband, George Blair, served in World War II. We had one daughter, Martha Louise, and two sons Gary Blair and Ronald Harris Blair who was better known as "Footsie" Blair because he never would wear shoes. He is still called that today.

As a child, I remember that my parents had a very hard time making ends meet as did most of the other families in Fullerville. We had no indoor plumbing; we had an outhouse in the backyard that was our bathroom. All of the houses of that time had outhouses because there was no sewage in Fullerville until years later.

All of the children had chores that were their responsibility to complete while Mom and Dad worked. My chore was to carry water from the old well that was in the back yard.

The water from this well was used to cook with, bathe with, clean house with, and wash clothes with. I remember having to carry so many buckets of water everyday from the well to the house that my arms ached. My other chore was to help Mother do the laundry which we did not have a washing machine, so I would have to fill up a round tin tub and Mother and I would use an old scrub board to scrub the clothes on to get them clean and then hang them on the clothesline to dry. That was a lot of scrubbing for our large family, and it took all day to get the clothes washed and dried.

As a child, I only attended school until the third grade and I had to quit. My sister was ill and my Mother needed help taking care of her. I never got to finish my education and when I was old enough, I went to work in the Villa Rica Hosiery Mill for many years and then later I worked at the Villa Rica Hospital until I retired. The Villa Rica Hosiery Mill employees were paid $6.00 per day for working 12 hours each day. We only worked 5 days a week so we earned $30.00 a week to take care of our families.

In the early years there were no benefits such as medical, life, or workman's compensation insurance, offered to the employees. My father bought a T–Model car but only the boys were allowed to learn how to drive, so I never learned to drive a car and had to walk to work and anyplace else I needed to go.

My family attended the Fullerville Baptist Church and I was there the day my father shoveled the first shovel of dirt to build the church. I still attend Fullerville Baptist Church when my health allows me to attend.

My husband and I had gone our separate ways and when my Father died he willed the house at the corner of Pate Drive and Old Stone Road to me and my sister and I have lived in the same house I was born in for many years. I am almost 90 years old and growing up in Fullerville in the 1920's and 1930's was hard. It still is hard to live on social security and get by, but I consider myself a blessed person. God has richly blessed me with a long life and a wonderful family.

Morris Brooks, a Black Man's Story of Fullerville

By Morris Brooks

Let me introduce myself to you. I am Morris Brooks and currently live in Villa Rica, Georgia. I was born 77 years ago on July 1, 1933 in Villa Rica, Georgia. I was delivered at home by Dr. Hogue, who in those days would make house calls. When I was eight years old, I went to live with my grandparents in Fullerville who raised me.

I really enjoyed living in Fullerville and compared to other people in Fullerville, I really did not have a lot of struggles to overcome. I was an only child and my grandfather had a job at Fullerville Cotton Mill and worked everyday to provide for our family. He went to work there in 1932. I was one of only two colored children that lived in Fullerville at that time, but we played with all the white children in the community also. We lived in one of the two houses down behind the cotton mill plant, Banning Cotton Mill, where the road dead ended. The switch track ran right in front of our house. Henry and Nellie Carter lived in the other house. We always had a garden every year and fresh hog meat for Thanksgiving and Christmas. The hog killings were held adjacent to the Banning Cotton Mill in Fullerville.

All of the children loved to go to the Lumber Yard in Fullerville and play in the huge sawdust piles that were left after the wood had been cut, stacked, and was ready to be sold. We would climb to the top and bury ourselves up to our heads and then slide down the sawdust pile. Boy were we a mess, but it was better than playing in the dirt and mud! We could just shake ourselves off and go home without my Grandmother being too upset.

We also played a lot of ball on the Old Fullerville Ball Park that was the original ballpark before the second ballpark that is now a soccer field. The original ballpark was located down from the Fullerville Lumber Mill. This was the original Fullerville Ball Park. Not only did we play with the white children but we were always welcome in their homes to eat, play games, and sometimes spend the night. The people of Fullerville did not treat us differently.

I remember when I got my first bicycle. My grandmother had it ordered from Sears Roebuck and my uncle, who lived in Atlanta, had brought it out on Christmas Eve and put it under the tree. That was some more bike, and even more special because in those days there was no money for gifts, but my Grandfather and Grandmother had saved and got me my dream bike!!!

All of the children in the community liked to pool their change together and if they had enough money, they would buy a pack of hot dogs and hot dog buns and go out in the woods and build a fire to roast their hot dogs. We did not do this very often because money was scarce; but when we did, we had a ball!!! We also used to pull Gene Lanning in a wagon to the old ballpark so he could watch us play ball.

Mr. Henry Carter's nephew would collect Prince Albert Tobacco cans and make them into little cars for us to play with.

You have to remember that I grew up in the period before the Civil Rights Act was passed in 1964. I went to school and graduated from Villa Rica Colored School which was located in Villa Rica. We were bussed back and forth each day. That is the school that all the colored children went to from 1st grade to the 11th grade. There was no 12th grade at that time. Schools were not integrated until the 1965-1966 school year.

Before the Civil Rights Act was passed in 1964, if you went to the theatre colored people had to sit in the balcony which actually were the best seats in the house. If you rode the bus, the colored people had to go to the back of the bus and sit before the white people got on the bus. If the bus was full, most of the time the colored people had to give up their seats to the white people and stand up for the trip.

At the old hospital in Villa Rica there were rooms set aside for the colored people only. The Villa Rica Clinic had separate waiting rooms for the colored people and the white people. Dr. Hogue was the only doctor that I know of who did not have separate waiting rooms. It did not bother me at the time that colored and white people were segregated because it was all I knew.

All of the houses were owned and maintained by the mills. They all had outhouses and once a month the "Honey Wagon" would come by and clean out the outhouses. The Honey Wagon was pulled by a mule and had 2 large metal drums on the back along with a shovel. Mr. Henry Carter drove the Honey Wagon for many years, and later on Harvey George drove it. He was the last man to drive it before sewage came to Fullerville in 1978 or early 1979. The story goes that Mr. Henry Carter liked to carry a gallon of white corn liquor with him. This was eventually found out by the Mayor and two city councilmen who took his corn liquor away from him so he went on strike until they let him have it back. During the period while he was on strike that Ernest Gattis drove the Honey Wagon for a short period of time. The mule was paid $4.00 a day. The metal drums were emptied in swamp land where Gold Dust Park is now located in Villa Rica. Later the honey wagon delivered its load to the city dump in uptown Villa Rica.

The only murder in Fullerville that I knew of was the stabbing death of Clarice Cole McClarty who was stabbed to death by her husband in a domestic dispute. This happened in the early 1960's.

Mr. Ben Matthews owned the Fullerville Planing Mill and went to Alabama to bring German prisoners to his plant to work. He went and got them each morning and took them back each evening. In 1948 or 1949 he bought another mill from Alabama and brought in other black children to work for him.

The lumber company had a whistle that blew each day at exactly 12:00 noon. It could be heard all over the community. The purpose of blowing this whistle was to let all of the workers know that they had 30 minutes for lunch. Most of the workers did not have watches, and the plant was so long that this was necessary in order for them to get a lunch break

All of the stores in Villa Rica and Fullerville closed on Wednesday at 12:00 p.m. in order for the owners and store workers to attend to their personal business.

Ben Rast and Ben Fuller were the Fullerville policemen during this time. Mr. Rast had a little truck, and he rode around the community. Sometimes he would park and walk around the community. Mr. Fuller had a car, and he always drove around the community. I only know of two men, Leon Massey and Bennie Wheeler, who were locked up in the old Fullerville Jail which still stands today. I would love to see the preservation of the jail by the City and the Villa Rica Jail Committee to continue. It is a piece of history that we do not want to lose for our city.

I graduated from Villa Rica Colored School in 1950 and went on to college at the Tuskegee School in Alabama to study engineering from 1950 to 1954. I returned to Fullerville in 1954 and was drafted into the army. I served from 1954 to 1956.

When I retuned to Villa Rica, I worked at several odd jobs and then went to work for The Bank of Villa Rica and retired from there in 1994 after 30 years. I now enjoy working in my church and community. Fullerville was a great place to grow up and I will always cherish the memories I have from there and my wish is that the city will get involved in this community and make improvements to make this historic place a better place to live.

My Boyhood in the Fullerville Mill Village--On the Hosiery Mill Side

By Bob Broom

The following is based on Interview with Bob Broom about his boyhood in Fullerville, GA – May, 2010

My parents Rob and Eva Gibbs Broom and my older sister Mildred, age 3 were living in the Fullerville Mill Village in 1930 on Rockmart Road. Both my Father and Mother worked at the Hosiery Mill. My Dad grew up around Villa Rica and Mama was from Alabama. I was born in 1932 at the "Old Gibbs

Home" Blount Co, Alabama but returned to Fullerville as a baby. We lived in several different mill houses and sometimes we just lived in one side of a house and other folks lived on the other side.

Thinking back, I guess my first memory of Fullerville is when I was about 4 years old when we lived on today's Pate Drive. I remember playing with the Millians brothers. The Farr family lived next door and Raymond threw a rock and it hit me right above the eye that *left a scar* that I still have. I also remember the *big snow* in 1936. When I was about 7 years old, a traveling photographer came through Fullerville taking pictures of children. He had a" Real Pony and Cowboy Outfit and Hat" that he would furnish for the Photograph. My Mama got my picture made on that Pony. A lot of my memories are when we lived next to the store on Rockmart Road right across from the Hosiery Mill.

When I was 5 or 6 years old, at the Hosiery Mill, some Doctors and Nurses came and gave shots for Typhoid Fever and the needle broke off in my arm. They could not get it out, someone had to go to town and get something to remove it with. It was about 2 hours before they got back and got the needle removed from my arm. This left a deep impression on me, over the years and even still, *I do not like getting shots!*

I attended Fullerville Baptist Church. When we went on Sunday afternoons to visit my Grandparents Broom, who lived outside Fullerville, I'd not like it because I would not have anyone to play with. In the Mill Village there was *always someone to play with* and we had some great fun times. We were always playing ball at the "1st *Fullerville Baseball Park*" (located going out of Fullerville, on the left side of Rockmart Road across from the Lumber Mill).

Some of my friends who lived in the Mill Village were: *Bobby Tolbert, Roger & Hoot Sauls, Vernon & Charles Harper and Bobby & Jimmy Matthews.* As boys would do sometimes, we did some dangerous things. When I was about 11 or 12, Roger and I decided we would climb to the top of the "Big Water Tank" at the Cotton Mill. We climbed up the ladder step after step and got up on the first walkway, it was *really high up there*! We thought we would climb the rest of the way up to the tip top, but after going up a couple more steps we decided to come back down. We then started going back down to the ground, I got so scared, I thought if I could just get back down to the ground, I would never go back up that high. To this day, I've never wanted to be that high off the ground again. I reckon no one saw us because we didn't get into trouble for it.

Another dangerous excursion was on a Halloween (*kids didn't go trick-0-treatin back then*) but young folks would go around *serenading,* making noise and throwing rocks on top of houses. Once a man came out of his house with a *gun* and started chasing us, he shot up in the air and we ran like everything and hid in the kudzu patch close to the Courthouse which was right past the hosiery mill on the left near **Ray Barber's** house and the railroad tracks. Later that same night, we went over on Sugar Hill and a woman came out with a *pistol* and we took off running through the big cotton patch and she shot at us and we could hear the *bullets buzzing* past our heads.

One time Roger, Hoot and I were playing near an old barn, down behind where the Barber's lived. We set a fire and Hoot started fanning the fire and it got so big, it got away from us. The field and weeds caught on fire and burned for a couple of days but we didn't get in trouble for doing it. Sometime we would "sneak" into the Cotton Mill and get some "yarn", then untangle it to make Kite cords but never got into trouble for this either. We would also go down to the Lumber Yard and play on the big piles of sawdust. We'd get some cardboard and make a slide out of it on the big piles. Those piles of sawdust would sometimes have "hot pockets" in them. If they caught you out there, they would run you off. I remember during **WWII**, at the Lumber Yard, they had "*German Prisoners*" working there. There was one man from Berlin, but he spoke English and a bunch of us boys would talk to him.

On Sunday December 7, 1941 Pearl Harbor was attacked and War Declared. I remember my Uncle Lyn Broom coming by our house to talk to my Dad. He was concerned that they might be called up to serve in the armed services and have to leave their families but they weren't called. My Mama got layed off from her job and she was so worried, because Dad only made $5 a week at the Hosiery Mill. She didn't know how we would make it, but we did. Some of us boys in the Village would gather "kindling" and sell it to make a few cents. There was food rationing stamps during the war and it was hard to get candy such as a *Baby Ruth* Bar but Bitsey would hold any candy behind the counter and sometime he'd let some buy a bar. When I was growing up, Bitsey Hamrick's Store was up on the hill at the corner where you turned to go to Fullerville Baptist Church. The Store across the road from the Hosiery Mill was run at one time by Mr. Goff and another time by Mr. Redding. Once when we lived in part of a house next to the store, my older sister was boiling some syrup candy on the stove and it splashed out on her, she screamed out in pain, Mrs. Aldora Williams was working in the other side of the house where we lived and she heard Mildred scream and came running over to see what had happened, immediately "she talked the fire out of that burn" and it didn't even blister up.

I remember in the 1940's, a Mr. Lee was a Policeman in Fullerville. There was a place down the tracks on past the Cotton Mill, where men would go to gamble and be up to no good. My Dad would go with the Policeman Mr. Lee, to try and catch some of them. I fondly remember Mr. Rayford Grubbs and his Barber Shop. He was a good man and he looked after us boys. Once I was getting a haircut and a man came in who was **AWOL**, he was cussing and carrying on and Mr. Grubbs made him leave. Later the Police got him for something and locked him up.

In 1940 or 1941 around Thanksgiving, they had a *Turkey Trot* near the Villa Rica Depot, *Governor Talmadge* was to be in Villa Rica. They let us out of school, we all went up there to hear the Governor's speech he made while standing up on *a flat box car*. It was a very *"BIG-TA-DOO"*, a huge crowd of people and all kind of things were going on, such as catching flying turkeys & greasy pigs and climbing of the greasy pole etc. It even made the front page of the Atlanta papers.

A big event in Fullerville was the *paving of Rockmart Road* 1948-1949. I remember it was paved before we moved out of Fullerville and we moved my senior year of High School which was Sept. 1949-May 1950. They first scraped and widened the road and then the large paving machines paved the road. The people in Fullerville would stand out and watch the process.

I started school at the Villa Rica Elementary in 1938 and graduated in 1950 (there was only 11 grades then). I went all through school at Villa Rica except in the fall of 1944, when we living on Sugar Hill, we went back to Alabama for a few months, then came back to Fullerville after the new year in 1945. Those were great school days at Villa Rica. My favorite *teachers* were *Mrs. Haygood* and *Mr. J.A. Ariail*. My favorite *coach* was *Sam McIntyre*, his first year at Villa Rica High was my senior year. In the summer of 1948 J.A. Ariail took a group of us boys to Summer Camp below Macon, Georgia. At the camp there was a large lake and some cabins. It was my first Summer Camp and we had a great time! In high school my friend Roger worked at Berry's Pharmacy. He got me a job there also, and I worked at Berry's from 1948-1950. We would walk to our jobs in Villa Rica and then back home to Fullerville.

My Dad bought a place out on the Carrollton Highway. In 1949, during my last year of High School, we moved out of Fullerville. After my graduation in 1950, I got a job in Atlanta at the Cannon Casket Company. I transferred to the Cannons Villa Rica Plant when they opened in 1951 and my Dad also went to work there that same year. In 1952 I quit at Cannon Casket and moved to Anniston, Alabama. Ever since then, I have made my home in Anniston, with my wife Louise, our daughter and 4 sons, (except 1-1/2 years when I was in the Army). After working 46 years with the C.M. Offray Company, I retired May 15, 1998.

I was a *very happy boy* growing up in the Fullerville Mill Village 1932-1949. Even though I left Fullerville over 60 years ago, the memories of my life in the mill village, the ball park, the families, and my friends in Fullerville still remain clearly in my memory.

Note: On December 5, 1957, Bob's Dad, Rob Broom was killed in the Villa Rica Explosion. He had not gone to work that day at Cannons; his daughter was sick and he had gone to Berry's Pharmacy to pick up her prescription. At that time Bob was in the US Army, stationed in Baumhoulder, Germany.

Doing business with the Rolling Store
Photo courtesy of Dorothy Seals

The Rolling Store

By Dorothy Seals

My husband and I owned and operated a grocery store on the corner of Old Town Road and Highway 101. The store was a block store owned by Mrs. Ida "Granny "McGuire, who lived across the street from the store in a large two story house. The barber shop was built next to the store. Other businesses that later operated a grocery store from this building were Petty's Grocery, Spinks Grocery owned by Paul and Ruby Spinks, Bryce Cole, just to name a few.

Mr. Lemuel Mitchell, a nearby neighbor, had a dry-cleaning pick-up route. He stopped by the store each morning as he began his route. He had chronic headaches. We would always say, "Good morning, Mr. Lemuel ", and he would answer with his gruffest voice, "I ain't got no good morning for nobody!" He knew it would make me laugh and that was as good as he would have! He would then buy a B.C. or Stanback headache powder and a coca-cola and take it for his early morning headache. Then he would stand around long enough to drink his coca-cola. This was always a pleasant visit for me.

Another pleasant thing that happened was with one of our regular customers, Vera Pate Williams, who worked at the Villa Rica Hosiery Mill. She would get home from work, come by the store and buy whatever she was going to cook for supper and many times, she would insist that Max and I come over when she got it cooked and eat supper with her and Billy. Since we lived in Temple about 6 miles away and couldn't eat our supper until we closed our store around 9:00 p.m., we really enjoyed the invite.

Aunt Clemmie Kilgore who just lived across the street from our store, evidently watched Max working around the store from time to time. She told her sister, Mrs. McGuire, that Max Seals beats all I ever saw a working; I declare, if I don't believe he would stay busy doing something all day even if he had to take something apart and put it back together again.

The years after WWII were hard. In most families, the husband and wife both had to work just to make ends meet. Max found out he needed me to help him at the store. Since we had one child in school (Julius) and another baby girl, (Judy) at home, I engaged a maid to stay with them in Temple and I stayed at home and cooked lunch, then carrying lunch in my hands, I caught the Southeastern bus in front of our house and rode it to the bus station in Villa Rica. Then I had to walk from there to Fullerville, to where Max was working in the store, give him his lunch and then help in the store all afternoon until closing time. Looking back on those days now and the way we lived, it is almost unheard of today. What I remember was that we were happy; we had good friends and relatives who helped to make living a pleasure.

We were operating our little store the year the main road from the City of Villa Rica thru Fullerville was paved. Mr. Ben Fuller was the chief of police of Fullerville during the years we had the store there. Grady Brown instituted his first hosiery mill right by the side of the building we occupied as the store.

After our years in the store in Fullerville, with the Rolling Stores, Max decided to put up another stationery store. We bought a store from my brother Albert Allen, just outside of Villa Rica. We operated that store for one year, then Max decided to change operations again. He made the statement that he wanted a cash business so that if he didn't have the money in the cash register he could have groceries on the shelf. He bought a plot of ground on Dallas Highway, which was Highway 61 in Villa Rica. Our store, which we named "E-Z Food Store" was directly across the road from the new Villa Rica City Hospital being built as we built the store. The store was also conveniently situated right next to the Villa Rica Housing Project, which must have had about 50 apartment units or more at that time. This was the year 1955. His idea for this location was that the families living in the projects could walk to the store if they couldn't to drive to the grocery store. The store turned out to be a good investment for us. It was so good that it encouraged Max to put up a second grocery store. This store was also a cash store, but more in the class of a supermarket and was right in the middle of the City of Villa Rica. We operated both stores for a while. My brother Charles Allen, who had been working for General Motors for a number of years, was looking for a career change. He decided to buy our E-Z Food Store. We continued to operate our larger store, which was now known as the Jitney Jungle Food Store for eleven more years. By then, Max's health was beginning to break, so we had to sell that store. Being the energetic person that he was, he bought a lot on Wilson Street in Villa Rica and built a 4 unit building and put up four stores in it, renting them out to individuals for their businesses. Now he was in the rental business. He still had time on his hands so he established a carpet and floor covering business.

My Pet Goat

By Sandra Matthews Smith

My parents were Robert (Buck) & Clara (Tince) Matthews. I was born July 20, 1943 in Fullerville, GA, on Rockmart Rd. My dad Buck, was another one from Fullerville who made it to a bigger ball team. Buck Matthews played baseball for GA-AI and then went to play in 1944-1945 for the Saint Louis Cardinals. He also served as mayor of Fullerville.

Buck Matthews   Photo courtesy of Sandra Matthews Smith

When my brother, Tony, was little we had a goat. Everywhere we went the goat was behind us. One day we went to Preacher Waldrop's Cafe and got ice cream cones. We gave our goat some and gave mama the rest. Our goat disappeared, we looked everywhere. We heard some men laughing; Tony and I took off and ran up Sugar Hill, wishing we had stayed home. They were barbequing our goat. We cried and cried.

We moved from Fullerville to Mableton on May 30, 1956. Mama and Daddy lived in the same house until they both died. You know, we were raised in the mill village. We were poor, but we didn't know it.

Walter Fields Family Story

By Gerald Fields

My name is Gerald Fields and I am the oldest of four children born to Walter and Mattie Martin Fields. My brothers and sisters are Ernest Fields (6/11/39), Reba Fields Maner (9/23/41), and Kenneth Fields (9/4/46).

My parents were married in 1936 and enjoyed 66 wonderful years of marriage before my mother's death in 2002. My father passed away in 2004. I remember that we moved around a lot when I was a child. We lived in Paulding County, Georgia for a while where my father farmed to make a living for his family. In 1942, we moved to Fullerville and my Father went to work in the Villa Rica Hosiery Mill and also worked in the Lumber Mill to make a living for his family.

He was a knitter at the Villa Rica Hosiery Mill. My father was called to serve in the US Army in 1944. It was World War II and he engaged in several battles in the European Theatre before he was honorably discharged as a PFC in 1945.

Times were very hard in those days for every family in Fullerville. There was no running water and no inside plumbing. Each house had an outhouse in their backyard because there was not sewage in Fullerville for several years. Everybody in the family had chores to do to help out. One of mine was to keep a trail cut in the back yard that led to the outhouse. The grass was cut with a manual push mower and that was hard work for a little boy. Mother had to wash our clothes in a round tin tub with an old scrub board to scrub the clothes on. It was an all day job for mother to get the clothes washed and dried for our family. We could catch the school bus but my friends and I liked to walk.

Some of my fondest memories of Fullerville are when we lived next to the old ball park, and I had one of the first peddle cars in Fullerville. My friends and I had so much fun with my car. I remember going to the Villa Rica Theatre and seeing a lot of western movies. We all used to sit around the radio and listen to the music. My father and I liked country and gospel and my brother Ernest like to listen to the mystery stories that were told on the radio. I liked to play basketball with my friends. I remember when my friends and I would walk up to Butler's Store get to pick out a treat if there was any extra money that week.

My favorite memory with my family was Christmas. We always had a live tree and we loved decorating it and seeing the lights playing on the walls. There were not a lot of presents to anyone; a few toys but fruits and nuts. My mother was a wonderful cook, and I remember the sweet smells of cakes being cooked and set aside for Christmas Day. Though there were not many material things, we were happy just visiting family and spending time with each other.

I would be remiss if I did not tell the story of the day I decided to sell my motorcycle which I had bought after I graduated and went to work at Sears. I had the motorcycle for several months when I decided to take it to the car dealer in Douglasville and trade it for a car. As I turned into the graveled drive the motorcycle slid and I lost control and down I went. We did not trade for a car with that dealer. On the way back home, the chain broke. When we got home I parked it for a few months and then when Mother and Dad were building their house on Old Stone Road, I let them have the motorcycle in return for $200.00 worth of kitchen cabinets for their new home.

That was the end of my interest in motorcycles.

Many friends and memories were made in Fullerville that I will cherish forever.

The Goat Man

Note: Ever wonder about the Goat Man? Perhaps more is known about him than may be thought.

Fortunately, this interesting character included West Georgia in his many travels across the nation.

Yes, a character; but he was a source of fascination to the local residents, old and young alike. His caravan, including a respectable number of goats, was always greeted warmly by the area people when his travel plans brought his unique procession their way.

Who is the Goat Man?

The Postcard Sold by the Goat Man as He Traveled His Way

Who "* GOAT MAN   IS *"

All the money I have over my expenses goes into mission work. I have a mission in Jeffersonville, Ga., and a church in Savannah, Ga. I try in my humble way to do the Lord's work.

It may seem strange to you that the one question I am asked most frequently is, "What is God?"

The same question was asked of Jesus Christ when he was upon this Earth, and apparently the people haven't gotten the word yet. Our preachers, rabies and priests are missing the boat. They should be preaching God and better living. I fear, however, that many of our ministers, whether Jewish, Protestant or Catholic, are more interested in the almighty dollar than they are in the Almighty God.

I am an ordained preacher, and I try my best with my limited education to explain God's work to the people, and if I can be instrumental in saving one soul I will feel amply repaid.

I see a lot of race hate during my travels, both in the South and in the North. And I can see more of it coming. It will end only when Christ returns to Earth, and I predict that this will be soon.

I feel though that preaching about the second coming of Christ is a bit foolish for too many people haven't yet heard about the first coming.

A parting thought—be kind to your neighbors, and your kindness will be returned many fold.

Postcard courtesy of Nancy McPhearson Bailey

The Goat Man

By Mrs. M. F. Word

"Mother, the Goat Man is here." When parents heard this, they knew it was time to load all of their children, plus some in the neighborhood, into the car to go find him.

Ches McCartney, the Goat Man, made Carroll County a yearly stop on his trips across the U.S. His birth date isn't known. He died in a nursing home in Macon, GA, in 1998. He is said to have been married and had a son who was murdered.

The Goat Man traveled with a herd of goats in a wagon filled with junk. Hanging from the wagon were all kinds of pots and pans. He had a long beard, was unkempt looking, and because of the many goats his surroundings were very smelly. But both children and adults were intrigued. He sold postcards of himself and his goats.

There were several stories about him, one that he was a wealthy eccentric. There was enough mystery about him that he was able to draw a crowd each year. And enough mystery that on the back hall wall of a home in Pensacola, the home of a former Carrolltonian, there is a portrait of him, found in a photography shop many years ago, a drawing of the square in Carrollton, and other Carroll County scenes.

The Goat Man Tells His Story

Courtesy of Nancy McPherson Bailey from the Goat Man's literature (transcribed)

My name is Chess McCartney, and I am known all over this nation as The Goat Man.

My new name was given me by my fans who me see along the highways and by-ways of this great nation with my 18 goats.

I have been called crazy, stupid, ignorant, and many other uncomplimentary names because of my way of life – herding a passel of smelly goats from Florida to Maine to Washington and California.

During my 30-odd years on the road, I have traveled well over 100,000 miles, and I have been in 49 of the 50 states of the Union. I haven't been to Hawaii yet, but the Lord willing I shall be there one day.

In order to make you understand my way of life, I feel that I should give some of my background.

I was born in Van Buren Township, Keokok, Iowa, the son of Albert McCartney and Louise E. (Russell) McCartney on July 6, 1901. Since Iowa is a farming country, I followed this profession until the 1930's.

At that time several misfortunes came to me. I lost my life savings in the bank failure and had to take a job on the Works Project Administration—the well known WPA.

While working at this I had the misfortune of having a tree fall across my body and shatter my left side. I was pronounced dead and sent to the morgue.

Luckily the undertaker was slow and by the time he got around to working on me the life came back into my body and I regained consciousness. It was as if I had been raised from the dead.

There was little left in this old body—I was crippled, tired and worn out. But hope springs eternal in the human breast, and soon I was well enough to walk.

A decision had to be made at this time. Should I give up and become a ward on the public, or should I try to make my own way? I decided to do what I could, and so my life with the goats began.

The goats have taught me a lot in the past 30 years. They don't, for example, care how I smell or how I look. They trust me and have faith in me, and this is more than I can say about a lot of people.

The Goat Man and His Wagon from the Goat Man's Literature courtesy of Nancy McPhearson Bailey

During my years on the road I have been reviled, cursed, beaten and shot at. I have been denied access to public accommodations, but I have survived.

I make my living by selling postal cards and booklets about myself and my goats. It costs a lot of money to travel from one town to another, but I manage.

The Goat Man Article

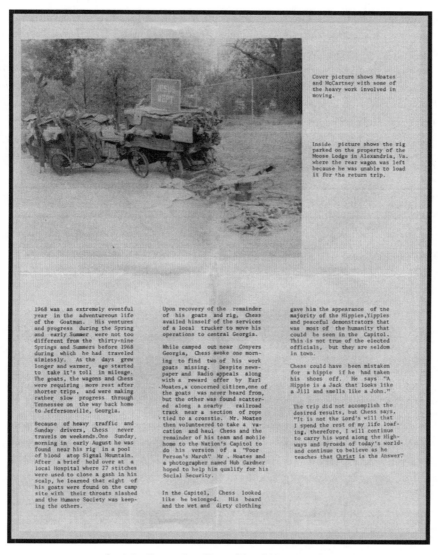

Cover picture shows Moates and McCartney with some of the heavy work involved in moving.

Inside picture shows the rig parked on the property of the Moose Lodge in Alexandria, Va. where the rear wagon was left because he was unable to load it for the return trip.

1968 was an extremely eventful year in the adventureous life of the Goatman. His ventures and progress during the Spring and early Summer were not too different from the thirty-nine Springs and Summers before 1968 during which he had traveled aimlessly. As the days grew longer and warmer, age started to take it's toll in mileage. The goats, the wagons and Chess were requiring more rest after shorter trips, and were making rather slow progress through Tennessee on the way back home to Jeffersonville, Georgia.

Because of heavy traffic and Sunday drivers, Chess never travels on weekends. One Sunday morning in early August he was found near his rig in a pool of blood atop Signal Mountain. After a brief hold over at a local Hospital where 27 stitches were used to close a gash in his scalp, he learned that eight of his goats were found on the camp site with their throats slashed and the Humane Society was keeping the others.

Upon recovery of the remainder of his goats and rig, Chess availed himself of the services of a local trucker to move his operations to central Georgia.

While camped out near Conyers Georgia, Chess awoke one morning to find two of his work goats missing. Despite newspaper and Radio appeals along with a reward offer by Earl Moates, a concerned citizen, one of the goats was never heard from, but the other was found scattered along a nearby railroad track near a section of rope tied to a crosstie. Mr. Moates then volunteered to take a vacation and haul Chess and the remainder of his team and mobile home to the Nation's Capitol to do his version of a "Poor Person's March". Mr. Moates and a photographer named Hub Gardner hoped to help him qualify for his Social Security.

In the Capitol, Chess looked like he belonged. His beard and the wet and dirty clothing

gave him the appearance of the majority of the Hippies, Yippies and peaceful demonstrators that was most of the humanity that could be seen in the Capitol. This is not true of the elected officials, but they are seldom in town.

Chess could have been mistaken for a hippie if he had taken his shoes off. He says "A Hippie is a Jack that looks like a Jill and smells like a John."

The trip did not accomplish the desired results, but Chess says, "It is not the Lord's will that I spend the rest of my life loafing, therefore, I will continue to carry his word along the Highways and Byroads of today's world and continue to believe as he teaches that Christ is the Answer".

Article from the Goat Man's Literature
Photo courtesy Nancy McPhearson Bailey

Fullerville: The Life I Knew There No Longer Exists

By Jimmy Matthews

My name is Jimmy Matthews. I'm the oldest son of Ray and Rozzie Lee Matthews. I have two deceased brothers Bobby and Larry, and a sister Kathy. We all grew up in Fullerville. Mother and Daddy both worked in the Hosiery Mill. Daddy was a fixer and Mother was a looper.

We lived in a series of four mill houses. Rent was $4.00 a month. I remember a well on the back porch and a wood stove in the kitchen. This changed later when a water line was laid. Each house had one tap in the kitchen. The ice man came periodically putting huge cubes of ice in the icebox. We had no refrigerator until much later. Milk was delivered to the front porch twice a week. During the summer when we were not in school, one of my chores was to ensure the milk got in the icebox. There was no indoor toilet. We made do with an outhouse that sat some distance in the back yard. Winter time found this arrangement very uncomfortable.

Dad raised and slaughtered two OIC hogs each year. Another of my chores was to slop the hogs. I did not like it when they were killed. I would never take part in the slaughtering of my pets. This also happened when a steer I raised as a 4H project was slaughtered. I refused to eat any of the beef that was canned at the canning plant at Villa Rica High.

My granddad, E.W. Redding, had a grocery store across from the hosiery mill. I earned show fare delivering groceries to customers in the village. We got our hair cut at Rayford Grubbs barber shop located next door to the pool hall which previously had been a grocery store.

Looking back, growing up in Fullerville was great. We didn't know we were poor. Everyone in the village was earning about the same so the standard of living was the same. There were lots of kids to play with. We had a ball-field located where a nursery now is located. The field was across the street from Matthews' Lumber yard where German prisoners worked during WWII. I remember some of us daring kids picked plums and gave them to the prisoners.

We walked from Fullerville to school in Villa Rica. No school buses for us back then. The road each morning was filled with kids of all ages heading for school. Rivalry between Fullerville kids and V.R. kids at school was great until high school where kids from the village dominated athletics. We were finally accepted as equals at this time. I even got to be captain of the football team and president of the senior class.

Saturday was "picture show" day. After getting an all over bath in a galvanized tub in the back yard, we headed in mass to the Villa Theatre to see a cowboy movie. We each got 25 cents. It cost 10 cents to get in the movie and a coke, popcorn, and candy cost 5 cents each. 25 cents went a long way in those days. We usually watched the movie twice then headed for home playing cowboys and Indians all the way.

Looking back, I'm amazed at how well the kids got along with each other. I remember few fights. We shared our toys and play things. My best friends were from the other side of the track that separated Cotton Town from Sock Town. There might have been a rivalry among the adults but not among the kids.

In 1950, Daddy was promoted to Foreman of the knitting department. So we moved to North Ave. in Villa Rica to a house for the foreman. I was 16 and just learning to drive the family car, a 1939 Ford. The 16 years I lived in Fullerville have given me wonderful memories of growing up there. I am proud to say that I'm a product of Fullerville.

I drove through the village last week and it was sad to see the mill closed. Daddy Redding's store and Grubbs barber shop are boarded up. The mill houses are no longer in the condition they were in my days there. The way of life there is like "Gone With the Wind". The life I knew there no longer exists.

Cannon Casket Story

By Kate Elliott from interview with Ann Broom

I went to see Kate Spinks Elliott today, visited with her almost 3 hours. She will be 85 this year. Kate and my Mama were close friends and neighbors, they also worked at Cannon's together. I gave her some pictures I had, that were made on her 80th Surprise Birthday Party, some muscadine jelly I made and a dozen of fresh brown eggs from my daughter Ellie and Darryl Farr's brood. Of course we talked about a lot of different things but following is what I learned about Cannon Casket from her.

She thought Cannon Casket started business in Villa Rica/Fullerville around 1949-1950.

She went to work there about 1951 in the Interior Department (the cloth/material parts). She was Floor Lady (supervisor) in the Interior Department for a while but suggested to her boss that Mrs. Iona Morris (not my mother but an older woman who worked there) would make a good Floor Lady and that she'd help her all she could and Mrs. Iona Morris was Floor Lady until Cannon closed.

John Jenkins was Manager and Hugh Bone was a boss when she went to work there.

At one time there were about 300 employees at Cannons.

The Union organizers did come there and "they voted the Union in" (I don't think she voted for it because someone told her that if the Union came in the plant would probably close down). As she put it "the union came in and it didn't last long". She couldn't remember what year the Union was voted in but not too long before Cannon's shut down, maybe 1964-1965. (From my memory, I believe my Mama was for the Union coming in but I didn't really pay much attention back then to all the talk about it).

When Cannon closed, some of the employees were offered jobs in the Atlanta Cannon location and she took a job there but it only lasted a few months and one day they went to work and the doors were padlocked.

She thought Cannon's closed in Villa Rica about the Fall of 1966 because she worked a few months in Atlanta but Atlanta closed in 1967. (I think Cannon's went bankrupt.)

I mentioned to Kate, that it seemed like that my Mama and some others went to see Lawyer Duffey (a new lawyer in VILLA RICA at that time) to try and get their "Profit Sharing". Kate said yes, some of them did but she didn't. This was probably because she kept working for them in Atlanta. I don't remember any of them ever getting anything. I can recall the names of many of the women who worked there but they are all dead now.

My Memories of Fullerville

By Patricia Kinney Pope Robinson

I lived with my grandmother and grandfather, Fred and Etta Bagwell. I remember living in the same house all my life. We had a nice porch, and we almost lived on it. We lived in the city limits, and I had to walk to school every day because there were no school buses then. It was only a mile, but, in bad weather, it seemed a lot farther. I remember one particular Saturday afternoon we had a special football game at school, and it was sleeting and raining. I decided to go anyway, and, of course, I had to walk. By the time I got there, my coat was frozen stiff, but I stayed for the entire game anyway.

I had friends who lived farther on into Fullerville, and we all walked together to and from school. Sometimes, we would go down a little dirt road in front of the school and go across the railroad track there at the end of the road. When we walked that way, we always walked by the mills, and I enjoyed that. Usually, though, I cut through at Fullerville Baptist Church and went on home. My grandfather, Fred Bagwell, worked at the Tatnal Prison as a guard, and he only got to come home every other weekend. I would walk to the bus station to meet him and then walk him back to the bus station on Sunday afternoon. When he retired, he was a night watchman at Cannon Casket Company.

My grandmother, Etta Bagwell, worked at Raymond Seal's in his furniture store in town. After that, she worked at the Shamrock Café as a waitress. My grandparents worked hard, but, unfortunately, they still had little money. I'm not sure how, but we always got by.

One day, Papa Fred told me to go to town with him to the Western Auto store. There, he bought me a Western Flyer Bicycle! It was blue and white. Papa Fred told me I'd better take good care of it, and I did. I even kept it in the house at night. I now had "wheels" so I rode everywhere. I went to Barbara and Sarah Fendley's house. Barbara's and Sarah's mother would sometimes take us to the fair. Then, the fair started coming to Fullerville near their house. I can remember having wonderful times at the fair and with them.

It was about that time that the goat man started going around, and he went to the same place as the fair had been. Frances and I would go every year. Then, he began to stop along the Carrollton Highway, and Mother and Daddy would take us to see him.

There were a number of kids who lived near me: Jimmy and Ted Bone, Gloria Ann Hulsey, Dorothy Jean Wix, Betty Pate, Charles and JW Pate, Jeanette Smith, Patsy Johns, and Kay McCurley, to name just a few. We kids didn't stay in the house like kids do now. I think we must have played ball every single day. We also would take two cans, make a hole in each one, run a string through the hole, and play *Walkie Talkie*. We walked on sticks, and we played "jump board" quite a bit. Our jump board was just a big plank laid across a block. One person would stand at each end and when one person landed on the board, the other would fly into the air! We entertained ourselves with these kinds of activities, and we always hated it when it became too dark to play.

I remember when Frances was born. Mother (Dorothy Leathers) was at Mama Etta's house, and we sent for Dr. Hogue to come deliver the baby. However, it was snowing so badly that Dr. Hogue had to walk to our house. He came anyway.

Mama Etta and Mother worked at the hosiery mill when they were young. Mother had a looper and Mama Etta had a table that she used to turn socks. I helped Mama Etta turn socks sometimes, but I never learned how to use the looper. I remember that Bitsey Hamrick had a grocery store nearby.

I remember so many people around us, people like Ben and Pearl Fuller, Ralph, Ray, and Clifford Fuller, and Rhena Fuller. The Brown's were their kids. I also remember Artie and Florence Taylor, Gladys and Eva Dobbins, the Thompson's, the Farr's, and many more. My memories are mostly about things around home, I guess. Maybe this is because we stayed home. I don't remember taking any vacations or anything---I just remember playing with friends in the neighborhood. My memories are wonderful, and I'm glad I had the opportunities I had. It was a good time and a good place to grow up.

The Curtis Farr Family

By Paulette Farr Crutchfield

Dad: John J Farr, B September 9, 1871 – September 26, 1949

Mom: Evie Mae Sewell Farr, B Dec. 30, 1882 – Feb. 10, 1958

Sons:

JAMES Henry "Crip", GUY, JODY, DURELL FARR, RADER Jefferson "Bulldog", HOWARD, WILBURN "WATTY", Paul LEONARD, and CURTIS Daniel "CURT"

Yep... nine boys. Enough for their own baseball team. Can you imagine being the only female in the house with 10 men? Bless my Granny's heart.

My story will be on the baby boy, Curtis Daniel Farr; my daddy.

Being the baby, my Daddy used to joke that Granny wanted a daughter so bad that by the time he came along, she made him wear dresses until he turned thirteen.

They, the boys, all had to help Pappa John in his cotton fields. They ate out of Granny's garden and the animals they raised and hunted. It was a hard and simple life, but a big family with lots of love to share.

He often spoke of his boyhood adventures with his brothers. He, Uncle Watty and Uncle Windy loved to play "Cowboys & Indians". Pappa John had gotten a new yearling bull, a very rambunctious one at that. Daddy and Uncle Watty being the Indians, captured Uncle Windy (the Cowboy and tied him to the seat of Pappa John's wagon. Rather than hitch up the horse, they hitched the wagon to the yearling bull; put the reins in Uncle Windy's tied down hands and slapped the bull on the hindquarters. The bull took off, ran under Granny's clothesline which caught Uncle Windy under the nose. Uncle Windy almost lost his nose that day, but Daddy and Uncle Watty lost their feathers, not to mention their bottoms and their dignity.

Most all the Farr boys played baseball. My daddy loved playing baseball and actually played for the Atlanta Crackers for a short time. Most all of them also served their country in the military. My daddy served over 9 years in the U.S. ARMY and in WWII (France, England, Italy, and Germany). He began writing to an old classmate (Oree Williams) while away. Actually, I think my mama, Oree, and some of her girlfriends began sending letters of encouragement to the local boys serving in WWII. Thus, began Mama's and Daddy's "courtship". Upon Daddy's return, they began dating and married on November 23, 1950. Coincidentally, that day was my daddy's 29th birthday and Thanksgiving Day. They married in a simple ceremony by Preacher Moon at his home.

Of course, they set up housekeeping in Fullerville. To my knowledge, they lived on Rockmart Hwy (Where my Aunt Vannie now resides) when I was born, then on N. Dogwood St.; to Third Street for most of my childhood, then into what was the former office (turned house) by the water tower at the cotton mill.

One of the detriments of WWII was that many young men came back scarred mentally. Many had turned to the use of alcohol and gambling in their off-time to deal with the perils of war. My daddy, never an angel by any stretch of the imagination, became an alcoholic and a gambler. Back in those days, the word alcoholism wasn't a recognized term. Alcoholics were just labeled as "drunks." My daddy knew all the folks who worked at the Villa Rica Police department and had occasion to spend the night there. He often came home on Friday, broke or with very little of his paycheck left. Still, my mama loved him beyond measure and he loved her. Mama worked at the cotton mill to pay our rent and to put food on our table. Their best friends were Curt and Esma Sauls. Some of my earliest memories were sitting on daddy's knee at the table while the four of them played Rook until the wee-hours of the morning.

On Third Street, we lived next to Granny Farr. That's where we lived when one very cold night in January of 1958, Granny backed up too close to the fireplace in her flannel gown. Neighbors hearing her screams awoke Daddy who broke down the door and put out the fire that was consuming Granny. She lasted 6 weeks in Villa Rica hospital. That was such a sad time for all of the Farr family. I adored my granny and living right next door, spent many hours in her company. I still recall sitting on her front porch in that old glider, eating buttered sugar biscuits. As an only child, I was privileged to have all the attention of my mama and daddy. They would play in the dirt with me with my Tonka toys (yes... my dolls rode on graders and in dump trucks. Daddy would push me for hours on my swing hanging from the old oak tree in the front yard.

Daddy even took me hunting with him in the Slickum's; Daddy with his shotgun and me with my BB gun, less the magazine, of course. He, Mama, and I often took Sunday walks back into Slickum's to pick berries, kill a rabbit or get

Sweetshrub. Oh that Sweetshrub; it made the house smell so good. Mama knew how to take a stick and make a toothbrush. I can remember her using one for just that reason.

The Temples and the Wheelers lived across the street from us on Third Street. The Temples were known for raising the best hunting dogs. Curly Temple, the oldest of the Temple boys was the good son and adored by all the neighborhood girls. Mama tells me that even at three years of age, I fell under his spell and hounded him constantly for attention. After Granny passed, "Tentil" (Mrs. Temple) took charge of spoiling me with buttered sugar biscuits. The Wheelers were a sweet family also, but were known for their rambunctious sons, who kept us entertained with their brotherly "love scuffles" in their front yard.

On one occasion, (my fifteen minutes of fame) at age three, I'm told I caused quite a stir in Fullerville. As I understand it, I went missing. , Mama was called home from the cotton mill (along with a number of other workers and neighbors, who came voluntarily). Daddy was called home from his job in Atlanta, and the Villa Rica police came out to help search for me. When Daddy got home, he began calling my little dog, Blackie. Blackie came running and led them to me down in Slickum's. Where they found me with my old BB gun and the entire lot of Mr. Temple's hunting dog. My explanation was, "I was just trying to kill us a rabbit for supper."

Sadly, Mama, Daddy and I left Fullerville and moved over to Old Town in 1963 and then to Dallas, GA in 1964.

We lost my daddy to Acute Lymphoblastic Leukemia on January 21, 1967, at the young age of forty-five. I only just turned fourteen. As a daddy's girl, to date, that was the saddest day of my life. But, I thank God every day for my sweet mama who is still with us and will be eighty-nine on October 16th. She now resides at the Douglasville Nursing and Rehab Center in Douglasville, GA.

Oh, the simple days of life in Fullerville. Those of us who had the privilege to live and grow-up in that small mill village have a treasure that could never be bought for all the gold Villa Rica had to offer.

The Legend of Peggy Cole Bridge and Creek

By Perry "Bill" Bailey

The Peggy Cole Bridge and Creek, located off Harlan Lane Road, was supposedly named after a young lady who drowned there. Many people had their own ideas about the cause of her drowning. Some say that she fell in after having a little bit too much to drink. Others say she jumped in, and some say she was pushed in. I don't know what the Coroner's report said, but reports from those I have interviewed say that she dove in and never came back up.

Peggy Cole Creek   pictured Ruth, Olin, and Andy Bailey in 1948.
From the Bailey family album

Over the years, a lot of people from the Villa Rica area have enjoyed swimming and fishing in Peggy Cole Creek. Many catfish have been caught there. My dad was the one who caught the big catfish that the fishermen had named Charlie. After trying to catch old Charlie for so many years, my dad decided to throw him back in, just like Howard did on the *Andy Griffth Show*. The creek is still there, but the Peggy Cole Bridge is gone. I wonder:

Is Charlie still there?

My Childhood in Fullerville

By Alan Dobbins

There is not a lot that I remember about my childhood, but do remember the good ole days in Fullerville. Some of the things that I do remember are as follows:

Summer nights at home – When we were young, we would all play outside till 9:00 or 10:00 pm at night. Most of the time we played under the streetlight and threw rocks at bats when they would fly by. Other times, we would be able to go to the ballpark and watch ball games. Many a time I got hit by foul ball line drives right up side my head. Guess that's the reason all my marbles are loose.

Fox and Hounds - During ball games or sometimes even afterwards, all the kids would get together, dividing up into two groups, one foxes and one hounds. The idea was the foxes would get a head start running, and then the hounds would be in pursuit. I think we use to run all over the place, down roadways, through yards; lying low in ditches, hiding in bushes. Whatever it took not to get caught. We would do this for hours without getting bored. I wouldn't last 2 minutes now!!

Fullerville Sawmill – What I remember most about the sawmill was playing in the sawdust. We would climb up into the chute after hours and jump into the big pile of fresh sawdust from the day's cuttings. There were many nights I went home with sawdust shavings all over me.

Throwing rocks at train cars/flattening pennies – Whenever trains would come by, normally three times a day, we would hang out beside the track and throw rocks at the cargo cars. That's a simple thing to do, unless you're standing to close to the track. I launched a rock at one, and wouldn't you know it came back at me. Hit me right smack in the nose! That's when I decided to just flatten pennies instead. A train could really flatten out a penny!

Family: I remember that lots of the Dobbins family lived in Fullerville. I know Jimmy Causey and I had many days of playing army out in his yard. Whenever we wanted something good to eat, it was a trip to Aunt Gladys's house across from Felix Leathers store. Now that woman knew how to cook! Just thinking about one of her strawberry cakes makes my mouth water today!

Cannon Casket: Where our house on Sugar Hill was located was directly behind Cannon Casket. I remember when it caught fire; my mother gathered me up and walked me to Aunt Gladys's home to stay the night. I remember her taking coffee with milk, crumbling up a biscuit into it, and then sprinkling sugar over the top. I don't know what it was called, but it sure was good.

Sugar Hill: My daddy use to grow our own food, be it vegetables from the garden, eggs from the chickens, meat from the chickens and hogs. Any pork that was killed was always kept in the salt box that we had in the house. Chickens of course were always fresh!

Now the little house we lived in didn't have indoor toilets and no bathroom. We took our baths in washtubs, the kitchen sink, or, during the summer through the water hose tied to the clothesline. The house only had 4 rooms total. One living room, one kitchen, and two bedrooms. Daddy, mother and myself shared one bedroom. My grandmother, and my four sisters, shared the other. And no one complained about not having privacy! I must admit though, I did hate having slop jar duty the next morning. It was a long walk to the outhouse!!

Daddy used to raise beagles. In the summer time they would lay underneath the house where it was cool. They had the right idea, and there were many times I crawled under there to join them. One day, I was bored and was pretending to fish with an old cane pole in the backyard. Not having anything to fish for, I took aim at the beagles under the porch. Sure enough, zip and one was on the line. I had hooked a poor beagle right in the lip! He was screaming and carrying on, argghhhh, argghhh, argghhh! I thought the poor dog was going to have a heart attack and me along with it, before I got that hook out. Sometimes, late at night, when it gets real quiet, I can still hear those screams.

Other firsts in Fullerville:

> I had my first beer at the ballpark. There was a bunch of us who sampled an unopened beer. I know it was me, Jimmy Silvey, Ricky Hancock, and others whom I can't remember.

> I had my first crush and my first kiss in Fullerville. You know who you are, and I will leave it at that!!

> I experienced my first taste of religion in Fullerville. Horace Wilson would scare the devil out of anybody!!

> I had my first bicycle in Fullerville. I could ride all day long, then when I got home would be asked where I was. I would only say, "Right over there." Of course my daddy had seen me half way to Dallas or Legion Lake when I was ask, but never said anything.

I hope that this helps in some way. I have many stories that I could tell, but most occurred outside of Fullerville. -Al Dobbins

My Memories of Fullerville, Georgia

By Margaret Washington Henry and Alton Washington

I started to school at five years old in Bright Star's one room building that was once Bright Star Church. The year was 1937. Our teacher was Miss Henderson, if my brother Alton remembers correctly. He went to school there in second grade. We lived on Sugar Hill and according to my brother; we lived there about eight years. Mr. Charlie Causey's family lived next door to us and Maurine was my best friend. I also liked Tom. I guess he was the only boy on Sugar Hill that wasn't kin to us. According to my brother Alton, our grandpa Washington was Mayor of Fullerville in the early years and Ben Rast was the policeman of Fullerville.

Fullerville had a restaurant and it was sort of a gathering place for the young and the old. One evening, our policeman Ben Rast got into a fight with another gentleman and it turned out to be a pretty bad fight. Many Fullervillians had gathered to watch the fight. Both men were bleeding badly. I think Sam Skinner was the owner of the restaurant at the time. The fight finally ceased after both men wore themselves out.

At the time we lived in Fullerville, everybody in Fullerville had outside toilets. Henry Carter had a one mule wagon and he kept the outhouses cleaned out once a month. He had two drums, a shovel, and a bucket of lime. The two big drums were for him to dump the waste into from the outhouses. Then he would sprinkle the lime to kill bacteria.

Grady Roberts was a boss at the hosiery mill where daddy and about all his family worked. I remember as kids we would stand in line at the mill to get our shots for school, which were furnished by the county who would send a nurse out to give the shots. The shots were very painful with those big needles and very sore arms. Uncle Lee Phillips ran a small store in the building where the restaurant was. I guess the only way I can remember that is because me and my sister Frances Washington George, use to go in and buy candy and put it on daddy's bill. But when he found out, he sure put a stop to that because back then a few pennies was like a few dollars now. Alton said Rayford Grubbs ran the Barber Shop and Shrimp Thomas was a boss at the cotton mill.

Norene House Broom: Her Life in Fullerville, 1924 – 1962

By Ann Morris Broom

Norene was my husband Charles H. Broom's Step-Mother and we lived next door to his Dad and Norene the last 28 years of their lives. Over the years Norene and I became close friends, and many times she and I would sit looking at her picture books as she told me of her life in Fullerville. Although, I can't remember all she told me in full detail, the following is based to the best of my recollection on those conversations.

Norene House was born September, 1910 in Paulding County, Georgia. In 1924 she moved with her Mother, Mrs. Mattie House, older sister Nellie and half brother Hulon Moon to Fullerville, Georgia. Hulon would join the U.S. Marines and Nellie went to work at the Hosiery Mil. On *September 26, 1924* at age 14, Norene started her first job with the Hosiery Mill in Fullerville and would work there continuously for almost 50 years. In the mid to late 1920's the country was economically depressed and having a job of any kind was certainly a blessing. For this 14 year old girl, it was very hard work and long hours but having a job, a house to live in and a little money to buy groceries and a few clothes and a pair of *slippers,* seemed wonderful to the daughter of sharecroppers who was just off the farm. Norene's Aunt, Sallie Dobbins, and her children moved to Fullerville. Her cousins also went to work at a very young age in the mills. It was good to have *kin folks* living near-by in the Mill Village.

Even though it was "hard times", the mid 1920's seemed like a happy time for the teenage girls in their *hats, hair bobs and roaring 20's dresses.* The young teenage girls that worked at the mills became quick friends. There wasn't really any kind of entertainment in the Mill Village, so on Sunday afternoons Norene and other girls would meet up and walk all around the Fullerville area together and take pictures of one another. Those pictures were a treasure to Norene, and it showed her life in early Fullerville. There were some people in the village that could "*make music*" and young people would get together at someone's home to listen to the music and sometimes they would have dances. If lucky, someone with a car would take them to places in the Villa Rica area, like Willis's Lake, Kinney's Lake or Boyd's Pond. Sometimes they would go as far as Marietta to "All Day Gospel Singings", or Pine Mountain near LaGrange for a picnic. A few years later, she would go to Stockmar's Lake, where she actually went up in an airplane ride. *She was a very brave girl! In* 1928 Norene's first "Beau" started "*courting*" her. They thought a lot of each other and he gave her a "*wrist watch*" on her birthday, but later they "*busted up*". In 1929 the stock market crashed and "The Great Depression" was rampant across the nation. It was a very hard time for the whole country and widespread unemployment of so many Americans including those in Fullerville, Georgia, but by being very frugal, somehow they persevered and made it through those very hard times.

By 1929 Nellie and Hulon had both married, leaving Norene and her *Mama* alone. They would live together in mill houses for 38 years. At times they would live in one side, and another family would live on the other side, of a mill house, but they lived the longest period in a four room house directly across Rockmart Road from the Hosiery Mill. In the beginning they had only a few basic household furnishings: wooden table and straight chairs, wood cook stove, cabinet, iron beds, chest of drawers, etc. Norene worked for a meager wage at the mill, her Mama did most of the cooking and indoor chores.

There was no electricity, plumbing, sewage or gas. After work Norene would do chores such as; draw water from the well shared by several mill houses, (this was before water lines were installed in the village), take out the ashes from the stove, bring in the wood or coal, trim the wicks and fill the "oil lamps", empty and clean the "*chamber pot*" (she never had a bathroom), and tend to the yard work. Sometime in the 1930's Norene bought some furniture which included a "*settee set & china cabinet*" from *Uncle Bud Taylor* who had a furniture store and was an undertaker in Villa Rica. After the village got electricity in the early 1940's, she got a refrigerator and an electric stove. After Fullerville was annexed into the city of Villa Rica in 1956, the residents of the mill village were taxed on their household furnishings. Norene and her *Mama* made a home for themselves and became very good friends to many of their neighbors. At times the Village seemed just like *one big family*.

The Early 1930's was a difficult and unhappy time. Norene became acquainted with a "*good looking, fast talking man*" and they married in the early 1930's. Sadly, the marriage was short, her husband turned out to be "*of very bad character*", they separated and Norene obtained a "*legal divorce*", she had no children. For the next 25 years she would be so busy working, making a living for herself and her *Mama,* she had no interest in any other man!

Norene joined Fullerville Baptist Church in the mid 1930's, there she taught Sunday School for several years. In 1939 she had 36 children in her Card Class and she loved each child very much. These children were from the Mitchell, Woodham, Mathews, Goff, Shelton, Thomas, Blair, Walker, Ferrell, Dial, McCalmon, Waldrop, Luther, Butler, Roberts, Wix, Millians, Tolbert and Skinner families. Her church was a very large part of her life. She served several offices of the church and with her best friend and fellow church member Sally Blair, cleaned the church and helped with the preparations for Communion. Norene was faithful to Jesus Christ, her Lord and Savior. She seldom ever missed a church service, prayer meeting, revival or baptism. Perry was a dedicated member of *The Eastern Star,* a charity organization. The Rev. Harold Wilson described Norene as a "*virtuous woman*" (Proverbs 31, Ruth 3:11); anyone that knew her would certainly agree.

On Sunday, December 7th, 1941 came the news that Japan had viciously attacked Pearl Harbor and the United States of America declared war. This war affected every family in some way. Husbands, brothers and sons went off to War with some never to return. Food rationing was enforced and money was short, but with some *"Government Sock Orders for the Service Men"*, the Hosiery Mill kept running.

Norene's life revolved around her mother, work, church, friends and neighbors in the Mill Village. After the war ended life seemed to get better for folks in Fullerville. In the 1940's and 50', most folks walked where they needed to go. Sometime Norene and a friend would walk the two miles to Villa Rica catch the bus to Atlanta to shop, returning later that day by bus and walk the two miles back to the village. Although they worked very hard in the mills, on occasion, someone with a car would take groups to "The All Night Gospel Singings" in Atlanta, Grant Park, Kennesaw Mountain and once to Lookout Mountain. Some of the ladies who worked in the Looping Dept. at the Hosiery Mill would get together at their village homes and have birthday parties for one another and sometimes they had tacky parties.

In the 1950's Ms. Mattie fell and broke her hip. To help with her care, a girl named Bobbie Jean was hired and Norene's cousin Carolyn also helped them. A few years later Norene had to have major surgery. On those two occasions, the mill moved a *Looping machine* to her village house and brought her sacks of work. Right there in her home, she looped and helped care for her Mother and then later after her own surgery, worked several weeks at home until she was able to return working in the mill.

Fall of 1961, a widower and a good Christian man started calling on Norene. He asked her to marry him, she had been independent and made her own way for a long time but after prayerful consideration, she said yes. Her Mother would go live the next 5 years with her other daughter Nellie. Norene sold or gave away most of her household furnishings as she prepared for marriage. March 1962, at age 52 Norene House married Herman T. Broom, and left the Mill Village but continued to work at the Hosiery Mill until the early 1970's. They were married 37 years. Norene loved the Broom family and all the Brooms loved her, especially Herman's 10 grandchildren who had a special *love* for their *Maw Maw*.

Those first years after marrying, she did so very much miss and grieve for her village home, church, neighbors and friends. Over the years she would clip and save newspaper pictures or articles about anyone she had known at Fullerville. That last year of her life in 1999 at almost 89 years old, her mind had gotten bad. We had to keep a close eye on Norene because many times in the evenings, she would get a sack and put some of her clothes in it and start out the door. We'd have to stop her and she would say, *Mama will be worried about me, I've got to be going, and I've got to be getting home.* **She wanted to go home. Home to her Fullerville!**

The Leathers Store   Photo courtesy of the Leathers' Daughters,
Fran Newton and Diane Wilson (See Fran and Diane in Part 2)

Growing up with Hope, Confidence, and Ambition

By Fran Leathers Newton

Hope, confidence, and ambition were three words that would readily describe my family in 1948 when I moved to 502 Jones Street, which was on the outer edge of Fullerville. I was six years old one Saturday morning when my parents did the most bizarre thing of my life up to that time. We went shopping for a home! I remember how excited I was to learn that we would be the only people in town who lived in a house that had wheels! My mother explained to me that we would live there until enough money could be saved to build a big house across the street. Living in that little house on wheels was a big adventure for me and there was no doubt whatsoever that we might not get to build that big, fine house. My parents talked in terms of "when" not "if". America had just proven itself in a war to end all wars and everyone in my small world was looking forward to better days.

In 1920 the hosiery mill by the railroad tracks in Fullerville had provided a life for my grandmother. Her husband had gotten killed while working on the railroad, leaving her to raise a six-week old child and tend a sick mother alone. Instead of staying on the in-law's farm, she chose to move to town to try to survive. She had a small amount of money from the railroad, but not enough to buy the house on Jones Street. She signed a note with Mr. Tom Matthews that allowed him to take her house if she failed to meet her responsibilities. She got a job at the mill. She got up at daybreak every morning and after feeding her animals and milking her two cows, she cooked a big country dinner. She left breakfast on the stove for her mother who would watch the baby until lunch time. At 12:00 the lunch whistle would blow and my grandmother, Mrs. Etta Pounds would actually run home from the mill to get the dinner on the table before her dinner boarders got there for lunch. After work in the afternoon, Miss Etta, as everyone called her, would go home, clean what Grandma had missed, tend her baby, milk her cows, feed her animals, and get supper on the table for her boarders. At night she sewed and made clothes for the neighbors, while her three or four lady full-time boarders laughed and talked to her about their lives. One of the women would tend the baby while another would snap beans or shell peas for dinner tomorrow. Miss Etta paid for her house right on time.

By the time my dad and my mother, Miss Etta's daughter, moved us into the house on wheels, Miss Etta's mother was old and in need of around the clock cares. That was the real reason our family moved. During the day my mother and grandmother worked at the mill, but they also did so at home. History books call this a time of "cottage industry". Every morning a man from the mill would pull up to the back door, pick up yesterday's work and leave three or four sacks of socks for my mother and grandmother to "loop" and "turn" for that day. Aunt Mandy, the maid, would take care of the cooking while we children kept an eye on my little sister, Dianne and watched to keep Grandma in the house and out of the road. The house was still full of laughing women, because Mama Etta still kept a boarder or two. It was a pleasant place. I can remember curling up on a pile of socks at night while the women worked and told stories. Mother would wake me up many nights and we'd stumble out to our little house on wheels where Dad had been asleep for hours because he had to get to Atlanta for work early in the morning.

Every member of our family had a job. My mother, Dorothy Leathers, taught me early in life that all of us had to work together if we were going to get where we were going. And we were going somewhere! We were going to move on up! Felix and Dorothy Leathers felt a strong responsibility to provide a good life for their children. By the time I was in third grade though, I recognized that we were not there yet. I noticed that the town children dressed much better than I. I noticed that many of them took dance and music lessons and went to scouts and parties. There was no one incident that led me to believe it, but slowly I learned that the people from Fullerville were not city folks. City folks didn't seem to think much of us. I tried to determine why, but all I could see was that we had outdoor toilets and they had indoor bathrooms. The mothers in town stayed home and made cookies all day while my mother worked at her home "looper". The town children wore better clothes and had more money. I can remember thinking that we had a long way to go before we got where we were going, but Mother and Daddy talked about getting there, so I knew I had to do my part.

My great-grandmother died when I was in second grade, so there was no use in our living so close to Miss Etta now. We moved across the street, not into a big house, but into a mill house that was about to fall down. I remember being cold all that winter. I also remember that one morning I got up to check on my gold fish and found him frozen in his bowl. My best friend, our sixteen year old maid, suggested that we wrap up Goldie and put him on the heater to thaw. I thought that was sort of dumb, but I really did want him to live, so I agreed. I stood right by the cold heater as it was heating up and sure enough, Goldie began wiggling! I put him into some warm water and he made it!

I remember adding another point of contrast to my life as a kid from Fullerville that year. Our next door neighbors had some big fights on the week-end. My mother said it was because of alcohol. Then alcohol became a reason for fights in our household too. I learned from my Fullerville friends that alcoholic disturbances were a way of life. I didn't see that kind of life from my friends in town or who lived out in the country.   My mother felt that Dad was holding us back by spending too much money on alcohol and since I noticed that my Fullerville friends were poor like us, I began to equate alcohol, fights, lack of money, and out houses with living in Fullerville. I was anxious to get out.

One summer my sister, Patricia, came running into the house shouting that the fair had come to Fullerville. I didn't exactly know what a "fair" was, but I decided since she was making such a fuss over it that I needed to go too. Mother gave each of us a dollar and told us to not stay long. We didn't think a thing about any dangers as we walked about a mile north from our house to the ball field to see the fair.

The ball field was then located on the left just before the three-way stop on Rockmart Road. When we got there, I saw the most amazing sight! A big wheel that was high as the sky that had seats and people were in those seats riding on that thing! There were fake horses going around and round and one could sit on a horse and ride! Oh my! I had wondered into a paradise of which I'd never dreamed! Patricia met some of her older friends and ran off with them leaving me alone, but I didn't care. I walked around and smelled the popcorn, the cotton candy and the horse manure, and I was in heaven. Soon, a man yelled at me to come on over and get myself a prize. Well, I thought, OK! I went over to talk to him and he told me to pick up one of those little ducks that were floating along and I'd get me a prize and all for the low cost of a dime. That seemed like a good deal to me, so I did it. Got myself a pretty ring. I put it on and moved on to the gun stand where I tried to shoot a balloon. I missed, but it only cost a dime. I moved on to the other booths and it didn't take but a minute for me to spend all my money and become broke. Just then, Patricia came running to get me to ride the swings with her. Oh my, I hadn't even had time to see them! But Patricia wouldn't give me any money! "Wait right here," I said. I suddenly remembered the purse Mother kept in the top of the closet with pennies in it. I ran home as fast as I could and got me a whole handful of pennies. Patricia and I had a wonderful time, but then when we got home she told Mother I had more money that she. That brought about a big problem of whether to tell the truth or not...

I must have been about eleven when the Medicine Show came to the ball field. It was hot and dry that summer, and by July I had just about worn out every idea of something adventurous to do. I was excited about the medicine show, because I had seen their wagon all opened up. It made a stage and at one end it had a sort of machine that played songs that sounded a lot like the fair. That night they had put little benches out for us to use as seats and I arrived early and sat on the front row. It was love at first sight. I suppose I should explain. At that time going to the movies was about our only form of entertainment. On Saturday there was always a cowboy show, but on Sunday the great musicals would be shown. I loved those classic musicals and knew the words to all the great songs. I'd practice singing them just as the stars sang them in the movies. So when this beautiful man walked out on that medicine stage and started singing all those favorite songs, I just melted. Never had I heard a real live person sing like that! He seemed to be singing just to me. I was on the edge of my seat mouthing the words and as he sung them to me, I sung them back to him. Oh! It was my first taste of romance! After the singing (I don't remember much else of the show except there was a girl who sang too, but she was nothing compared to that wonderful young man) they began telling us about their medicine. They had medicine for everything. All my family was pretty healthy though, so I didn't figure we needed any. But then glamour boy lowered the boom. He said if people didn't buy the medicine they couldn't stay long. He promised they'd be back the following night though, so we all needed to bring at least fifty cents for a bottle of something that would help us. My heart dropped. I couldn't see my Mother giving me fifty cents for something we didn't need. When I got home I told Dad about the show and told him they probably had some medicine that would help him. He readily agreed, which surprised me a lot. So, I got my fifty cents and went to bed happily awaiting another wonderful day in Fullerville.

I remember that as a happy week. Daddy would give me fifty cents every day to buy him some medicine, but for some reason he didn't want Mother to know he was taking it. I figured I had something to do all summer. But alas, one night I got there early and found that the show was gone. All that was left were the tracks of the heavy wagon as it left the ball field.

But there were ballgames! If there was a person named Sauls around, there would be a ballgame. Two things that have not changed much about Fullerville is this: The Sauls family plays ball, and ball is played in Fullerville.

In 1956 I was twelve years old when my daddy lost his job. Actually, he could have kept his job if he had agreed to move to Alabama to work at the Redstone Arsenal. I didn't want to move to Alabama. I had played ball myself since I was big enough to hold onto one, and we had a team who was already on its way to being great. I fussed and fussed and even threatened to move in with Miss Etta if the family decided to move. One day I came home from school and found a lot of machines in our front yard. They were digging and I saw a big square lined out with string. Mom told me that I had to keep a big secret, but we were building a grocery store in the front yard. "Get otta here!" I couldn't believe it! I was so excited and relieved that I wasn't going to have to move to Alabama. Mom also told me that it was my fault that she and Dad had mortgaged their house to do this. She let me know real quickly that I had to help our family make a go of the store. Oh, yes, yes, I would work my heart out!

I did, and so did they! From the time the stock started arriving we were there day and night getting the store ready. People would see us working and stop to see what we were doing. If any of my friends hung around, my Mom had them working in no time. We had happy days and evenings getting everything ready for business. I never gave a thought to what poor Mr. Petty must be thinking. He had a store right up the street from us and had always been real handy when I needed a snack. But now, the snacks started arriving and my mouth started watering. Mother announced that I could have one snack a day. Daddy overruled that though. He said I could eat anything I wanted to eat as long as I was there to help them. I'm telling you, I ate until I couldn't. I remember Mrs. Anne Anders was my health teacher that year and she weighed us every month. She gasped when she found that I had gained twenty pounds in one month! That was fine with me though. No longer was I called Long, Tall Sally!

Soon, we were so busy we didn't have a moment's rest. We had finally been able to build us a house, but we didn't spend much time in it. My Dad opened up at 5:00 A.M. and sold gas to the Atlanta commuters. My Mom worked late into the night looping her socks in the store while I waited on the customers. I did homework between customers. Our store was more like a meeting place than a place of business. Our regular customers came in every day and we could almost have their milk and bread waiting on them, they were so regular. They told us about their families and we told them about the latest sick people and the news around town. I learned how to talk to people and count change at the same time. My Mother was the personality of the store and my Daddy did the business. They were a great match. I spent many happy hours with Daddy cutting up chickens on Friday afternoon. We would try to beat our time each week. We got to where we could cut up and box sixty chickens in sixty minutes!

Because Daddy had had polio when he was a child and was crippled, Mother and I tried to take as much of the heavy load off Daddy as possible. But I never heard him complain. In winter he would kill hogs and grind them into sausage.

We'd fry some in the store and sell a whole hog in a day. The smell would drive people into buying and hurrying home to cook! Dad went to the farmer's market to get fresh produce every week. He would get up at 3:00 am to get it back in time to open. People knew when the fresh stuff was coming in and would be there waiting on him. Sometimes our customers would help unload the truck.

We had a bench at the front outside and I always enjoyed sitting out there talking to all the old men who gathered to visit. They would pump gas for us and watch to see if anyone ever tried to drive off. They also washed the windshields for all the pretty women. They let the men do their own. My parents never minded the people who hung around. We'd just take them into the family and put them to work. If a person ever came by begging, I knew exactly what to put in their box. I wonder how many boxes of side meat, dried beans, shortening, meal, flour, sugar, oatmeal, potatoes, onions, cabbage, and redlinks my Dad gave away. We also sold a lot of sugar and cans of hops. I remember I asked one day what a man was going to do with all that sugar and those hops. He said he was going to get things hopping! Mom explained later that he brewed beer at home.

One day Rev. Camp came into the store and went looking for something. Finally, he said he couldn't find what he wanted. Mother asked him what he was looking for. He shyly said he needed a little sugar. Mother laughed, grabbed him by the arm and said, "Come on Rev. Camp I've got all the sugar you need in the back room". Scared that poor man to death and gave us all a big laugh. We had one man who was really bad to steal after shave and rubbing alcohol. He would get drunk and come in to call Clyde Jones, the local undertaker to carry him home. Clyde would drive up in the hearse and take him home. We finally had to tell the man we couldn't sell him any more alcohol. But he would catch us all busy and grab a bottle and throw a quarter on the counter for it. One day he went out the door after paying for a bottle. I told Daddy he'd done it again. Dad said, "I thought we were out of rubbing alcohol" In just a minute here came the man again, spitting and wiping his mouth and cussing. He set half a bottle of mineral oil on the counter and said, "I want my quarter back!"

I began to notice that every morning more and more cars were arriving at the store early, about the time we opened. My Uncle Lewis began coming every day and I knew he, too had a store to run, so I got sort of curious. One morning I got up early and went out to see what was going on. I walked in and no one was around. I walked toward the back of the store and found the bread man, the milk man, several customers, Uncle Lewis and Daddy all crowded into a circle. And they were throwing dice on the floor. "Oh, I'm telling Mama", I said. All the men rose up and looked at me, eyes big and guilty. My Uncle Lewis said, "Here's a dollar for her" as he handed me two dice. I threw them on the floor and won all their money! "Now, who you *gonna* tell?" laughed my uncle. Every time I got a chance I played with the men!

Happy Hudgins was named for his personality. He was one of the happiest boys I ever met. One summer Daddy went to Fort Valley to buy a truck load of fresh peaches. Dad told me if I would peddle them in Fullerville and in the Crack, he'd give me a dime a basket. I went and got Happy.   We had hundreds of little baskets and Happy would fill them up as I drove from house to house. He would jump down and run to a house and greet the homemaker with his happy smile and collect a dollar for a basket of peaches. No one ever turned Happy down if they had a dollar. I paid him by the day and made lots of money. Daddy started bringing whole truck loads of watermelons for us to peddle. Soon, the local supermarket owner went to the city council and asked them to pass a "No Peddling" law. He said Happy Hudgins was about to put him out of business!

With churches all around us Daddy was subjected to a lot of criticism for having the store open on Sunday. He used to laugh and say if the church people didn't stop after church to buy something he wouldn't need to stay open. If we were ever closed and someone needed something, they would simply come to our door and knock. My Dad wouldn't ever turn anyone down. We never had a Christmas morning that we didn't share with some of our customers who might have forgotten the batteries or even worse, the coffee!   But back to the church people, one lady kept telling Daddy he needed to close the store and come to church with her. He gave her every excuse he could come up with, and finally one day he told her he just plainly didn't want to go to her church. She asked him why. He said, "Because your church is full of hypocrites. That is why." She was a really old lady. She put her little hands on her little hips and sweetly said, "You know you are right. There are a few hypocrites in my church, but hadn't you rather go to church with a few of them than to go to hell and be with all the hypocrites?" Daddy didn't have an answer to that one!

As I grew up in our store, I came to love the people who traded with us. I came to see that people were people and it really didn't matter where a person lived. Where we live might influence us, but it doesn't define us. I met some wonderful people who lived in Fullerville. Those people helped my family reach our dream of overcoming poverty. The people of Fullerville spent their money in Villa Rica, so ultimately they helped build our community and our town. Many of them influenced me, corrected me when I needed it, and contributed a lot to the values I learned.

Born and Raised in Fullerville and Proud of It!

By the Reverend Charles Williams

Charles Williams was born May 16, 1926 in Fullerville, Georgia. The youngest son of Homer Lee and Sarah Frances/Fannie (Browning) Williams. He had two older sisters, Oree and Pauline. His Father's parents were Jack and Becky Willliams, and Homer's siblings were Monroe, Pearl, Vinnie and Garfield Williams.

When he was a child, he never dreamed of ever leaving Fullerville. Charles joined Fullerville Baptist Church and was baptized by Preacher M.B. Moon 1937-1938. He went to school at The Fullerville School grades 1 - 3 in one room, the teacher was Ms. Effie (Alfie) Henderson (the school building was previously The Bright Star Church). It was located, second house down from the Cotton Mill on right side of road (now there is dirt piled up against it).

Tubby Rainwater and Charles Williams
Photo courtesy of Charles Williams

The mill office was on the left as you turned in to go to the mill. He said the *"first Jail"* was wood and they had locked somebody up, the prisoner set a fire and burned his way out! So, then they built it back, out of some kind of block or concrete (that couldn't burn) and it is still there today. He remembers Ben Rast and Ben Fuller being Policemen in Fullerville and when he was a little boy, the Fullerville Court House was located in a side room (about 12' x 18') connected to Mr. Florence's Store.

Just about everybody in Fullerville had *Nicknames,* his was *"Easter".* He *picked a guitar* and his buddy, Tubby Rainwater *blew a jug.* He said "the railroad tracks were sorta like a dividing line between the Cotton Mill and Hosiery Mill Folks and sometimes, *they'd get to feuding over something, like the Hatfields and McCoys"* . In Fullerville, everybody knew just about everything about each other but they all cared for one another. When he was growing up you would keep your distance from *"The Honey Wagon"* because of the smell (this was the wagon that came around and cleaned out the outside/toilets in Fullerville).

In Fullerville when he was a *youngun,* there wasn't much to play with, but if somebody was lucky enough to get hold of an old tire, *they'd roll and roll that thing.* Once, some of them were playing, 3 of them had some tires and were rolling them and having a good time," Carl had a *"big ole tire,"* and Johnny wanted a turn at rolling it, and Carl said, "No!" So Johnny took the tire away from Carl and set fire to it, he then took the other boys tires and set them on fire also. Soon they heard the fire alarm and the fire truck coming. Charles and his buddy Tubby Rainwater *took off a running home,* as fast as they could. They ran into the house and got under a bed and stayed there for a long, long time. Johnny, who had started the fire, was fined one dollar. In Fullerville, if you were fined for something, the Mayor would let you work off your fine by cleaning out ditches, the sides of the streets and the like.

Charles got his first guitar from his Aunt Vinnie, she had been visiting friends and someone there had a guitar and she bought it. When he saw the guitar, he wanted it! His Aunt Vinnie said he would have to pay for it. He *picked cotton* for a whole week to get enough money to pay for that guitar and he taught himself to play it. He also helped some others learn. They would get together at one of their houses and play. One boy named Olin Bailey had a guitar and he could cord, but he didn't know when to switch cords, so Charles would signal him with some little gesture. Before Charles got his guitar, he and a couple of other boys, Tubby Rainwater and T.J. Butler had a little *"Jug Band",* Mr. Florence would let them play at his store right next to the railroad tracks and he would give them a *Pepsi Cola* for playing.

When the Village first got electric lights in the early 40's, he remembers they cut on the light bulb that hung down from a cord in the middle of the ceiling and his Grandmother said "cut off that bulb, it will burn all the gas out of it". She didn't understand electricity. His Grandmother could hardly hear at all and when WWII started in 1941, all the young boys in the village started collecting "scrap iron", his grandmother couldn't figure out what was going on with all the boys running around. His Grandmother kept saying, "What's going on, somebody tell me what is going on, his mother spoke up real loud and told her that *war had broke out and the boys were gettin up scrap iron to help make bullets for the soldiers to shoot,* then Grandmother said "Well, they got my shovel!"

There were lots of boys in the village but Charles best friend was Tubby Rainwater. When Charles was a young boy his Dad made him a swing with a rope and old tire on a tree in their yard. Once a boy they called *Slick* came by and wanted to swing but Charles didn't want to let him swing right then, so *Slick* went on. After swinging for a while Charles went into the house, later returning outside to swing again. Unknown to him, Slick had climbed up in the tree and cut the rope and when Charles began to swing, it broke with him and fell. Slick got into trouble and said his Mama *like to have killed him* for cutting that rope. Kids in the village really didn't have any toys, but one thing they made and played with was a ball. They would get some scrap thread and soak it in kerosene for a week, and then they would wrap the thread around and around making a ball from it.

Kids playing pranks on one another in the mill village was common. Drawing water from the well shared by several village houses was his sister Oree's chore, every evening she would go out and draw two big buckets of water for the night. Carl Tapley would hide in the bushes with his buckets waiting for her. She'd draw her water and fill the buckets, and Carl would sneak out of the bushes and pour one of her buckets of water into his bucket. Also when he was just a little boy, Charles remembers that Mr. Spinks would come thru the village and take his false teeth out of his mouth and it would "just scare him to death."

When Charles was about 10 years old in 1936, the building of the "Big Water Tank" at the Cotton Mill was a very big event in Fullerville. Before the Big Tank was built, the hosiery mill had a Wooden Tank and some sort of water pool, but after the Big Tank was finished, it served both the Cotton Mill and Hosiery Mill.

Charles's Dad worked at the Cotton Mill, his job was as a "Fixer in the Spinning Room" and his sister Oree, worked there on the Spinning Frame. His sister Pauline worked as a Practical Nurse at the Villa Rica Hospital. Charles got a job at the Cotton Mill as a teenager in 1943 as a Doffer, he made $16 for a 40 hour week.

There was not any kind of employee medical insurance in those days and Charles' Mama was sickly a good bit and had to have the Doctor. The Doctors B.C. Powell, Earnest Powell Sr. and Earnest Powell, Jr. and Dr. Hogue made house calls. The regular charge for having the Doctor was $5. If you couldn't pay all right then, you'd pay later. You could buy your groceries at the Mr. Florence's store on credit and pay when you got your pay from the mill and get your hair cut at Rayford Grubbs Barber Shop next to the store or Carl Hicks would cut your hair in his home, they both charged 25 cents.

In 1944 at the age of 17 and weighing less than 100 lbs, he knew he would be drafted soon. He went to his Daddy and told him that he didn't think he would be able to carry the big back packs the Army boys had to carry and he asked his Dad to let him join the Navy. (When he got out of the Navy, he weighed 135 lbs.).

He was in the U.S. Navy 1944-1947 and remembered well the day *The Japanese Surrendered*, when his time was about over in the Navy, his Captain (who called Charles "Willie") said, "Willie, I'm going to be going down toward South America next, why don't you just stay in the Navy and go with me".

Charles told his Captain, "Sir, I don't think so, cause I sure am *a wantin* to see that *Red Light* in Villa Rica." He wanted to go *Home.*

He came back to Fullerville and married Jean Smith later in 1947. He was called to preach and was ordained in 1954. He and Artis Busbin started having Tent Revivals in the mid 1950's. He has pastored many Baptist churches in the Villa Rica Area including New Georgia, Star of Bethelhem, White Oak Springs , Abilene, Harmony Grove, Callie Harbin, West Carrollton and also in Riverdale. After pastoring 13 churches, he is now retired from preaching.

Some boys from Fullerville Baptist Church that became preachers are: Charles Williams, Guy Rainwater, Carl Tapley, Ralph Tapley, Jesse Howell, Joe McMichen, Tubby Woodham, Ollie Shadrix, Carl Shadrix, Don Butler, Terry Butler and Kenneth Johns. Garland Odom was the pastor at Fullerville Baptist Church in the 1950's and is still living.

Charles Williams said he was born and raised in Fullerville and he is proud of it, "I moved out of Fullerville in the mid 1950's, but over the years when I would be riding through with some of the fellows, I'd always say," OK now, take your hats off, we are passing through Fullerville, and it is *Holy Ground*!"

The Johns Family in Fullerville

By Kenneth Johns

In 1916, John W. Johns could see the "handwriting on the wall" for his blacksmith trade. He operated a blacksmith shop directly across the road from New Georgia Baptist Church, as had his father, James Jackson Johns. John had owned an automobile himself as early as 1912, and understood that the days of horses and buggies would soon be over. Although farmers would still need their farm implements and their mules shod, but the days of the blacksmith were numbered. And so he moved his wife, Mary Magdalene (Maggie), and their four sons to Fullerville the same year it was incorporated. He took a job in the cotton mill. His four sons, Comer, Cliff, Carl, and Hugh would all eventually work in the mills also. In 1919, he was licensed by the city of Fullerville to operate a "jitney", or a taxi. They also had a small store at one time.

From 1916 to 1924, the family lived in the mill village. He then moved them to Griffin, to Atlanta, and, in just a matter of months, back to Villa Rica, They lived in Villa Rica for a short time, while he worked in the blacksmith shop located at the current intersection of old Highway 61 and Wilson Street. Soon, however, he bought a house in Fullerville on Rockmart Road (now 502 North Dogwood Street), and went to work again at the mill. In the spring of

1926, he was diagnosed with stomach cancer, and died April 10, 1927. He had continued doing light work at the mill almost until his death. During this time, he put together boxes that were used to ship the yarn.

John's son, Carl, married Jewell Swafford from Douglasville in 1924. They had two children. Doris was born in 1926, and Robert in 1930. Carl and Jewell lived in Fullerville, and worked in the mill until the 1940's. They then moved to Atlanta, and started the Dixie Auto Seat Cover business. Carl died in 1974, and Jewell in 1998.

John's son, Cliff, married Lena Mae (Sis) Matthews in 1936. They had one daughter, Patricia Ann, who was born in 1937 and died in 1970. Cliff worked in the cotton mill and Sis in the hosiery mill all their working life. They built a house directly across Rockmart Road from the family home. They were lifetime members of Fullerville Baptist Church. He followed his older brother, Comer, as pianist for a number of years. Cliff died in 1970 and Sis in 2008.

John's youngest son, Hugh, married Ruth Odom in the 1930's. He worked in the mill, and played on the mill's baseball team. In those days, cotton mill teams were a source of great community interest and pride. During the Depression, Hugh was recruited to "work" and play for the Hogansville mill team. He also had a tryout with the Atlanta Crackers. Hugh served in the U. S. Navy during World War II. He served on a destroyer escort, the U. S. S. Foreman, during the Battle of Okinawa. The ship was hit by a Japanese Kamikazi plane and a bomb during this action, and he was awarded a Purple Heart. Following the war, he moved to Atlanta to work for General Motors. He and Ruth had one child, Ricky, who was born in 1948. Hugh died in 1982 and Ruth in 1998.

John's oldest son, Comer, who was born in 1899, was my father. Except for a short time in 1929-30, he worked in the cotton mill until his retirement in 1965. In 1929, he and a partner (Mr. Veitch) set up a mill to grind corn in the now historic Barnes Hardware building in Mableton. This building is next to the railroad. The idea was to grind the corn into corn meal, and transfer it directly onto railroad cars for shipment. However, the stock market crashed in October, 1929, money "dried up", and the business soon failed. He then returned to Fullerville, and the cotton mill. During the Depression, the mill's first shift never shut down. However, when he returned, only the second shift was available. Work for the second shift was "off and on" during the Depression years.

Comer, Cliff, and Carl all worked as "fixers" at the mill. Down time meant lost money, and it was their job to keep the machinery running. According to Edmund Sauls' book, The Linthead, Comer was also his foreman in the late 1940's. In his younger years, he had played on the mill's baseball team. He served as pianist at Fullerville Baptist Church, beginning in the 1930's

103

when the church was located in the mill village, and known as **Bright Star Baptist Church.**

In 1946, Comer married Ruth Andrews. She, along with her sisters Ruby, Bessie, and Christine, had moved to Fullerville from their Dad's farm in New Georgia a few years before. She worked at the hosiery mill until her retirement in the late 1970's. I was born in 1947, and my sister, Judy, in 1953. During the years before we started to school, she "looped" socks at home on a machine provided by the mill.

In the mid 1970's, Comer finally sold the old family home, and built a new house a few hundred yards up North Dogwood Street. He died March 22, 1987, and Ruth on October 27, 1994.

Comer served as the Treasurer for the city of Fullerville from 1945 to 1950, and as a Councilman in 1948 and 1949.

Katie's Story

By Katie Marvene Bice

I was feeling quiet nostalgic about growing up in Fullerville after being at the reunion and seeing so many old friends. It brought back so many good memories. I wish more could be done to improve the conditions in Fullerville. They have no sidewalks, street lights, no improvements or upgrades at all. It is a shame it has been neglected in such a way. The families living there pay taxes just like everyone else and deserve more.

Growing up in Fullerville was the best experience a child could have hoped for. We had many parents watching over us and nurturing us, we could play all over the neighborhood without our parents worrying about our safety, we used our imaginations playing games and forming clubhouses, played ball until it was too dark to see the ball anymore, and every home we went into there was always good food (home grown, home cooked) and we were always welcome to eat. What we lacked in material things was greatly overshadowed by the genuine love, caring, and feeling of safety we were privileged to grow up with. I never realized I was "raised poor" until someone (not from Fullerville) told me. We were "rich" in every way that counted."

Fullerville and My Next Door Neighbor

By Joyce Massey Fain

Growing up in Fullerville was hard and had many challenges. Most of the homes in Fullerville were heated with coal or wood heaters and the houses were not insulated to keep the wind out thru the walls and the windows. Most of the floors were covered with linoleum rugs to keep the wind from coming thru the floor. As a child I remember that we moved a lot and I often wondered why. As I got older, I realized that we moved for a better house or lower rent. Business people of Villa Rica purchased the houses therefore the upkeep and the rent on each house was not the same. The houses on the cotton mill side were the oldest houses of Fullerville because they were built first and the houses on the hosiery mill side were not always a better house. Some of the houses on the cotton mill side of Fullerville were better conditioned than the newer houses on the Hosiery Mill side. I enjoyed living on the cotton mill of Fullerville because the yards looked so much neater and cleaner. This is still true today. I love the old trees, the flower beds, and the well kept look of the houses.

On cold winter mornings, the children would have to get up to a cold house and get dressed in the warmest clothes they had. The boys could wear pants and shirts with their socks and shoes but the girls were not allowed to wear pants and could only wear dresses or skirts and blouses. The girls only had short white socks to wear with whatever shoes they had. A lot of the boys and girls had nothing like a sweater or jacket or warm coat to wear and we would have to walk from our house to the nearest bus stop and wait on the bus in the cold wind and sometimes rain. There were no bus shelters where the children could get out of the cold and the rain as we see today. The buses were not very warm

Joyce Massey Fain & Dad
Photo courtesy of Joyce

and so the ride to school sometimes seemed forever. I remember that the most popular shoe that both the boys and girls wanted was the black and white saddle oxfords, but you did not see many of those on the children who grew up in Fullerville as a place to live and food to eat were much more important than a pair of fancy shoes.

I also remember that some of the men in Fullerville were bootleggers and made corn liquor in the woods behind some of the houses and the mills. This corn liquor could be bought from under the counter at one of the stores in Fullerville. It was sold behind the counter of one of the stores located in

105

Fullerville. The bootleggers were dirty, long hair, smelled and scary. The men of Fullerville would meet at this store and buy the corn liquor and sit around and talk. These family men of Fullerville had no right to spend their hard earned money which should have been used to provide for their family. Alcohol should have been voted in a long time ago. Just think of the tax dollars that could have got sewage in Fullerville years before the 1970's by stopping the bootleggers and voting in alcohol. I have wondered many times if the churches had any idea that by preventing the legalized alcohol was only going to help the bootlegger. It would have also depended on the establishments of our fair city who were the powerful and wealthy that controlled our city and who more or less looked after the special interest groups that have held Villa Rica back from progress for so many years.

People had to buy the things they needed on credit most of the time because working and making an average hourly wage of 50 cents an hour was the only way they could survive. I remember things like the Dutch Oven Bread Truck having a route and stopping in the Fullerville community and you could buy fresh bread, pastries, etc. if you happened to have enough money for a treat that week. Stubbs and Hobbs Furniture had a route that came thru Fullerville also and Lee Tuggle from Temple drove this route for as long as I can remember when I was a little girl. I always loved for him to come because he would sit down in the rocker Mom was buying on credit and paying weekly and get me up in his lap and give me the bag of candy that he and his wife Ruth had fixed for me. People paid their life and health insurance weekly or monthly to an insurance agent who came by to collect and mark their premium books showing they had paid. A lot of these families never benefited from the life insurance policies because most of the insurance was term insurance and was no good by the time some of the people passed away.

I have saved the best memory of most of the children in Fullerville for last. That is the scary memory of the legendary "ROGER"! The legendary "Roger" was said to be half man and half animal. Some called him just Roger and some called him white Roger! Legend has it that "Roger" was made up by the night watchmen at the old mills to discourage kids from coming over to the mills and lumber yards at night for safety reasons. It has been said that Ben Rast, the Fullerville Police Chief, encouraged this story to keep the children of the village safe and off the streets at night.

Roger's hangouts were in the woods behind the Fullerville Ball Park, now the soccer fields, and also Slickum's because of holes and caves in the ground where gold mining was attempted in these two locations. The gold mining in these two locations was not as successful and very little gold was found in these mines. Gold mining was more successful on the Flying S Ranch which was owned by the Stockmar family.

You don't hear much about the legendary "Roger" by the generations today but occasionally conversation about Roger pops up by some who are well familiar with the "Legendary Roger".

As many as have claimed to have seen UFO's today, the same holds true with the legendary "Roger". Many say they would swear on their grave that the "Legendary Roger" walked the woods and village of Fullerville at night.

DOES THE "LENGENDARY ROGER" LIVE ON? YOU DECIDE!

My Next Door Neighbor

I lived in Fullerville from my birth in 1950 to 1953. We then moved to my father's hometown, Grantville, Georgia and later moved back to Fullerville in 1954 until 1967. Little did I know that the author of the book would be Perry "Bill" Bailey, my next door neighbor. I knew Perry from my childhood as my neighbor, going to school together, and a friend and playmate as were many of my other Fullerville friends. We rode the same school bus and Perry was always a special person to me and maybe that was because we were neighbors or maybe because we were just close friends.

I don't really know how to explain it, but Perry was different from most boys that I went to school with. He was courteous, mannerly, just a little gentleman. My Mom and Dad always liked Perry and he was their pick of the four boys. They would see Perry working in the yard, hanging out clothes for his mother and I was always thinking why it was always Perry doing the chores. I remember the four boys, Jimmy, Andy, who was the 3rd boy, and Doug. I would always see Perry or Doug pushing the lawnmower, not Andy! Ha-Ha!!! I always saw Andy on the porch or playing music with other boys. Sometimes, my parents and I would sit on our front porch and listen to them play.

I remember one time in particular when things were not going so well with Mom and Dad. I was sitting on the back porch crying. Perry saw me and came over and talked to me trying to comfort me and get me to stop crying. He said everything would be okay! Many times I could see Perry under the shade tree with notebook and pencil, writing for hours. Of course I was just thinking he was doing homework. I did not know that he was writing a journal. What got my attention was that he continued to write in his journal in the summer months when there was no school. Many times on an overcrowded city school bus that we rode, he was lucky to find an empty seat. After sitting down, looking and seeing me or another girl standing with an armload of books, he would get up and say, take my seat. Of course I always hugged his neck and kissed him on the cheek and thanked Perry and he would turn red as a beet with a big smile on his face. Other guys would whistle and tease him by saying,

"Oh, Perry got a kiss!" I will never forget the day that Perry and I were walking home after school on the day I had given him a kiss and Perry said, "Hey Joyce, you don't have to thank me or give me a hug and kiss when I give you my seat on the bus." Of course, when he said that, I knew I was going to have a little fun with him, so we stopped a minute and I said, "Perry you're serious! I don't have to thank you or hug you and give you a kiss on the cheek?" As the school bus passed by us as it was leaving, I gave him another hug and kiss and all I could hear was Perry saying, "Joyce, the school bus is coming by !" and Perry's friends laughing and shouting, "Oh, Perry got a hug and kiss!"

Was I mean or what? (Smile!) I got the biggest kick when I could embarrass Perry, but he was a good sport and took it well. Of course because I had started something, some of the other girls started it too just to aggravate and get a laugh, but Perry had caught on and started walking to school rather than ride the school bus. Most guys would have considered themselves lucky, I would think, but Perry and his friends were at the age of being little boys and when the girls would tease them or kiss them on the cheek, they would say "YUCK" and wipe the sugar off.

I guess my heart went out to Perry as a child when I realized that he was seeking an education and he came to me to help him with his schoolwork. My reply to him was "Perry, can Andy not help you or your Mom or Dad?" He replied to me that his schoolwork was over their heads and they would not even know where to begin. Andy, who was his older brother, was too busy with the girls and music because he was a teenager. I could relate to that because I was in the same situation.

As I began to try and explain some of the math problems and English that he had asked me to help him with, my heart went out to him even more because I realized how much he was struggling to understand as I explained and tried to get it into his head how to work the problems out. I even questioned myself that maybe I wasn't explaining it well enough. Then it hit me that Perry had been placed by the school system up a grade when he should have been held back and I have seen this in the school system during the time I was in school with other children. If there was any fault that I had with the Carroll County School System at that time, it was that the teachers needed to put the children who were having a hard time in a front row seat instead of the back row so that they could see and hear better to pay attention to the teacher. Perry said they always put him in the very back row. Teachers should never have placed children in a higher grade if they were not ready.

Although we had good teachers at Villa Rica School System, we also had teachers who should have retired or should not have been teaching at all. I am referring to the time period that we were in school, not today, because I am not aware of what the school system is doing today.

I wanted to help Perry, but I did not know how. I could tell that he was a late bloomer that needed confidence, direction, and someone to take the time to help him. He did not have a dictionary or encyclopedias and was overloaded with chores, the responsibility of taking care of a younger brother.

I've never seen anyone his age doing washing and hanging out clothes, sweeping and mopping floors and doing dishes from the time he got home from school to when his parents would come in from work at 11:00 p.m. at night. Even his play time was limited.

Then our paths crossed again 43 years later at a Fullerville Reunion that was held on May 22, 2010 and I had already heard that he was writing a book.

When I got that news, the first question that entered my mind was could this be the same Perry Bailey that was struggling through Villa Rica High School to learn? Then I thought maybe he did what I did. He found some help and went back to become a radio broadcaster and now an author of a book about a Community that he grew up in.

I met him, and he introduced his beautiful wife Rhonda. Then he pulled his wallet out and showed me a picture of their beautiful daughter, Kassey, who is also in college to become a commercial arts and graphic animator. Of course I hugged Perry and Rhonda's neck and told him how proud I was of him because I thought Hey, another Fullervillian has succeeded and done something with their life. I know other Fullerville people can relate to that thought because there are others who have succeeded.

I think one of the messages the author is trying to express in this book, is that there are other children struggling, although we are living in the 21st century and should be updated to educate our children better. The system is still poor. When it comes to educators, parents, grandparents, brothers and sisters, and citizens in general, an effort is needed to ensure a better and stronger education system for our children and a better America.

I think that there will always be people in need, but the more we can educate and provide more jobs for Americans, there will be less poverty, welfare and dependency. As I have heard Perry say many times, "Education is the key to Success" and one of his favorites, which he uses often, is, "What you don't know is what can hurt you!"

Finally, as I write this about the author, I think he has touched so many. Fullervillians and Villa Ricans live once again. Because of the book, the Fullerville Jail Committee was founded by the author to preserve the historical Fullerville.

The Jail which would be a plus if the city officials of Villa Rica would take more interest in what the Fullerville Jail Committee is trying to do. The author is trying to bring out the history of Fullerville which was not included in the book written by Mary Anderson, (The History of Villa Rica, The City of Gold).The author of this book organized a Fullerville Reunion which was held on May 22, 2010. He even personally invited another author, Hoot Sauls, to the reunion who wrote a book about his life in Fullerville. He allowed this author, Hoot Sauls, to speak and to sell his book at the Fullerville Reunion and this really impressed me and other people as well of Perry who shared the light of another book with his book.

Just when you think one event is over, he comes up with another surprise by honoring a special lady who Perry refers to as the "First Lady of Fullerville" because her husband, Cecil, had served as mayor of Fullerville at one time, Perry honored her with two plaques, one that honored her as "First Lady of Fullerville" and a second plaque honoring her for her contributions to the Fullerville Ball Park and its players. Little did anyone know that Perry had yet another rabbit to pull out of his hat. As Mrs. Sarah walked up and sat down in her chair, Perry said, "Ladies and Gentlemen, the First Lady of Fullerville, Mrs. Sarah Sauls." As the applause was finishing up in her behalf, Perry spoke into the microphone and says

"Ladies and Gentlemen, I am about to make the suggestion that the Ball Park Road sign be taken down and replaced with a new sign with a new name, Sarah Sauls Drive." Perry no more than got the word drive out of his mouth that the crowd was cheering him on in applause for about five minutes or more. This is what I mean about how Perry has brought Fullerville back together again and touched so many lives in a good way.

The Edwin Busbin Story

Interview by Joyce Massey Fain and Ann Broom
Written by Rhonda (Hovater) Bailey

My name is Edwin Busbin. I was born in 1931 in Douglas County to Edgar and Eva Busbin. In later years we moved to Conners Road in Villa Rica, Georgia. In 1943, we moved to Fullerville, Georgia where I lived until 1952. I married Willie Tee Hicks and we moved to a house we built on Dallas Highway in Villa Rica, where I still reside today. My wife and our one daughter, Brenda, are both deceased.

Although my time in Fullerville was a simple time, there were hard times as well. My father was a farmer and because farmers were needed to grow food for the country, he was not allowed to work in the mills. During World War II, my father grew crops to sell as a means of providing for our family. My mother worked in the Villa Rica Hosiery Mill. But during the war, you had to have a special release to work in the mill if you were a farmer because the country needed crops to feed the people.

When my family moved to Fullerville in 1943, we lived in a mill village house across from the Villa Rica Hosiery Mill. These houses lacked running water inside. People, fortunate enough to have a well, shared their water with the less fortunate. Each house had an outhouse in the backyard. The houses were hard to heat due to no insulation and no underpinning. Most of the houses were heated by either coal or wood heaters. And in some cases, the same heater used to heat the house was also used to cook on. So it was not unusual to have a pot of beans cooking on top of the heater for supper.

During the war, people had to buy what little they could afford on credit. On payday, they would go to the store and pay their bill. Mr. Carnes and Mr. Redding ran the store not far from our house. At the end of the week when people would come to pay their bill, Mr. Carnes would send me to the bank on my bicycle to see Mr. Knight in order to pick up a bag of money. This was so that money would be on hand to cash people's checks allowing them to pay their bill. Unlike today, I never had any trouble carrying the cash back and forth to the bank.

While growing up, I did a number of things to earn money. I would buy and fix up old bicycles and then resale them. I worked at Mitchell's Grocery for $4.00 a week and at Sutton's Drug Store for $6.00 a week. Sutton's Drug Store was located where Berry's Pharmacy is today. At age 16, I worked at the Villa Rica Hosiery Mill for forty cents an hour. I worked many different jobs in my search for one that I enjoyed. I finally went to work for Sears and worked there for 31 years before retiring.

I remember the fairs that would come through Fullerville twice a year that everyone loved to attend. The fairs were located in two places, one in the clearing between the Pearson home and the Butler home and the other across from the Villa Rica Hosiery Mill. I remember having a crush on a girl and asking her to go to the fair, hoping to steal a kiss from her. I never could stand to ride the swings but that's the ride this girl wanted to ride. So ride I did. I didn't get that kiss until I took her home but we had a great time at the fair.

Other fond memories were swimming at Willis Lake. It only cost five cents to swim but you better not get caught trying to sneak past Mr. Willis without paying! Turkey Trots and Squealed Pig contests were always fun to go to at the depot in Villa Rica.

I also remember the first funeral I ever helped with. One of my brothers worked for Uncle Bud Taylor, an undertaker and store owner in Villa Rica. I was about 13 or 14 years old. The funeral was to be in Bowdon Junction. The graves had to be dug with a shovel at that time, and it had not rained for quite a while. When my brother and I saw how hard it was going to be to dig that grave, we paid someone else to do it--a wise decision on our part. Bud Taylor owned a funeral home in Villa Rica on Wilson Street where later Dr. Guy Davis had his dental business. The building is still standing today.

I played ball one year on a team managed by Leon Massey. One other ball player on my team was Bobby Matthews who pitched for the team. We had uniforms and traveled to other places to play ball with other teams. I wasn't all that good but one day a player didn't show up, and I got to play in my first and only game.

I built a building next door to my home on Dallas Highway for my wife, Tee's florist business. When she closed the shop, I opened a carpet shop. I sold it in 2004. I also operated an ambulance service in the mid sixties. I joined my grandson, Jay Collins, at his funeral home in the year 2000, where I still work today. J. Collins Funeral Home and Cremation operates from the Malone Home, one of the oldest homes in Villa Rica. It was built in 1892 by W. H. Malone and was one of the first houses to have electricity in Villa Rica.

I have been blessed in many ways over the years and try to enjoy every day to its fullest.

Roses Store   Photo courtesy of Paulding Roots

Christmas – 1950's Style

By Kenneth Johns

Below is an article I put in the Newsletter a few years ago. I enjoyed reading it again. I thought others might like it also.

Christmases of long, long ago evoke fond memories for many people. Most of us like to revisit our childhood memories of Christmas. And so, in the words of a popular TV Western of the 1950's, "Go with us now back to those thrilling days of yesteryear". (For those of you under 50 years old that program was The Lone Ranger!)

In the 1950's, Villa Rica was a "sleepy little Southern town" located about 30 miles from the big city on U. S. Highway 78, the main highway from Atlanta to Birmingham. It was situated along the railroad. Its population was about 3,500 people. The downtown area consisted of a grocery store, two drug stores, a 5 & 10 cent store, a jewelry store, a dress shop, a theatre, a couple of restaurants, and a handful of other stores and businesses scattered on both sides of the railroad.

In those days, most people decorated their Christmas trees with a few strands of large, multi-colored lights, colorful balls, "silver icicles", and a star on top. The tree was most likely a real fir tree, usually a cedar. We would go to the woods and cut our own tree, and bring it home in the trunk of Dad's old '50 Chevy. A few of the wealthier people in town would also string up lights outside their home. Sometime during December, we would ride around town to "look at the lights".

Shopping trips to Atlanta were all day affairs, and were few and far between each year. However, a trip to Atlanta was always a highlight of the Christmas season. Going to Atlanta meant driving down U. S. 78 through the little towns of Douglasville, Lithia Springs, Austell, Mableton, and on into West End. From there we would continue on Marietta Street to the vicinity of Five Points. All the major department stores were located around Whitehall Street (which became Peachtree Street north of Five Points). There were Grant's, Newberry's, McCrory's, and, of course, the "granddaddy" of all the department stores, Rich's. Rich's had the famous "Pink Pig Flyer", which carried kids on an elevated ride around the store. Sliding up and down the counters was better than looking at the Sears catalog because you could actually see and touch the toys you thought you wanted for Christmas. Of course, you never knew for sure you were going to get what you wanted until Christmas morning!

As December slowly rolled by, Christmas vacation from school would finally arrive. Christmas Eve would be a night of anticipation, and then the long awaited Christmas morning would come. Our house was cold since we didn't have central heating and air. The floors were like ice; only rich people had carpeting. But none of that mattered! And I can never remember waking up late on Christmas morning. It was always at the "crack of dawn". Sure enough, under and around the tree would be the very toys I had wanted. Mom and Dad always made sure it happened! In the 1950's "toys" usually meant cowboy outfits, toy guns, footballs, basketballs, BB guns, bicycles, and board

113

games (also dolls and all their accessories were big with the other half of the human race).

Christmas morning was spent trying to play with all the toys at once! We always hoped the weather would be nice enough to get outside. It's difficult trying to ride a bike or play football in the hall, even if it is a big hall! Christmas afternoon all the aunts and uncles would bring all the cousins to see the grandparents. Everyone wanted to take every toy they could to show what they had gotten for Christmas! Now it was the adults who were hoping the weather was nice so all the kids could go outside. In addition to the toys, there might be some firecrackers to "shoot" also.

Somewhere along the way there was Christmas dinner. (In those days dinner was served in the middle of the day, and supper was served at night.) By the end of the day, everyone was worn out. All the aunts would call all the cousins to "wash up" to go home because you "never knew when you might have an accident on the way home and have to go to the hospital." Goodbyes were said, and we sadly went home.

Christmas had come and gone. That night there was always a little let down now that all the excitement was over. But then came December 26. No school until after New Year's Day. Serious playtime!

Fond memories? Yeah, Mom and Dad made sure it was a happy time. They had lived through the Depression when a Christmas gift sometimes meant an orange or an apple. They wanted their children to have more. They were not rich, just hard working, honest, God fearing folk. Life was simpler, slower, but filled with love, family, neighbors, and friends. It was a good time to grow up, and in a good place with good people.

Praise the Lord for Christmas—1950's Style!

Christmas Time in Fullerville

By Perry "Bill" Bailey

As I pondered over what I had read from my contributors, I wondered if there was anything that was being left out. I decided to go outside and just take a walk in my yard. Two maple trees in my front yard caught my eye, and I thought how this is my favorite time of the year. I remembered planting the two maple trees when they were just little seedlings and admired how tall and beautiful they had become, their leaves turning a vibrant yellow and orange. I just had to go inside and get my camera and get a picture of them because I knew their beauty wouldn't last long. I looked around my home and thanked God for all that he had blessed me and my family with. I started thinking of all the Christmas holidays that my family and I had enjoyed here.

I started daydreaming a little and tried to visualize me as a child in my present home, my mother and father being the owners of this house and land. I thought how we would have enjoyed playing in such a big yard and hunting in the woods behind it that actually belonged to us. My mom, dad, and brothers would have been thinking what a big step from the Fullerville way of living.

With these thoughts still in my mind, I continued my walk in the yard and caught myself starring at a cedar tree that I had planted years ago which now has the shape of a perfect Christmas tree. This took my thoughts back to Christmas time again and back to my Christmas times in Fullerville. Then it dawned on me what was missing in the book, recollections of past Christmases.

My Christmases in Fullerville as a young boy were not like the Christmases of today. Christmas in Fullerville was quite different and probably more enjoyable than I sometimes give it credit. I've had to set aside the material things that I wanted that my parents could not afford and focus on the happy times. Today, Christmas is so commercialized with holiday decorations being on sale in stores as early as September. In my day, you didn't even see anything Christmas related around Thanksgiving.

Thanksgiving Day was something to look forward to as well as Christmas because the city of Villa Rica would always put up the big Christmas tree in front of the old train depot and the Villa Rica High School band would play Christmas songs while everyone sang along. This was something the whole town came out to see. Plus the school children got an extra couple of days off from school. A lot of parents also had Thanksgiving Day off. But if your mom and dad worked for the mill in Fullerville, Thanksgiving Day was just another work day. They only got one day off for Christmas and that was Christmas Day, unless the mill was on what they called 'slow time' in which you had to be laid off. If that happened, you could count on not getting much for Christmas.

I remember one Christmas when Mom and Dad were working second shift. The mill would usually work only half a shift on Christmas Eve and be off on Christmas Day. On this particular Christmas, the mill hands were having a covered dish dinner. My dad asked the superintendent of the mill, Curt Sauls, if he could bring his boys to play some music. Mr. Sauls approved for us to play music while the mill workers ate their dinner. This meant that we three boys had to learn some Christmas songs so that the mill workers could sing along. My oldest brother was already married, so we had a trio, Andy, Douglas and me. We learned Jingle Bells, Silent Night, We Three Kings, and other popular Christmas songs. We even did "Blue Christmas" by Elvis. It all turned out great, and everyone enjoyed it. Some of the mill hands even gave us money that we didn't expect. But best of all, we made our parents proud of their boys.

Many of the children in Fullerville, when they could afford it, would buy fireworks at Christmas time, since fireworks were legal in Georgia at that time.

115

We would pop some of the fireworks on Christmas Day and save the rest for New Years Eve and New Years Day.

My favorite part of the Christmas season was looking for a real Christmas tree out in the woods. Mom, dad, and boys would load up in the car and go looking for a real cedar tree to bring home for Christmas. Now that was fun. We would be together as a family and doing something as a family. We would agree on one that looked like a perfect Christmas tree and bring it home. We always put the tree in a huge bucket filled with dirt and a little water. A lot of people cut their tree early, but we always cut and put up our tree a week before Christmas. My dad didn't want the tree to dry out too quickly and become a fire hazard. We would take the tree down the day after Christmas just to be safe.

Our Christmas tree was not surrounded by tons of presents, both big and small, as they are today. There were times when the only things we got for Christmas was apples, nuts, oranges, and a few cheap toys. Douglas and I got cap guns one Christmas; and Andy, being older, was always tickled to get clothing items. But at least we didn't wake up on Christmas morning with nothing under the tree.

Our Christmas was blessed with a mother who was a wonderful cook. I believe that was my favorite part of Christmas was my mother in her kitchen cooking her cakes, candy, and other special treats. The aroma in the house would make anyone's mouth water. She would always fix three or four cakes--everyone's own favorite. There was usually a homemade fruit cake, rum cake, chocolate cake, and a fresh homemade coconut cake made from scratch (my favorite!). While mother cooked, we were all together helping her by licking the big spoons and bowls clean for her to use again for another cake--after being properly washed, of course. We would all stay up late, talking, playing music, or just watching TV. We would stare at the Christmas tree, watching the lights and just looking at the tree decorations. We were all together and happy and blessed and there was always a warm feeling inside.

Another fond memory of Christmas was when my dad would announce to everyone that we were going to get ready to look at Christmas lights. We would ride down streets and look at everyone's decorations and at the trees lit up in the windows as we passed house after house. We would ride to nearby towns and compare their town's decorations to those in Villa Rica. Once again, it was being together and doing something as a family that meant so much to me. Christmas time to me is family time. It's a time to laugh together and give to each other, especially since the most precious gift one can give is love from the heart.

Fullerville Mill Village, a Poem

By Diane deVault Wilson

There she is. Can you see her: the girl
on her front porch?
She cuffs her hands around her mouth
and yodels some strange sound.
Soon, there are children with
expectant eyes laying down their
spoons and forks,
For the call to play has been made,
and it's outside they're bound.

Where is this you ask? This place
where children call each other out to play?
It's Fullerville, from the early 1900's to the
1960's –just a small mill village of people.

Photo courtesy of Catherine Burns

Yet, the kids have a place where they can play, where wherever they are, they're safe.
And where on every corner lot, there's some kind of church with a steeple.

These kids were born on the wrong side of the tracks, but maybe nobody told them?
For, they think they're rich; they are loved, and they love. They're happy and content.
If it takes a village to raise a kid, then these dear children can follow their whim.
For each kid belongs to one and to all; It's as if all the parents were heaven sent.

If there is one who is hungry or sick, then the whole village gets involved.
They scrape and they search and they find a way to lend a helping hand.
They all work together and find a way for any one's problem to get solved.
It appears that there are as many helpers as there are grains of sand.

Everybody knows everybody, and even though nobody has much money.
They all are rich: these folks from Fullerville. They are blessed as blessed can be.
For they have each other, and they have their God and they see their days as sunny.
Because these folks from Fullerville, they've got what's important, you see?

They have their priorities, so they their lives with respect for one another.
After all, they're just good village people who consistently try to do what's right.
And these children of Fullerville, wherever they play, they know they have a mother.
Because there's always someone who's watching them---who keeps them in her sight.

I am so blessed that I am one of these children—these children from Fullerville.
Does it take a village to raise a child? All I know is I'm glad for my village with its mill.

Part 3

Perry's Story

Rockmart Road   Photo courtesy Charles and Ann Broom

Chapter 1

How It All Came About

My name is Perry Bailey. Those who never knew Perry call me by my professional name which is Bill. When in the fourth grade, I started a journal recording the events in my life along with the events happening around me. I have memories, great and small, and many of them.

My community of Fullerville was in the town of Villa Rica, Georgia. It was this small village that supplied the work force to the mills of the surrounding west Georgia area.

These are my memories.

Let me begin by saying that I come from the salt of the earth: good, hard working Southern stock that was one of the major foundations of our country.

Now, it all started a long time ago in the British Isles. To put it politely, the Irish had long been a thorn in the side of the English. As early as the 1500s, a system called plantation (planting) was devised by the English to bring settlers from Scotland into Ireland. The purpose was to dilute the native population by bringing in those with the English language, culture, religion, and loyalty. This system was carried out with varying success over a period of approximately two hundred years.

This era was followed by a span of 58 years, between 1717 and 1775, dubbed the Great Migration. During this period, there were five waves of migration of, as they are called today, the Scotch Irish to America. Georgia and the Carolinas received a goodly share of these new arrivals. Indeed, some families left Ireland in search of religious freedom, but most left because of severe economic hardships.

Those who founded the southern branches of the Bailey family left Ulster just before the start of the last migration period. Their progenitor, Nathaniel Bailey, was born at Ballybay in County Monaghan, Ireland. His son Nathaniel, wife Jean, and their children emigrated from Ireland by way of the sailing ship, the Lord Dungannon, in February of 1768. They entered America through the Port of Charleston, South Carolina. At the time they arrived, there was no United States. They were staunch Presbyterians and were the forbearers of all the Baileys in Gwinnet County, Georgia.

In later years, Baileys and their extended family members answered the call to duty when the War Between the States was declared. Needless to say, they joined the Confederate Army fighting under the Georgia banner. David Bailey, the great, great grandfather to our current Bailey family of Fullerville, Georgia, was born in 1832 in Gwinnett County, Georgia. He and four of his five brothers were in Company H 35th Georgia Infantry. He was taken prisoner at

Gettysburg. He died a month later when a measles epidemic swept through Fort Delaware, the notorious Yankee prison camp located in the middle of the Delaware River on Pea Patch Island. His brother Elijah was killed at the Second Battle of Manassas and is buried in one of the mass graves there.

It is only because of the interest and hard work of family historians that extremely important parts of the past are preserved. A salute is given to my cousin, Lamar Wadsworth of Rockmart, Georgia, for his meticulous research. He has made it possible for the Bailey family of Fullerville to know its roots.

Grandfather George Shelton Bailey, Papa Bailey, of Villa Rica, Georgia, began his working life as a sharecropper. Married to Katie Tant Bailey, they produced 9 children, all of whom were raised in or near Fullerville, Georgia. The children were named Estelle, P.C (Clyo), Gladys, Shelton, Claudie, Olin, Ozelle, Andy Lease, and Earlene. All the children labored at sharecropping. At that time, it was necessary for the children to work in order to help their parents provide for the family. As a result, they were able to get very little education. Without education it was, as it still is, impossible for them to ever seek the better employment opportunities.

George Bailey left the grueling hardships of sharecropping for a better life in the cotton mill industry in Fullerville. The cotton mills were a God send to the rural people of Georgia who relied on share cropping as a way to support themselves and their families.

The Hard Life...Photo courtesy of Melvin Fain

The mills offered a better life than share cropping, and there was no problem recruiting workers from the rural areas of Georgia. Every one of Papa Bailey's sons eventually came to the cotton mill industry and worked there until retirement.

According to family history, Papa Bailey served as the mayor of Fullerville, Georgia, sometime between 1920 and 1930.

According to the 1930 Federal Census for Fullerville Town, there were 96 households and 491 individuals living in Fullerville. These households provided 211 people to the work force: Cotton Mill-116; Hosiery Mill-79; Farmers-7, Carpenters-1; Mechanic/garage-1; Presser/own shop-2; General store-2; Servant/private family-3

Three sons out of the 9 siblings served in the military; my father, Olin Bailey, and my two uncles, Claudie and Andy Lease Bailey.

Cold Mountain, the book and the movie, is a true story based on my mother's family, the Swanger family. My grandmother was Margret Matilda Swanger George. Descendants of the early Swanger family are found today in both Paulding and Carroll counties. These include the families of Donald and Gene Swanger and the late Jim and Matilda George of Carroll County.

Although *Cold Mountain* by Charles Frazier, is fiction, it is based on actual people, places, and events. It is set in the mountain country of North Carolina near Waynesville in Haywood County. The names used by Frazier, Esco and Sally, are fictional.

The Swanger family was indeed very real and their descendents live on today. John and Margaret Swanger were the parents of fourteen children. Two of the girls married into the Inman family.

In tragic occurrences during and shortly after the Civil War, the Swanger family lost John, the father of the family, two of his eight sons, and two Inman sons-in-law.

My parents, although living elsewhere at various times, always retained very strong ties to Fullerville and Villa Rica. Return trips were made constantly for both the trivial and the important things of life.

A word about my parents: Theirs was a true love story. They were very young when they met; and marry they would, in spite of the objections of the Bailey family.

Olin and Ruth Bailey
Photo courtesy of the author

Everything they ever did, at work or at play, they did together. They always remained devoted to each other and stayed very much in love for the rest of their lives.

And now my story begins

Chapter 2

My Beginnings

I was born on August 9, 1952, in the old Villa Rica community hospital, which was located off of Carroll Road. The building still stands to this day and has been turned into a church. Although my family was then living in Tallapoosa, Georgia, this event was one that sent them back to Villa Rica.

My family was made up of my father, the late James Olin Bailey Sr., my mother, the late Ruth George Bailey, my eldest brother, the late James "Jimmy" Olin Bailey Jr., my second eldest brother, Andy, Earl Bailey Sr., myself, and my youngest brother, the late George Douglas Bailey. Douglas was also born in Villa Rica in 1955 at the brand new hospital there. It was named the Villa Rica City Hospital and was located on Dallas Highway.

My father was a very active person who enjoyed life. In his early days, he played ball for the Villa Rica Cotton Mill, which was sold to Banning Yarn in later years. He was what most people would call a go-getter.

Often young men chose to serve in the United States Military as a means for providing for their families because they couldn't afford to go to college. The same holds true today. My father served in the United States Army during World War II, from December 28, 1942, until January 29, 1946, leaving the service with an honorable discharge. He had served as a Military Policeman and Fireman. Some of the medals he received were the following: American Service Medal, Asiatic Pacific Service Medal, Good Conduct Medal, and AR 600-68 World War II Victory Medal.

While serving in the Army, he would often bring oriental rugs and unique items home to my mother from his trips around the nation and the world. When my father's term of service ended, he returned to Fullerville to work in the cotton mills. On returning to civilian life, my father took advantage of the G. I. Bill and attended night school in the old school house in Fullerville, finishing his high school degree. In 1948, he served as a city councilman of Fullerville.

Research provided by Jeanette Harlow, Director of the American Hospital Association Resource Center provides a concise overview of the bill.

The G.I. Bill of Rights (Servicemen's Readjustment Act of 1944) provides federal aid to help veterans adjust to civilian life in the areas of hospitalization, purchase of homes and businesses, and education. The goal of the bill is to "see that the veteran is not punished by reason of his service, but is given a fair break in winning for himself those traditional American privileges to which he is entitled, and which he fought to preserve for us at home."

Ruth and Perry Photo courtesy of the author

The family relocated to Tallapoosa, Georgia, shortly before I was born. I remember only a few experiences I had while I lived in Tallapoosa, Georgia. But my family members filled me in with all sorts of stories about life there to make up for what I can't recall.

While we lived there, my father and mother were both employees of the American Thread Cotton Mill Industries. Although most mill employees at that time chose to live in mill villages, mine did not. Instead, my parents purchased a 2 1/2 story house that was once used as an orphanage home. (see appendix D) They bought the house in 1951, and I can remember the huge pecan trees in the yard. It was painted white both inside and outside and was beautifully decorated inside as well. My parents remodeled it and rented the extra rooms to senior citizens or families with no more than two members. They were very particular about their renters. Wisely planned, the money from the rented rooms covered the house payments. I also remember the stories about my father's work life there. He worked the third shift at the cotton mill and got off at seven in the morning. When he arrived at home, he was greeted by a delicious hot breakfast that my mother always cooked for him. After eating, he would load up his push mower and cut yards for friends and neighbors from nine in the morning until three in the afternoon as a means for bringing in more revenue. During the fall, he harvested and sold the pecans that fell from the trees.

In 1956, my parents sold our house and moved to New Georgia, Georgia. There we rented a home from a Mr. Chambers. Not long after we had moved away, we learned that the orphanage had been completely destroyed by fire. No one ever knew what had caused the fire.

Going from life in the city to life in the country was a major change for us. It was a step back in time because, unlike the city, there was no inside plumbing in the country. It didn't bother me that we left the city for the country since I was young and accepted life as it came. It did bother my two eldest brothers because we had left a home that we owned, located on a street that was once considered to be uptown. Most of the houses on the street were modern, neat, and clean. People that lived in this part of the city were also well respected. Jimmy and Andy felt that my parents had made a great mistake when they sold our city home and moved to the country.

This was my first experience with life on the farm as well. We had many farm animals including two milk cows named Lucy and Maybelle, chickens, pigs, a rooster and even turkeys. I didn't really like the turkeys except around Thanksgiving time. Those feathered monsters would chase me. At my young age, I was terrified by them! We also had a family dog and a few cats.

My parents continued to work at American Thread Cotton Mill. It was one of the few mills in the area that offered high wages, good healthcare, paid vacations and retirement. However, the majority of the mills in the area didn't offer such benefits as retirement, healthcare, or paid vacations. To escape vacation pay, these mills would close down production during the week of July the Fourth for vacation. They would lay everyone off so that if people needed the money they could apply for unemployment pay.

I remember little about life in New Georgia because I was only about four or five years old when we lived there. I do remember the old Chambers Saw Mill behind our home. I also remember my two eldest brothers, Jimmy and Andy, often arguing over girls. They once told me that they had to be very quiet when getting ready for school in the morning. If I woke up, I would follow them onto the front porch and begin to entertain. I'm told that I would go out on the front porch scarcely dressed and sing Elvis Presley's song, "You Ain't Nothin but a Hound Dog", to the children on the school bus on Dallas Highway. I would embarrass Jimmy and Andy terribly, but I'll bet that the other children got a kick out of it. I was young at the time and didn't really have a care in the world.

Eventually, my mother took some time off from work to be with my youngest brother, Douglas, who was only a year old and still needed her attention. She would get up early during the week and make sure Jimmy and Andy did their chores before heading off to school. These chores included milking the cows and feeding the animals. When my father arrived home from work, he would help my mother churn the milk. We always had fresh buttermilk and butter. We always had plenty to sell to relatives and neighbors. On occasion, we would give some away, especially to the needy families.

My parents had purchased the family's first television set while living in Tallapoosa, Georgia. I have no memory of watching television while we lived there because I was so young that I preferred to play instead. In New Georgia, I can remember watching shows like Tennessee Ernie Ford and Captain Kangaroo on the black and white television set. On weekends, friends and relatives would come over to watch the television shows because few people owned a set at this time. The children and I would play while our parents watched programs like The Jackie Gleason Show and western movies.

In late 1956 or early 1957, my parents decided to move once more to be a little closer to town. Sadly, we had to sell every single one of our farm animals. We lived in New Georgia for only a short while, and it was a great community. Jimmy and Andy loved going to the school there. I enjoyed gathering the eggs from the hen house--a very important job for a youngster. We moved from New Georgia to the Old Town community in Villa Rica, Georgia.

There were two houses located off of Dallas Highway that were straight up the hill behind Cecil Leather's Grocery Store and Dan Barber's house. Both buildings were quite upscale being made of brick with brown siding. When visitors came to our house, they would turn into our driveway, which was located on the right. Both houses were side by side on the left of the driveway. The first house was occupied by my uncle, the late Joseph "Shorty" George and his wife, my aunt, Frances Washington George; the second house was ours. Both houses were owned by J. W. Taylor. We lived in that house until one tragic day.

It happened on one cold, brisk Saturday morning. My family made a trip into town for groceries and to pay off a few bills. We never suspected that while we were in town, our house had caught fire. Emergency teams responded quickly because several people believed that we were still in the house. Finally, a relative was able to locate us in town and rushed over to us to tell us that our house was burning and that emergency teams were already on the scene trying to save it. We dropped everything we were doing and dashed toward home. It was too late. The fire was out of control! Unlike Fullerville that had no fire protection at all, Villa Rica had a volunteer fire group that was called into action in emergency situations.

Unfortunately, they were unable to save our house. The exact cause of the fire could never be determined. It was surmised that it could have been started by anything from faulty wiring, appliances that may have been left on, or even a cigarette that hadn't been properly put out. Only God knows what really happened on that fateful day.

My family was devastated. We had lost everything our parents had worked for so hard. After the fire had finally been put out, we sifted through the rubble searching for anything that was salvageable. This search proved to be fruitless, and we found very little to save. Sadly, we lost our family pets; the parakeet we kept inside, a pet squirrel, and a small puppy we had just bought that we kept on the back porch. We lost the many items that my father had bought overseas while serving in the Army. We lost all other things that my parents had bought; a cedar chest, wardrobe, an antique trunk, and the old black and white television set that had been purchased in 1949. In fact, everything we owned had been swept away.

My parents had collected pocket change and old money that they stored in mason jars in the house. The collection included Indian-head pennies, silver quarters, mercury dimes, half-dollars, even paper money from one dollar bills to twenty dollar bills. We even had original two dollar bills. We were able to save some of the money, but most was burned beyond recognition.

It's easy to look back and feel sorrowful about all the material things we lost that awful day. We may have not realized it at the time, but God had His hand on us. We could very easily have been in the house that day and lost our lives. We then realized the truth of many of the life's lessons that our parents had taught us. It's true; you never know who your real friends are until you are in a time of need.

That day we found we had many friends, some we didn't even know. My parents were not rich when it came to material things, but they were very rich when it came to being blessed with many true friends. We received food, clothing, and shelter from the compassionate people of Villa Rica. We even received help from people in the Villa Rica community that we didn't know and from churches that we had never attended. It amazed us that so many wonderful people were there for us during our time of loss.

My parents always said, "God will take care of you if you have faith and believe that He will do so." I can truthfully say that God always came through for us.

They always taught us to keep our name clean, and stressed that since we weren't rich, a good name was all that a working man has going for him. I took this to mean to always pay the bills and treat others as you would want to be treated in return. If one wants respect, one must first earn it. A working man who pays his bills, feeds and clothes his family, and loves his family will automatically be given the respect he deserves. I can honestly say that my parents had that respect. They never asked, much less looked for help of any kind. Any help we received came on its own. They never forgot it.

Less than a week after our house burned, a second tragedy struck Villa Rica. On December 5, 1957, Berry's Pharmacy, located in the center of town, exploded. This time both lives, and property were destroyed in a sudden, chaotic burst of noise and flame that shook the area for miles around. A detailed account of the explosion may be read in Elaine Bailey's book, *Explosion in Villa Rica*.

Our next move was to a ranch house in Villa Rica that my parents rented from Buddy Stockmar. I remember enjoying the days living in the ranch house on Stockmar Road. My father still worked at American Thread in Tallapoosa. My mother continued to stay at home and care for me and my two year old brother, Douglas. Day care was a rarity at this time. The house had plenty of privacy, and it also had the marvelous convenience of indoor bathroom facilities. Unfortunately, our possession of a home with this so very important attribute was all too short lived.

We packed our things and moved back to the Old Town Community into the house that was next door to our house that had burned. As I mentioned earlier, my aunt and uncle lived next door. They moved into a house across the road from Cecil Leather's Grocery Store, and we moved into their old house. We rented from J. W. Taylor once again. What I disliked most about this house was that it didn't have indoor bathroom facilities. I had to use a flashlight at night to go to the outhouse. Being a young child at that time, I was afraid that I would come in contact with a snake or some other loathsome creature.

Eventually, my father bought a brand new car, a 1957 Ford. The bright, sleek colors of red and white made it look really sharp. He also owned a 1955 Ford pick-up truck. He and Jimmy built shelves on the back of the old pick up that were used when they sold produce from the back of the truck.

Later on, my father bought a brand new television set. Once again, I must brag on my father because when he saw something he wanted, he would work even harder to get it. My parents were not materialistic people, but that didn't mean that they didn't enjoy having nice things. If they saw something they wanted and could afford, they would buy it. If they couldn't afford it, they did without. My father never purchased anything on his credit that he couldn't commit to. He knew his limits, and he stuck to them. If production at the mill happened to be slow and we were barely getting by, he would go to the people to whom he owed money and negotiate some sort of payment plan until things made a turn for the better. My parents always believed in taking care of responsibilities first and taught us to do the same.

I'll never forget my parents saying, "Don't ever burn bridges! You never know when you might have to cross them again."

130

In 1958, I started my first year in school. I never went to school on an empty stomach. My mother always made the family large, wonderful breakfasts serving up freshly made biscuits hot out of the oven, gravy, cheese, eggs, her homemade apple jam, and ripe cantaloupe. Since my parents sold so much produce, they encouraged me to take an apple to my elementary school teachers. Instead, I gave them to a different classmate every day.

I only received paddlings from two teachers while I attended school, and my first grade teacher, Mrs. Lawson was one of them. Sometimes Mrs. Lawson would take me out in the hall to paddle me. Other times she would beat my hand with a ruler until I couldn't feel it anymore. My parents certainly never shrank from the responsibility of using the rod, but they refused to go along with something that they felt was unjustified. Mrs. Lawson was confronted by not just one set of parents, but by several including mine. No doubt you heard the song, "The Harper Valley PTA". Well, my mother had words with her. My mother told her before she walked out the door that if she ever paddled her child again, she was going to bring a ruler back to school and give her a taste of her own medicine. I didn't witness the confrontation between the teacher and my parents but they told me what had happened when I was older. After my mother had her say with Mrs. Lawson, I was treated nicely until the end of that school year.

The greatest thing about first grade was that there was no such thing as snobbery. All the children got along well together. Maybe this was because we were all too young to understand what a social status was. This was a time when children played together because they liked each other and did not care if their friend or classmate was from a rich family or a poor one. I often think about how great the world might be today if this were true among adults.

Unfortunately, a few of us failed first grade. Some believed it was because the teachers didn't work with us as they should have done. Others would argue that the parents were to blame for not preparing their child for school. At that time, both parents in each household usually worked long hours. At the end of the work day, they did not have the time or the energy to work with their children on school assignments. My own mother had returned to work by the time I started school. Most of the children that passed first grade had a mother that could stay at home and work with their parents who had enough money to send them to kindergarten. Kindergarten was not a requirement when I was growing up, and a lot of schools didn't even offer it. It was also quite expensive, so usually only those parents who were fairly well off were able to send their children. Unfortunately at that time, there was no preschool evaluation made to determine if a child was mature enough to begin school.

We didn't stay in the Old Town Community for very long. My father suffered a nasty accident, losing his little finger while he was working at American Thread. During this time, it wasn't uncommon for someone to get a body part cut off or even to die while working at a mill or a factory. If a worker got caught in the machinery, and if there was no one around to turn it off, the victim could literally be chewed to pieces. Most of the mills and factories at this time didn't have a bit of protection of any kind for the employees. By hook or crook, employees who were hurt on the job were usually terminated. This happened to my father.

Before the incident, my father had advanced at American Thread from an entry level position to being a machine mechanic or fixer, as they called it back then. The next step up from being a machine mechanic would be supervisor. The accident changed everything.

My father never filed workman's compensation because he knew full well that doing so would cost him his job. Perhaps one of his supervisors felt threatened, afraid that my father would take his job one day; or possibly, it was feared that my father would change his mind and file for workman's compensation. For whatever reason, one of the supervisors started giving him trouble. He spread rumors that my father was going to file workman's compensation and even went to the company's personnel office with this false report. It was all lies. My father expressed on several occasions that he was satisfied with the company for covering his medical expenses due to the accident and had no intention of ever filing workman's compensation.

Three months later, the supervisor, who had already caused my father a great deal of upset, found a minor reason to fire him. That's right, a minor reason that other supervisors would overlook unless, of course, there happened to be a grudge of some sort involved. There were no laws or unions to protect the employees at that time. If there had been, my father, along with many others, could possibly have had better, safer working conditions and job security. The sad truth is that this sort of thing still goes along today.

There are many states in our country today, Georgia being one of them, which have a Right to Work Law. This means that employees cannot be required to join a union. Controversially, some refer to the right-to-work laws are as the right-to-fire laws. With the misuse of these laws, employers have the right to fire or terminate an employee for unjust causes or without any cause at all. Unfortunately, it has not been unheard of in right-to-work states that employees ready for retirement are fired the day before they qualify, losing all of their money and benefits.

After my father lost his job at American Thread, he looked for employment elsewhere. He was quickly hired right away by Banning Yarn Mill in Fullerville because of his experience with the workings of a mill. So we moved to Third Street in Fullerville in 1958. The house had only four or five rooms, but they were very large. The houses were built well for that time.

However, there was a problem with these houses because there was no sheetrock to cover the walls, just plank siding. There was no insulation in the walls, in the attics, or under the floor. None of the houses were underpinned to keep cold air out, and this made it just about impossible to keep a house warm or cool. Frozen water pipes were the norm during the winter.

One of the worst ice storms that could ever be remembered occurred while we were living there. I'm not sure of the date, but I believe it was sometime around 1960 or 1962. The entire Carroll County area was without power for weeks on end. The whole community was shut down, including schools and stores.

It looked like a frozen waste land, but the beauty of the landscape soon took second place to the hardships it created.

Those who had natural gas in their home were fortunate because they could continue to cook and stay warm. I remember my mother had an electric stove. This was our only means of cooking other than the coal heater we had for heat. Thanks to that coal heater, we were able to stay warm and fed. My father always left the water running during extremely cold weather so that the water wouldn't freeze inside the pipes. I remember a huge build up of ice on our back porch which was about four feet from the ground. The water faucets on the back porch could be turned on from the porch instead of the ground. My father had left the water running so the pipes wouldn't freeze. The water froze just below where it exited the pipes, making a wide frozen puddle across the deck. This looked very tempting to children, especially one particularly active five year boy. Of course, I had no ice skates, just my little PF-Flyers on my feet. What did I do? I started ice skating on my own back porch. I fell, and it took 13 stitches to repair my chin. Thank God that I had Someone up above looking after me. I somehow managed to grab the water pipe and kept from falling the four feet to the ground below. This would have been a big fall for me, and it would probably have caused even more damage.

During the ice storm, our neighbors worked together to help each other through this tough time. We had good friends there including the Farr family, Padgett family and other neighbors.

We shared eggs, sugar, flour, corn mill and even coal because the coal trucks couldn't make deliveries. The community made sure that everyone had plenty of heat and plenty of food.

The Olin Baileys 1958   Photo courtesy of the author

Since there was no electricity, we had no television or radio for entertainment. We all gathered together and shared stories. My father brought out his guitar, and family and neighbors joined him in singing. We sang gospel, country, and bluegrass songs. By the way, bluegrass music was a gift of the Scotch Irish to their new homeland of America. My older brother did imitations of Elvis because he too played the guitar. Andy always kept his hair combed like Elvis.

Our home generated entertainment, kept our spirits high and gave us hope. Perhaps families today would do well to set aside one evening a week and enjoy being together without all the modern distractions. Of course, all the children loved not having to go to school. We did miss our favorite television shows like Captain Kangaroo, Sky King, My Little Margie, I Love Lucy, and The Andy Griffith Show just to name a few.

My older brothers, Jimmy and Andy, escaped the house taking their pellet rifles into the frozen woods behind our outhouse. This place was called the Slickums, and boys hunted there for rabbits, birds, and squirrels. They always had the best luck killing squirrels, but we never did clean and eat them. Our father had a problem eating anything that resembled a rat. I think that the rest of the family felt the same way, so squirrel killing was just for sport.

Living on Third Street in Fullerville wasn't so bad. There were plenty of children to play with. The bigger kids would often pick on the little kids because the little ones wanted to play with them. Of course, the older kids were always saying, "get lost" to the smaller ones. I remember playing softball and baseball many times at the old ball park that was across from the lumberyard in Fullerville. The excitement of carnivals and circuses would often come to that old ball park since it was large enough to accommodate them. Religious groups would also set up tents and run a week long revivals at the old ball park.

We lived by the Padgett family on Third Street, and I remember playing with the Padgett girls who they were close to my age. I remember that their brothers, James and Junior, were musicians and played in church. Jerry Padgett sang in church and later formed The Gospel Quartet which traveled around singing for the Lord. The Padgett boys were outstanding musicians and singers. Andy had learned a lot about playing the guitar from our father and by participating in the church at the Congregational Holiness Church of Fullerville where the Padgett family attended church services. The late Jerry Padgett was elected to city council of Villa Rica sometime in the 1970s. As far as I know, he was the only one raised in Fullerville to actually run for office and serve as a city councilman. Jerry was well liked by all that knew him. His Christianity always shone through.

I remember well the summer and winter months living on Third Street in Fullerville. I would have to take a bath in a wash pan or tub. As I grew older, I was assigned the additional chore of emptying the chamber pot, a necessity for the convenience of the family at night. Unfortunately, the chamber pot was often to full to carry in the dark, or the weather was too bad to get it to the outhouse. I would then have to walk to the outhouse regardless of the weather or time of day. The winter days were somewhat better as far as the outhouses were concerned. The hotter days were always the worst since the outhouses attracted a lot of flies. I know that today people will shake their heads in wonder at the ignorance of former generations in the matters of public health; not to mention the simple esthetics of the situation.

The worst part about the cold was that all the children who lived on Third Street had to walk to the bus stop to meet the school bus. The path led from our house to what once was the Fullerville City Hall in earlier days of Fullerville, Georgia. Later it housed a store, barber shop and café, all occupying the old building together. This building is still located by the switch tracks and the historic Fullerville Jail building.

Often boys would wash their hair and put on Brylcreem, "A Little Dab'll do Ya!" Sometimes I put more on than I should have and that gave my hair a remarkable greasy shine. Then all the kids would laugh at me as I walked to the bus stop. They would feel of my hair because it had ice cycles in it from the cold. It always seemed that it took forever for that school bus to get to our bus stop, especially since I was one of several kids waiting in sub-freezing temperatures who did not have a coat.

135

Around the first part of 1960, we moved to Rockmart Road in Villa Rica into the old school house that once served as a church. I remember the big oak tree out in front and the cool shade it offered in the summertime. My mom worked at the Golden City Hosiery Mill in Villa Rica, and my dad worked at the Banning Cotton Mills in Fullerville. During this time, peddlers came through Fullerville every Friday evening selling fresh produce, candy, fruit, and other goods. I knew that it was definitely Friday when the produce man came by selling his wares. It was such a pleasure going to the television set on Friday nights to watch the Flintstones, Route 66, and other programs even though they were in black and white.

The family menu was another thing that made my weekends so special. We always had hotdogs, hamburgers, banana sandwiches, potato chips, and real, old fashioned Coca Cola. The best came on Sundays; we were blessed with my mother's good, old home cooked beans, fried Irish potatoes, stewed cabbage, your choice of cornbread or her good old fashioned homemade biscuits. Believe me; I would rather eat my mother's homemade biscuits any day than canned biscuits! But then, who wouldn't?

When the weather was nice, J. W. Keeton and others would drop by the house on Sunday afternoons. They would sit on the front porch and sing and play with my father. It was amazing! Neighbors would come to listen and enjoy. Some would join in singing away at the old country and gospel songs.

Some of the songs I remember were, "I'm Moving On" by Hank Snow, "The Great Speckled Bird" by Roy Acuff, "Give Me that Old Time Religion" a traditional gospel song dating back to 1873, and "I Wonder Where You are Tonight" recorded by Del McCoury. My father and my mother both sang in church. He usually did solos for the crowd at home. In his early days, my father had played with other musicians including J. W. Keeton and Billy Williams, and they would often sing on the radio. J. W. Keeton and Billy Williams were very fine musicians and great backup singers with my dad.

I guess my brothers and I inherited our father's gift of music. My brothers were guitar players. But my father decided we needed a drummer, so I became a drummer. Some fathers worked with their children to be football players and baseball players. Our father pushed music, and we were made to practice and to play.

We certainly have no regrets about this. I've played drums for several quartets, rock and country bands as well. My other brothers Andy and Douglas sang in church and played with gospel, rock and country bands. Jimmy decided just to fool around with his guitar at home. He lost interest in the guitar and never got up to par as Andy and Douglas did.

I still fool around on the drums, but I do not play anywhere professionally any more. Douglas died in June of 2006, and my older brother Jimmy passed away in March of 2009. Andy continues to play his guitar at his church in Chickamauga, Georgia.

Olin Bailey   Photo courtesy of the author

Perry's Union Home Revisited   Photo courtesy of the author

In the beginning of 1961, my parents built a house in the community of Union in Paulding County, Georgia. They bought forty acres from my great-uncle, Mack George, who owned quite a bit of land. This was like being in heaven to me. It was a nice four room house with an inside bathroom.

We enjoyed the quietness of the nights at our new home. It was quite different to fall asleep without the sounds of the trains, cars, and sirens of Villa Rica. I remember our first snow. It was so beautiful! The clean countryside smelled of the pine trees which gave the air a wonderful, refreshing scent.

I was in third grade going to a new school called Union. It was different from the city school that I had attended in Villa Rica. The Union school was laid back and didn't have the social pressures that the city school did. In the months that followed, I began to catch up on my studies learning more in the months that I was there than I had learned in the two years I attended school in Villa Rica. The Union school had what all schools need to promote learning. While I was there, the teachers at the Union school made sure that the parents were aware of the grade status before report card time. They put pressure on the students and the parents when grades began to slip. The parents were urged to help their children themselves or to get help. We just didn't have this kind of concern at Villa Rica.

While I was in the fourth grade in 1962, I started keeping a day to day journal. I quietly recorded things that took place in school, at work, at home, and while at play. I refer to my journal from time to time and read about how people believed, how they lived, their morals, their likes and dislikes, and their fears. I notice that things back then compare pretty much with life today, though some would find that hard to believe. My journal has been a big plus in bringing memories back to me for this book. I have continued to keep my journal until this very day.

My father worked at Cannon Caskets in Villa Rica after being laid off from Banning Cotton Mill. Jimmy, still lived at home; and he also worked with my father at Cannon Caskets. They were both making better money than my father had made at the cotton mill. My mother was employed at the cotton mill in Douglasville, Georgia; and Andy, Douglas, and I were in school.

My family still had most of the older generation with us at this time. My grandmother, Matilda George, was known as Granny George; and she was still living at the time we were in Union. She passed away in November of 1968. My grandfather, Jim George, had passed away in 1949. His funeral was conducted by the Taylor funeral home in Villa Rica. He was buried at Powell's Chapel in Villa Rica, Georgia.

On my father's side of the family, Mama and Papa Bailey were still living while we lived in Union. My grandparent's names were George S. Bailey and Katie Tant Bailey. One brisk Saturday morning my father pulled into the driveway after a trip to Douglasville to pick up my mother from work. He had informed me that Mama Bailey had passed away on February 24, 1962.

Unbelievably, the night before, I had dreamed that my Mama Bailey had passed away. In the dream, I remember her coming to my bedside; and it was as though she were real. I could feel her cold hands touch mine. She said to me, "Perry, I'm going to be going away for awhile. No need to worry, I'll be okay."

I never said anything to my parents or family fearing they might think that I was just making it up. So I kept quiet until I was older. Still, I'm not so sure that they believed me even then. The important thing is that I knew it was true.

Times were getting hard, and the Cannon was slowing down. Because of the slow down, they began having layoffs. My father knew that if he got laid off that we would lose our home, land, and that would cause him to have a bad name on his credit. So dad called a meeting with the family and informed us that we must sell the house and land before he got laid off; otherwise we would lose everything. By selling out we would be able to make a little bit of a profit and keep our good name. He found a buyer, and our place was sold. This was hard on me because I had to leave the place that I had grown to love so much. The friends that I made at Union were boys and girls I enjoyed. They helped me catch up in school, and they spent time at my house playing. I enjoyed being a kid who was accepted.

Chapter 3

Return to Fullerville

The Fullerville homes were sold over and over again by the wealthy owners of the mills. If one bought a home and got laid off, no matter how long you had been paying on your mortgage, they foreclosed. No one knows how many times the Fullerville houses were sold, foreclosed, and resold.

After my father had been laid off from Cannon Caskets, he returned to Banning Yarn Mills. So once more, we moved back to Fullerville living at 529 Rockmart Road. Right across from our house was Dogwood Street and Villa Rica City Hosiery Mill. From the front porch of this house, looking to the left of the street was a small gravel vacant lot where mill workers parked. On the left of the vacant lot was an old tin building.

Although our new home was a shack compared to what we had just moved away from, it was on the uptown side of Fullerville. So, we were back in a small five room house.

One room was already rented to a gentleman named Prude Waldrop, the brother of "Preacher" Malt Waldrop. He was a World War II Veteran and had been injured at Pearl Harbor during the Japanese attack. Prude told Douglas and me his war stories as we sat on the front porch on hot summer days. His stories were terribly exciting and educational as well.

My family didn't like living in a house with anyone else, because we all liked our privacy. However, this house was the only one vacant in Fullerville at the time; there wasn't any choice. The fact that they knew that Prude Waldrop was a very good person eased their feelings about having to move into a shared situation.

My parents worked second shift at Banning Yarn Mill. Jimmy was now married and had his own home. Andy was still in high school. After school, he worked until 10 P.M. at night at the Bay Service Station in Douglasville, Georgia. My mom and dad felt at ease knowing that Prude looked after both of us. Every evening Prude invited us to watch the 6:30 P.M. Amos and Andy television show. We enjoyed watching many of the episodes with Mr. Waldrop. He would always get a kick out of King Fish. Everyone knew Prude Waldrop remembering and respecting his service to the country as a soldier in the United States Army.

In spite of Prude's kind attention, Doug and I were at home alone, so I had to look after him and do the chores. Things did occur due to the fact that a child was caring for a child. One cold, sunny afternoon after school we were bored and were looking for something to do. Somehow playing ball or watching TV just didn't sound like fun. We decided to pretend that we were dipping snuff. During this time period it was common to see older folks, both male and female, with a mouth full of snuff. We knew better than to try to dip the real thing, so we hunted for some cocoa and sugar. Mom was either out of cocoa and sugar, or she had hidden it really well from her two mischievous little boys. Our next option was flour. My late grandmother, who we called Mama Bailey, had left us a cabinet which had a flour bin to the left side of it. Ironically, I still have that old cabinet as I write this today.

We each grabbed a chair and pulled it up to the cabinet. I got a huge tablespoon and dipped it into the flour. I told Douglas to open his mouth as wide as he could. Then I poked the spoon deep into the flour and came up with the biggest heaping tablespoon full of flour possible. Douglas was patiently waiting with his mouth wide open. I carefully and slowly turned the spoon in Doug's direction and said, "Douglas, here it comes." When he closed his mouth, I announced that he was officially a "snuff dipper" for life. Douglas looked as though he had the mumps or something. Each cheek was so full of flour that he looked like he had a balloon on each side of his face. His lips were white with flour. I couldn't help laughing at how funny he looked. If only I had had a camera, because it definitely was a Kodak moment. He gave me a questioning look as if to say, "What now Perry?" As I was laughing, I decided to take both of my hands and clap them against each of his cheeks at the same time to see what he would do. He quickly climbed down from his chair. He couldn't talk. "Puff" was all he could do. Every time he "puffed", flour spewed out of his mouth resembling the smoke coming from a choo choo train. I've never seen Douglas run as fast as he did that day. He ran through every room in the house, then out to the front porch and away looking like a steam engine every time he "puffed" and leaving a trail of flour scattered behind him.

Prude Waldrop was sitting on his porch, and he asked me where Douglas was going in such a rush and what was wrong with him. I told him I really didn't know. I followed the trail of flour to Bitsey Hamrick's Store. Douglas had run inside, still puffing flour like a train. Richard Hannah was running the store at the time. By the time I got to the store, I knew I was going to be in deep trouble because I knew Mr. Hannah would surely tell my mom and dad. Mr. Hannah patted Douglas hard on the back and gave him a free chocolate milk. I'm sure the people in the store and Mr. Hannah had a good laugh about it later. Of course, I learned my lesson by getting a good whipping, and I never did anything like that again.

Legion Lake, a recreation area for veterans belonging to the American Legion, was in the process of being built while we lived at 529 Rockmart Road, My father and my Uncle Andy Lease Bailey, known as "Lease" to everyone, both served in the United States Army. Lease encouraged my father to join the American Legion because my dad's love of fishing. This would give the family an opportunity to enjoy the benefits of fishing, swimming, boating, camping, and other related outdoor activities. The cost was just five dollars a year. So my father joined the American Legion. We enjoyed so many wonderful evenings fishing, swimming, and boating at Legion Lake. My father was allowed to bring his family and a limited number of guests. It never failed, when we got the benefits, family members that we haven't seen in a long time suddenly appeared on our front porch wanting to go fishing, swimming, or boating. My father recognized this for what it was, and he always had a good excuse when they showed up on our front porch. He was no fool with people who tried to use him. I always admired my father for that.

While still living at 529 Rockmart Road, my father, Jimmy, and my Uncle Lease were employed at Cannon Caskets in Villa Rica. They all worked in the department that made metal caskets.

The back yard of the Rockmart house was larger than most of the yards in Fullerville. It was big enough to have a very nice garden, and that we did. We grew corn, beans, tomatoes, a few cantaloupes and watermelons. There was also an old tool shed there that the Hosiery Mill had once used to store old boxes and thread combs for resale or recycle. There was also another building beside our house that the mill had used to store broken machinery which was scavenged for parts as needed. Douglas and I painted the old tool shed and started a boys club which included the other young fellows from the Fullerville Community. Our boys club would play sports against other boys clubs in the area. We played army, football, baseball, and sometimes we would even have real fights. We were good kids, and we always made up afterwards.

The people who lived in Fullerville had a sense of pride about them. They didn't believe in handouts and welfare. However, back then folks looked after each other. They were generous in helping those who were really in need.

Sometimes this didn't work out quite right. A relative of my family would send hand-me-down clothes for me, but I never wore them because most of them were either outdated or too big. So my dad would take them to keep from hurting their feelings, and we would sneak them off to the Salvation Army or to a church. These kinfolks would then brag that they helped their family out, and one would never hear the end of it. Dad and Mom quit accepting their hand-me-downs because they were not given from the heart. The givers just wanted to brag and to have something to talk about. It's sad we have such people on earth, but maybe God put them here to be examples of how not to behave.

None the less, everyone in Fullerville looked after all the children of the community. If someone had told on me for something I shouldn't have been doing, my parents thanked them for letting them know so they could take the proper means of discipline. I have to admit that the system wasn't perfect. Unfortunately, there were one or two sick, malicious persons who would make false accusations getting the little fellows punished for things they had not done.

My parents and grandparents, as well as other old timers, shared their stories with me about how a kind and generous man, Bud Taylor, helped the folks that could not afford a funeral for their loved ones. Taylor Funeral Home served Villa Rica for many years. I'm not certain when he actually started his funeral home, but Taylor Funeral Home closed its doors around 1950 or 1951. Taylor Funeral Home buried my granddaddy, Jim George, after he died in 1949. Everybody thought the world of Bud Taylor because of his kindness to other people. One seldom finds men like Bud Taylor today.

The people in Fullerville did pretty well unless a set back came due to some sickness or tragedy. One summer I developed a toothache. My parents bought a bottle of red toothache medicine from the drugstore. It was called Red Cross, it had a red cross on the bottle, and it tasted terrible. Cotton balls were dipped in the medicine and then put on the aching tooth. I'm not sure if it was suppose to numb the pain or what. The next choice was putting a baby aspirin on the tooth. I used so many baby aspirin tablets that my blood probably got pretty thin. It's a miracle that my gum wasn't ruined forever. There I was with a fever and swollen jaw, but I went for four days without seeing a dentist because it cost five dollars to have a tooth pulled.

I don't know if dentists back then were encouraged to save a tooth. Maybe it depended on what your income level was. When I go to the dentist today, I usually get a free toothbrush, dental floss, and sample size toothpaste. It's probably supplied as advertisement by the companies that make tooth care products, but who cares. The only thing I got free from the dentist back when I was a kid was a great big lollipop, and that was only if I was a good boy. Just more sugar to rot the teeth.

Because the toothache didn't get better, my dad finally took me to the dentist, Dr. Guy Davis. What does the late Dr. Guy Davis do? He pulled my tooth while it was abscessed. That was a no-no. One doesn't pull a tooth when it is abscessed. The infection should have been treated before pulling the tooth. If my parents had taken action when my tooth was first giving me problems, it would have saved them a whole lot of money and time. I was excited about his pulling my tooth because I thought the pain would go away. However, the pain and swelling got worse afterward. I went home; but before the day ended, my parents rushed me to the emergency room at Villa Rica City Hospital. My jaw was so swollen that I couldn't open my mouth. I was admitted to the hospital, and Dr. R. L. Berry worked to get the swelling down without lancing. I was given shots and an IV. On the third day, the swelling began to get better. Dr.

Berry had succeeded. I was in the hospital for a week and two days. That one tooth cost my family a dentist bill, a doctor bill, and a hospital bill. For me, the cost was pure pain and agony.

There are many other stories like mine, simply because the insurance plans available paid so little on healthcare. Additionally, they were quite expensive for minimum wage mill workers. I understood why my parents avoided the dentist and doctor as long as possible hoping that things would get better. But in my situation, it didn't get better. It only got worse. I could have died from the infection. That would have resulted in yet another very costly expense-a funeral.

Unfortunately, I had yet another encounter with the heath care system during my childhood. It all began at school.

I will always remember the great lunches we had at school. On Fridays, we always had something good to eat like fish, hamburgers, or hot dogs. Everyone bought lunch on Fridays. Today one couldn't think of buying a meal at the price we paid for our lunches back then. We paid 25 cents for a hamburger, chips, baked beans, dessert, and milk. This was not a bad price for that kind of meal, and 25 cents is what we paid everyday.

In 1963 I may have paid for this enjoyment rather painfully and caused my family a great deal of financial stress. I enjoyed my wonderful lunch, and then I went out on the playground to run. I came down with a cramp. This was not an uncommon event among the school children considering the circumstances.

Villa Rica City Hospital built in 1955

Photo courtesy of the author

My parents were called, and I was taken to one of the doctor's office in Villa Rica. There were two waiting rooms there. One was for black people, and one was for white people. I insisted that I no longer had any pain, but I was given an emergency appendectomy that night at the Villa Rica City Hospital. Even though my father carried his company's health insurance, it took him two years to pay off the bill. Strangely two or three years later, people from the

State of Georgia Health Department came to our school and interviewed those kids given appendectomies between 1963 and 1965. Did the number of emergency appendectomies slack off after that? There is no way to know.

As a child, I would hear the grownups of Fullerville, who made low wages, knock people who lived in the housing projects along with anyone accepting any type of welfare. As far as health care went, the mill workers of Fullerville were in the same boat as those in the public housing. If low wage jobs did offer health insurance, it was expensive and didn't carry a good health plan. What confused me about all this was that the people in Fullerville may have been paying their own rent or buying their own house, but when it came time for their children to start to school for the first time, nearly every kid in Fullerville received their shots free from the county nurse. The expense, of course, was paid by the taxpayers. Was this socialism back in the fifties and sixties? No one seemed to care. I wonder if many parents would have been unable to afford the shots on their own. What is even stranger, many of the kids getting those shots had parents working at high wage jobs.

The Bailey Brothers   Photo courtesy of the author

As a student in Mrs. Mary Anderson's fifth grade class, I always had a fascination with history. She taught us a lot about the history of Villa Rica from the early settlers of Carroll County to Coca Cola. She always held my attention, and I believe that was because of the way she taught. One could tell that she really enjoyed teaching and that her enthusiasm drew the children in making them want to learn more. She was the elementary school teacher I admired the most and held the greatest respect for. In fact, it was in her class that I was inspired to become a radio broadcaster. As I mentioned before, we would have to report on a current event after lunch. Most of the other children in my class would pick a topic in the national or world news. I took my assignments personally because I made a mental contest out of it. Since I knew that the other children would get their assignments from the mainstream news networks, I chose the majority of my reports from the local news in Villa Rica and Fullerville. I even got my family and neighbors to help me out by giving me any news tips that might be of local interest. Mrs. Anderson seemed very pleased with this. The rest of my classmates started to catch on and tried to pursue me, but they never caught up. Good teachers, with a God-given calling, really do mold young minds and inspire. Bless them!

A major and most terrible event of national importance occurred while I was living at 529 Rockmart Road. I was in Mrs. Anderson's class. It was a typical cool, sunny day on November 22, 1963. It was a Friday, and all the children were looking forward to getting out of school for the weekend. We walked to the lunchroom.

After finishing our lunch break that Friday, we returned to the classroom and settled in for our next subject which was current events. Mrs. Anderson told us to get ready to present the topics which we had gathered from the news. We then had to tell what we thought about our subject. She called on the first student to come to the front and start the class off. He had no more gotten out of his seat when the principal came over the public address system and spoke saying, "May I have your attention please?" After repeating his request a couple of times, all the classes quieted down and listened. The very last thing we had expected him to say was that the President of the United States, John F. Kennedy, had been shot while riding in his motorcade in downtown Dallas, Texas!

All of a sudden a big lump had formed in the back of my throat, and I thought to myself that this couldn't be true. Why would anyone want to shoot the President of the United States? I was so shocked and confused. I felt as though I were moving in slow motion. I looked around at all my classmates watching their expressions. Some of my classmates were getting very emotional. With their heads down, they began crying quietly.

However, some classmates looked happy about the shooting, and even a few shouted that they hoped that he would die. Mrs. Mary Anderson quickly put a stop to those despicable outbursts. I didn't understand what to make of it all. I was just a fifth grader; still young and naïve. I had always been taught that wishing anyone ill was a sin. I didn't understand why some of my classmates hated the President or why they would wish a terrible death upon him. I knew that the United States of America was the land of the free, a country that believes in God; and yet, some of my classmates wished death itself on our

President. These same classmates attended Bible school and church services every Sunday with their parents. Questions began to pop into my mind such as, "What would their parents say if they could hear their children right now?" I wondered if Mrs. Anderson would tell their parents and what action would be taken, if any. Would these parents let their children know that it is wrong to hate or wish death on someone? I was too unworldly to realize that children just parrot things they hear from one adult or another without thinking. I understand that we have politicians that we don't always agree with, and that is why we vote. If we really care and are not just plain lazy, we can vote them out of office. Assassinate them? Never!

It seemed as if the world had just stopped. Everything from government offices to the local beauty shops closed up for the day. The entire town was practically a ghost town because everyone was at home watching their television set to learn what had happened on that dreadful day. Those without a television set stopped by our house. There were only three networks at the time and three local television stations. The networks were NBC, CBS, and ABC. The television stations that serviced our area at that time were WAGA Channel 5, WSB (TV) Channel 2, and WAII Channel 11. The Kennedy assassination was on every single channel, and it would be on every single channel until after the funeral on the following Monday. Unbelievably, the town would remain closed until then.

There would be no *Flintstones, Route 66, Sky King, Lone Ranger, My Friend Flicka, Fury,* or any other great television shows that weekend due to the coverage of the assassination. You could hear talk on the streets and from family members wondering if Russia, Cuba, or even Vice President Johnson were behind the assassination of the President. All kinds of theories have been developed since that time. However, I really don't believe that we will ever know the truth about the JFK assassination.

Another shocking and significant event took place right on our very own television set, right before our very own eyes, and before the eyes of the world. On the Sunday morning after President Kennedy was killed, we were sitting around with our eyes glued to the set for more news about the assassination. The Dallas Police were transporting Lee Harvey Oswald to another facility for further questioning on the assassination of President Kennedy. A man suddenly appeared out of nowhere and shot Lee Harvey Oswald dead in cold blood. This was history in the making, and we were watching it live as it happened. Everyone in my living room was stunned and horrified. None could quite grasp what they had just witnessed. This was the talk of the town for many days. I still have many unanswered questions about what really happened on those terrible November days in 1963. I believe that I am not alone in this and that many people also have questions.

There was just not much for children or teenagers to do in Fullerville or Villa Rica. If one wanted to go bowling, skating, or to see a movie, they had to go out of town to find entertainment. Fortunately, there were some activities available to us; but they were mostly available only in the summer season. We did have a recreation center which had a swimming pool and a tennis court. Sometimes local bands came to play for the teenagers so that they could dance on Friday and Saturday nights. Some of us had the Legion Lake available for swimming, picnicking, boating, and fishing. We also had the ball field in Fullerville shared by people in both Fullerville and Villa Rica.

Some children would travel as far as Mableton, Georgia, just to go roller skating. Finally, the Mableton Skating Center started its own bus route from Mableton to Villa Rica in order to bring the kids to skate and then return them home. One of the stops for the Mableton Skating Bus was in front of the house of our next door neighbor, Larry Shelton. All the kids from the Villa Rica and Fullerville Community would meet there to catch the bus which was a great convenience to both the children and their parents.

We still had just three television stations and networks to choose from. The television stations were based in Atlanta, Georgia. All of our shows were still in black and white. We watched shows like *Bonanza* which came from NBC, *The Fugitive* (ABC), *Gomer Pyle, U.S.M.C.* (CBS), *The Andy Griffith Show* (CBS), and *Bewitched* (ABC), and *Twilight Zone*. After the news on Friday nights, WAGA channel 5 aired the *Big Movie Shocker* hosted by Bestoink Dooley. Mr. George Ellis, who owned a theatre in Atlanta, was the mysterious Bestoink Dooley. He would present thrillers on Big Movie Shocker such as Frankenstein meets the Wolf Man, Dracula, The Mummy, and many others known today as classic thrillers. The show was really a really big conversation piece at school.

In the year 1964, people were pondering about the impact of both the Kennedy assassination and the effects of the newly enacted Civil Rights Act. On the ninth of February that year, the Beatles made their first appearance on the Ed Sullivan Show and performed, "I Want to Hold Your Hand" and "She Loves You", as 74 million people watched. No group has ever been able to compete with The Beatles when it comes to drawing the largest audience in the history of television.

In the spring of 1964, the Villa Rica Theatre, known as The Villa, closed its doors forever. No more Saturday mornings or nights at the movies. I'll never forget the long lines in front of that theatre when movies like *Elvis Presley's Jail House Rock and Love Me Tender, The Ten Commandments,* and *Gone with the Wind* came to town. The line for the really popular movies would stretch all the way to Chamber's Gulf Station on Bankhead Highway. I had enjoyed so many movies at The Villa. After all, there's nothing to compare with hot buttered popcorn from the theatre. I have never understood why a growing town like Villa Rica no longer had a movie theatre. Perhaps the people in Villa Rica did not go to the movies often enough to support a theatre. Of course, today with the wide spread ownership of video players, DVD's and entertainment centers, people are no longer limited to public facilities.

I was in class in the sixth grade at Villa Rica Elementary School. Of all of my school years this was the very worst year for me. All of the students were trying to get used to the changes that had been made by the new principal, Mr. Ash, who had replaced Mr. Hollomon, the elementary school principal. Even the high school principal, Mr. A. B. Duncan, was replaced by Mr. Max Crook. Thad McCoy, the school custodian for years, left with Mr. Hollomon and Mr. Duncan. Our school recesses were shortened and were no longer called recess but were referred to as breaks. We got a ten minute break in the morning, lunch break, and a fifteen minute break in the afternoon. This was the year we started changing classes and were assigned to homerooms. Many classmates didn't like the changes but it got better as time went on, and we adjusted. It just took getting used to.

Unfortunately one of my teachers was adverse to the modern day hair styles. With the invasion of the Beatles and other rock groups, the boys at my school had started wearing their hair a little longer. This teacher still wore his hair short and greased down. He would pick on the boys with longer hair, and I dreaded going to his class everyday because I knew my day was coming. And it did! I was sitting in class one day; and he said, "Bailey, I don't like the way your hair looks today. Go to the barber shop and get it cut. It had better be cut when you come in tomorrow!" My hair wasn't even long because I had just gotten a haircut the week before. In fact, it was neatly cut because my parents wouldn't allow me to wear long hair.

The next day, I was dreading his class. Halfway through the class, I decided he must have forgotten about my hair. He was walking around the classroom with a ruler in his hand. He stopped by my desk, stuck the ruler behind my neck, and started sliding it up and down the back of my head. He said "Bailey, I thought I told you to get a haircut!" I replied, "My dad said to tell you that I didn't need a haircut and that it was just cut a week ago." He then said, "You know what I told you. Now get up there to my desk and bend over." The class was laughing because Bailey was going to get "his butt whipped".

When this teacher put the paddle to you, it burned. When he paddled me, the first lick got me right smack on my backside. The next two licks fell between my hips and my back bringing me to the floor. I think by the look on his face that he knew he was in trouble. He knew I had an older brother in high school, but he had no idea that he was going to have to face up to my father. He did ask if I was hurt and started being nice. He apologized saying he that he didn't mean to hit me on my back. However, I was in tears; and I was hurting.

When I got home I told my parents about it. My parents told me to say nothing. At the beginning of class time the next day, whom should I see? Three family members arrived, my older brother and my mom and dad. As I started to walk into the classroom, my dad called me back out. He told me that I needed to be there since I was the one involved. When the teacher came down the hall, he walked past my mom, dad, and brother. He said to me smiling, "What are you doing out here? Do you want another dose of what you got yesterday?" My dad spoke up and said, "I don't think so. Your paddling days with my son are over. If you had a problem with my boy's hair, you should have contacted me since I'm responsible for giving him the money to get a haircut."

Now my dad had a way with words, especially when he was mad. He never used foul language or raised his voice. His facial expressions could be serious, but he would have a "don't give a rip" grin on his face. Dad told the teacher that he planned to talk to other parents from this class to find out if their kids were getting paddlings that they didn't deserve just so that he and the rest of the class could get a big laugh. I never thought I would ever see my dad directly point his finger in someone's face; but my dad pointed his finger in his face and said, "If you ever hit my son for the fun of it again, I will personally beat the hell out of you." My dad really meant it, and he could have carried through. Dad was a good boxer in his youth. He never started trouble, but he would stand up when he was confronted.

The teacher apologized, and my dad told him that he didn't have a problem with his paddling me if I deserved it. However, hitting me just for everyone's entertainment and almost sending me to the hospital was going much too far. From that day on, the teacher was a different man. He knew that he was in the wrong. Later we found out that he had been confronted by other fathers who had kids in his other classes for the same kind of mistreatment of his students.

My dad always said that the Carroll County School Board at that time sucked, and I have to agree with him. They always catered to the students with prominent parents and ignored the plight and abuse of the others. After all, they were elected to represent all students of Carroll County.

In all my years of going to Villa Rica School, I had never been bullied by anyone until I entered the sixth grade. Evidentially, a clique had formed within my sixth grade class. I began to notice that some of the guys that I had hung around with from first grade to fifth grade were beginning to ignore me. Even the girls were beginning to be unfriendly to me. I had always been nice to them, and they to me, until this point. These were all good, Christian, church going kids from good, Christian, church going families.

One morning I came into class. I sat on top of one of the classroom desks talking to a friend about the Friday night football game. Before I knew what was happening, I was pushed to the school room floor with the desk shoved on top of me. I had no idea what was going on. A gang of boys and, even more freakish, some girls joined into the fun of kicking me. They hit me from all directions laughing while they were doing it. I knew that I could not take on this crowd by myself. But I did remember each and every face. I knew that I could fight them one on one by myself without a problem, and that they were going to have hell to pay later. One big guy kept stomping my hand, and it was horribly battered. My eyes were blacked, there were large black and blue bruises over my whole body, and my nose was broken. My sixth grade teacher came in and stopped the attack. I was lying on the floor and could barely move. I had blood on my shirt and hands. The sixth grade teacher told me to get up and go to my desk. I could hear some of the kids holler, "He's putting on!" and "He's not hurt!" My teacher told me again to get up and go to my desk and not to start anymore fights. As I was slowly getting up without anyone helping me up, I looked at her and said that I did not start a fight and asked if she planned to do something to the ones that did.

"Are you going to allow me to go to the washroom and wash up?" I asked.

She excused me and allowed me to wash up. When I came back I went to her desk and whispered to her what had taken place. She told me to drop it and go to my desk. I held on as best I could through the rest of the day, lapsing in and out because of the pain. I should have been taken to the hospital.

At last, I finally made it home. I said nothing to my parents, or they to me. However, I did notice that one of my brothers and his friends became very protective toward me after the attack.

I got even with most of them one by one before the school year was over. This happened when I caught them alone. I didn't have a problem going up against the guys who beat me when their crowd was not around to protect them. However, this on my part did bring on continued bullying by the same rotten group of fiends. If one ever wonders how cynicism comes to the young, please realize that it is taught in very ideal shattering ways.

I'll never forget the day that I was jumped on for the last time. Luckily, I had made a new friend who was pretty tall and a couple of years older than my classmates. My friend's name was Olin Ivey. He pulled the boys off me, and we both started fighting. Between the two of us, we did very well. I never had a problem with any bullies after that. I have never forgotten that Olin came through for me. He was a true friend from that day on and the nicest person anyone could have ever known. Olin Ivey was also one of the best musicians in

Carroll County. After the fight, I asked him to come home with me to meet my family. Olin played guitar with us, either in the living room on a bad day or on the front porch on pleasant days. Nobody ever complained about our music being too loud. In fact, most of the time they would either come by to enjoy it, or they would listen from their porches. Olin usually played the guitar at that time, but later, he took on the keyboards. As a matter of fact, I can't think of a single instrument Olin couldn't play. I lost my friend Olin Ivey in January 2010. Fortunately, I was able to talk to him a week before Christmas. We spent an hour or so reminiscing about all those years ago. I failed sixth grade, so I had to repeat it. A lot of my buddies were also held back. I'm so glad it happened. It was a new beginning and the making of new friends. We all got along well. There were very few fights. It seemed as though we all worked together to help one another. The class of 1972 was good for us because it was a class that was made up of good, decent kids. I was very glad to be a part of the class of 1972. School was more fun, and we were all getting into the music.

In the seventh grade I had my second God-sent teacher, Mrs. Word. She was my homeroom teacher and taught science. If anyone recognized that I needed help and realized how far behind I was, it was Mrs. Word. While other teachers before and after her threw their hands up and gave up on me, she did not. She made me recognize the qualities that I had to offer and inspired me to do what was necessary to better myself. She was able to put words in my ear that have never left me. "Perry, you can do it!" And I believed her. She made me believe in myself. Unlike the Carroll County School system, I knew that Mrs. Word cared about every child's education. All her students were important to her. Perhaps those students who did not care for Mrs. Word were the kids who were favored by other teachers.

We listened to two radio stations, WQXI and WPLO. Both were AM stations. First they carried rock music. WPLO later changed to country music. It's a shame, but it is no more. It should not be confused with the current station now serving Atlanta under the WPLO call sign.
http://www.youtube.com/watch?v=5Od1MDGbkk&feature=related

Chapter 4

509 Rockmart Road

No matter where we lived in Fullerville we always had good neighbors, and we all looked out for one another. There was something special about 509 Rockmart Road. The neighbors around us were great. We lived next door to James and Ruth Sauls and their son Jimmy. Mrs. Ruth Butler, who lived there long after we moved away from Rockmart Road, and Mrs. Pearson each had a house across the road. The Leon Massey family and the Thornton family moved in later. The Causey family was our nearby neighbor along with the Bill Barber family, the Sarah Sauls family, and the Pate family. There was a basketball goal in Sarah's yard, and all the kids gathered there to play and have a good time.

Some fine athletes came out of Fullerville, especially during my time there. Let me just name a few, Bob, Terry, and Sheila Sauls, Terry Butler, Scott Swafford, and Jimmy Sauls; all did well. They were very good athletes for Villa Rica High School sports programs. I was proud to know them all and called them good neighbors. Those of us that were not active in the sports program at Villa Rica High School were very active as far as backyard football games. Jimmy Causey, myself, and others got up a football team and played against the housing project kids. I think we even had a few cheerleaders from Fullerville and the housing projects to cheer us on. Those were the days and good times.

Villa Rica F.F.A. String Band Competition: of 1964
John Lafitte, Jerry Kesler, James Cowan, and Andy Bailey
Villa Rica News Paper 1964 Photo courtesy of the author

At 509 Rockmart Road, music continued to be played in the living room and on the front porch of our home. My dad still played his music; and my brother, Andy, formed a band. Andy and his group also joined with the Future Farmers of America String Band. In 1964, they won first place for Villa Rica High School.

Douglas also started a band. He and his good friend, Jimmy Wald played their music many times at 509 Rockmart Road.

The common thing for most people in Fullerville, and maybe a few in Villa Rica, was that we ate what ever was put on the table. We were not wasteful. We would warm leftovers on a stove, not in a microwave, and have them the next day. The first microwave I ever saw was on the Jetsons, a cartoon show on television. Luxury items were considered to be a television, a radio, window air conditioner and a telephone. I can't imagine being without those items today. We had a television and a radio; later we got the two party line telephone. Dad and mom decided to get a private line after a month of sharing. After all, it was just $2.00 more. When we moved to Villa Rica, we did not get a phone until we moved to 509 Rockmart Road.

I guess the reason my dad and mother didn't get a phone until that time is because they would always visit the people they wanted to talk to, or they would visit you. Andy joined the United States Marine Corps in 1966. I believe that his joining the Marines played an important role our getting a phone. He was not able to call home until he got to his first station which was at Camp Pendleton, California. After Andy left for the Parris Island, South Carolina Marine base, just two of the Bailey boys remained at home, Douglas and I. The war in Vietnam was growing, and I remember how parents would stay in touch with each other and talk about their sons who were serving in the United States Military. I remember that when Andy got to the Camp Pendleton Marine Base in California, we could talk to him again and catch him up on what was going on in Villa Rica. Andy was trained for the tanks; and after finishing his training at Camp Pendleton, he was sent straight to Vietnam. It didn't take Andy long to move up in rank. He was a tank commander in Vietnam and was promoted to Sergeant. Andy Bailey served in the Marine Corps until 1970.

Jimmy and his wife Nancy and their two children, Lanette and Lynn, were living in Dallas, Georgia. Jimmy was in the flooring business laying carpet and tile. His wife Nancy worked at Sears in the administration.

We moved to 509 Rockmart Road, not realizing that this would be the last Fullerville house we would ever live in. It never occurred to me that my mom and dad would ever move away from Villa Rica. Villa Rica was their home. They knew everybody there and everybody knew them. I want to tell you more about 509 Rockmart Road. It was a good house, but none of the Fullerville houses had sheet rock walls. None of the houses had any sort of insulation. One would burn up in the summertime and freeze in the winter. The natural gas heater ran all the time in the winter, running up a very expensive bill. Of course, there were no inside bathroom facilities which made things very unpleasant in bad weather.

I remember the purchase of our first automatic washer. What a thrill it was to finally have one. Up until then we had to either wash our clothes at the laundry mat or in the old ringer washing machine which was kept on the back porch. People back then had to wait for a pretty day to wash clothes because they must either hang their clothes on the line outside or travel out to the laundry mat. We had to wait three days after purchasing our new washer to use it because our father had to dig a trench all the way to the ditch behind the house to carry away the dirty wash water. Alas, there were no sewage pipes or septic tanks in Fullerville at this time. Since we had not purchased a clothes dryer, my mother would wash a few loads at a time in bad weather and dry them by the heater.

I have so many memories at 509 Rockmart Road that I cannot count them all. I remember the apple tree. We children would gather apples and throw them at one another. We called these crab apple battles. On hot, sunny days we would splash each other with water from the hose. Sometimes a gang of us Fullerville children would go to Sarah Sauls' house to play basketball. She would always give us Pepsi Colas to drink. Sometimes I would just sit out on our porch on warm days just to watch the traffic go by.

I always looked forward to people coming over and playing music. I enjoyed the big Sunday dinners that mother would whip up. The table would always be full of fried chicken, biscuits & gravy, cream potatoes, and ice cold tea. She also made homemade ice cream on Sundays during the summer. I always looked forward to Thanksgiving and Christmas when the family would all be together. It was amazing to listen to their talk. It ranged over everything from politics, religion, sports, to music. It was interesting to just sit and listen to what my family members thought about these topics. I always found myself disagreeing silently with a great deal that was said because thinking "outside the box" was something they never did. Their thinking was strongly geared to the messages sent by the media.

Just about everybody in the Villa Rica and Fullerville community had some type of religious background from both sides of the family. I was always taught, as a little boy that I should never criticize another's religious background just because they didn't believe the way you do. I was also taught that it was not our place to judge another man's faith. It's amazing how things have changed since then. Now people are criticized for holding beliefs that differ from others.

Those with different outlooks are now accused of being un-American and having no morals or values what so ever.

As a little boy growing up, I always asked my parents and others a lot of questions about religion. They would tell me what they believed, but I never got a straight answer that I could understand. Rather than satisfying my curiosity, it caused me to become even more curious. I grew to wonder if religion were something to control people and make them fearful.

My brother Douglas and I often dreaded going to church. We would hear a fire and brimstone sermon that was scarier than watching a horror movie. People would shake all over and scream and holler and even cry while the preacher pointed at them and yelled, "Come out of their bodies Satan." Well, you could imagine what went through our very young heads. With our eyeballs about to pop, we feared that a devil with a long forked tail was going to jump out of someone's body. Each time this would happen, Douglas and I would crawl under the bench and close our eyes. Out of fear, we begged not to be taken to that particular church again.

I'll never forget the Sunday evening that we all went to an old country church in the New Georgia area. I remember the old cemetery beside it and the old wood stove inside. The people who attended services there were good, old fashioned country folks, work worn and most with sparse teeth. I remember thinking, "We left civilization to attend church." Not that we were any better than these people, but my family was much more sophisticated than most of those folks.

I don't know the reason we attended that church. Perhaps it was because my parents had been invited to sing that night. They had only one six string guitar, and my daddy had brought his along. I remember that my parents sang a hymn. I had never heard of any church serving the Lord's Supper at the night service, but this church did. Most churches serve broken crackers and grape juice at the Lord's Supper. This church had what appeared to be a homemade biscuit broken up and what looked like red Hawaiian Punch. I'm here to tell you that juice did not taste like red Hawaiian Punch. I choked down my piece of biscuit and drank what I think was really cranberry juice. I said right then that whoever made that biscuit made it with a crunch, and it was all I could do to get the juice down.

After the service was over, we went home; and I knew something wasn't right while on the way. All of a sudden I went from a high to a low and started feeling awful. It seemed as though it took forever to get home. I told my mom and dad that I was not feeling well. When we got home, I immediately went to bed. I slept for about two hours then woke up with a horrible cramp in my stomach. Then it really hit. It was the worst vomiting and diarrhea I've ever had, both at the same time. My little brother and my dad were experiencing the same awful thing. For whatever reason, my mother did not take the Lord's Supper that night, and she was perfectly well. Her first thought was that we had food poisoning. We all went to the emergency room. Maybe mom should have been a doctor because she had diagnosed us correctly. We did indeed have food poisoning. My dad laughed about it for years afterward and often told the story. I can still hear him saying today, "Who would have thought that one would get food poisoning from taking the Lord's Supper?"

On Sunday evenings, we would often ride around, and I would notice all the churches we would pass along the way. The churches would range from big churches to medium sized churches to very small churches. I can remember thinking to myself that of all these different sized churches, which one is the real House of the Lord. I asked my parents why there were so many churches and why so many different sized churches? I can remember their pointing to one church and saying, 'That's where all the rich people go." Other churches would be described as houses of worship for average people, and yet others were described as churches for the poor folks.

Does the Bible not state that there is only one faith and one church? Why are there so many churches with so many different faiths? Then I would wonder how so many people can read the Bible and find so many different meanings. I haven't been to a church yet that teaches much about the Book of Revelations. Some believe it has already taken place, some believe it's yet to come, and others believe it's symbolic.

I do know this, the rich, the middle class, and the poor can rest assured that all will be equal in Heaven. Will they all be happy about this?

I worked selling The Grit newspapers. In fact, I think every kid my age all over the country was selling Grit papers at that time. Now, for those who may be scratching their heads and wondering what a Grit could possibly be, I will offer a few words of explanation. The Grit was a small, very successful newspaper which served the small towns across America. Its distribution success was made possible because it was sold by an area's teenagers. However, I didn't make much money at it; and I didn't keep at it for very long. Delivering the newspapers wasn't so bad in the summertime, but in the winter you thought you would freeze to death.

The theatre had already closed, so there wasn't much to do in Villa Rica unless you wanted to play ball or go swimming everyday. We didn't have the bowling alleys, theatres, arcades, and skating rinks of today. Video and DVD hadn't been invented yet. Neither could one go to a computer and play games to pass the time away as can be done today. I have often wondered if life would have been different if the internet had been available in our time.

I'll never forget how we all heard preachers and others saying that the end of time was near when the first man headed for the moon. It was believed by some that if man belonged on the moon, God would have put him there or made a way for him to get there. It was actually feared that the moon would turn to blood when the space craft touched down. I have a friend who was a scientist working on Redstone Arsenal in Huntsville, Alabama, during the days of the Space Race; and she laughs as she recalls reading letters in the Huntsville newspaper predicting that dire things would happen if we invaded God's privacy. That was just at the thought of a satellite! Then Sputnik I started a time of thrilled anticipation and excitement! At last the dream of space travel was on the way! However, our very own southern bunch of space enthusiasts, lead by Dr. Werner von Braun, was held back from launching in order to give other agencies the first try at it. It is well known that when finally called upon, the South did indeed rise to the occasion and in no time at all. None the less, some were convinced that the moon landing would be an even bigger insult to God than the satellites were. I thought it was stupid to make such statements and even more stupid to believe them. I felt that God did make a way for man to go to the moon. The answer is, "It R us!" He gave man a brain which was the best computer ever invented. A problem with brains is that they can come down with a virus just like a computer and stop working.

The Bailey background has always been conservative in religious practice, but in the 50s and 60s the great majority of Fullervillians and Villa Ricans voted Democratic because of the fear of Hoover times. The old saying back then was that the Republicans were for the rich man, and Democrats were for the working man. We witnessed history first hand on our black and white television sets. Things started to change slowly as the liberal movement began taking over the Democratic Party starting with the protesting of the Vietnam War. With good reason, this didn't set well with people that had family members in Vietnam or with the veterans who had served in World War I or World War II.

In the summer months of 1966, I was age 14 and Douglas was age 11. I talked over finding a way to make money with my brother so that perhaps we could buy a bicycle. He was all for it! I called Mr. Stockmar.

Mr. Stockmar's parents had come to the area in search of gold. Gold was mined through out Carroll County, and mines existed at the Slickens and behind the Fullerville Ballpark. These mines yielded even less than that found at the Stockmar mine. The Stockmars found little gold, but their efforts led to something better. Their son, Buddy, established the Flying S Ranch which was a large farm, a guest ranch, an airport, and lake.

He agreed to talk with us. We walked the four or five miles to the Stockmar ranch, had short interview, and got our first real job. We worked five days a week. Our main tasks were washing the planes, burning old brush piles, washing dishes in the restaurant, and carrying the luggage of guests who arrived at the Flying S Ranch airport. Our everyday work clothes consisted of a pair of blue jeans and shirt for the dirty jobs, but we had to dress nicely in dress shorts and shirts when we met the guests.

Mr. Stockmar often told us stories about his wife and how much he missed her. He told us that she had been killed in a car wreck several years back. I think at times he had moments of loneliness. We had no problems with just sitting and talking to him. After all, he was the boss. We always did whatever he wanted.

Flying S Ranch was also the place where I learned how to drive. Buddy Stockmar would throw his keys to me so that I could drive the truck around the ranch and pick up trash and brush. I didn't know how to drive at the time or change gears. Unfortunately the truck had a straight shift. I would drive

Vera and Buddy Stockmar

Photo courtesy of Monroe Spake

the truck in first gear and then ease off the clutch to make it sound like I was changing gears because I didn't want Buddy to know that I didn't know how to drive. I was afraid he wouldn't let me drive the truck anymore if he found this out. I knew then I was going to have to learn how to drive the straight shift and soon. So I drove to Stockmar Road, which was a dirt road at the time. I drove up and down until I got everything going smoothly, but there was one more gear I had to learn and that was reverse. So I pulled over to a stop and started playing with the gears again until I figured out which one made the truck go in reverse. I was really enthusiastic about teaching myself how to drive a straight shift truck. The sad thing was I had no one to share my excitement with other than Doug. My parents had no idea that their 14 year old son already knew how to drive a straight shift. I certainly have never thought that there's anything wrong with self education.

Douglas and I enjoyed working at the ranch. My mom and dad would take us to work every day before they went to work at Banning Yarn Mills. My mother made sure we always had a lunch. We always had chips and Mr. Stockmar had a drink machine. At lunch time, Douglas and I would buy Fanta orange drinks. I'll never forget the time she fixed fish sandwiches for us. The fish sandwiches were cold, and we had yet to hear of a microwave oven. So I had an idea that was just fine for a 14 year old. We parked the truck on the landing field away from all the shade trees. Mother always wrapped our sandwiches in aluminum foil. I unwrapped the sandwiches, placed them on the foil, and put them on the hood of the truck. The sun provided enough heat on that hot summer day to warm them up nicely. In only a few minutes they were warm enough to eat. I'm not sure what she was thinking of. Perhaps she thought we could heat them up in the oven at the restaurant. I'm sure Mr.

Stockmar would have let us, but we never asked. Afterwards, we made sure that there were no more fish sandwiches for lunch. Instead, we asked for cold cuts like ham, turkey, and peanut butter and jelly.

I dreaded going home and having to take a bath in a wash pan. We always got very dirty by the late evening when we got off. So during the summer we wore our cut off jeans and took a shower in the back yard with a hose pipe. We would be covered from head to toe with the soot from burning the brush piles.

Dodgie Stockmar & Citabrita
Photo courtesy of Monroe Spake

When he wasn't busy on Sundays, Mr. Stockmar's son, Dodgie Stockmar, gave us free air plane rides. My family and I could attend the air shows, motorcycle races, and anything else being held at Flying S Ranch for free as well. I thought the world of Mr. Stockmar and Dodgie. But sometimes I felt like I didn't earn my pay.

161

I'll never forget the day that Mr. Stockmar drove us to an old house that belonged to him. The house was made mostly of fieldstone. Our job that day was to go through some old trunks. As we went through them, we saw all sorts of photographs, papers, and stuff that just purely blew my mind because it was so old. There was so much information from years ago. As I searched through one of the trunks, I saw something that looked like a small rock at the bottom of it. Mr. Stockmar had said to just lay things aside and not to throw anything away. I took him literally on that. I laid the rock aside and continued to work so he could place things in order.

When Mr. Stockmar returned to pick us up, I asked him about the rock. He said to bring it to him. Upon seeing the object, he asked me if I knew what it was; and I answered, "No.", believing it to be just a rock. He stated that it was, in fact, a gold nugget! My eyes got as big as saucers. I asked him how that could be because it wasn't the color of gold. He explained how nuggets form, and what some look like naturally. Once we got in the truck, he told us that since we had been working so hard, for the rest of the week he would take us all over the ranch and teach us all about it. So he told us not to wear our work clothes the next day. He said that he would cook some barbeque and that we would all have a good time. I had even asked him if I could bring a notepad. He let out a hearty laugh and said that he thought I'd never ask. I made many notes about the important and historical things he told us.

Often Mr. Stockmar wanted us to sit and talk with him rather than work. The old ranch house, the airport, and the lake were absolutely beautiful. He allowed us to fish in the lake anytime we wished. Douglas and I even went out on the lake in Mr. Stockmar's peddle boat. It fascinated us that Mr. Stockmar's guests flew in from out of town. These were very wealthy men and women, and some were dressed such a way that we wondered if they might be movie stars. They always tipped us when we carried their luggage.

The smallest tip was two dollars. Even a two dollar tip was a lot of money back then. Douglas and I saved some of our pay from the ranch, after giving part of it to our parents. We also had the money we collected from grass cutting and other odd jobs done for various people. Some of the elderly people paid us with old money. I remember one lady paid us with two silver dollars. It took me all year without missing a day to collect a silver dollar for having a perfect attendance in school.

We put our earnings in fruit jars because there was no place to hide it in the house without our older brother Andy finding it. Douglas and I each had a fruit jar. I had my name on mine and he had his name on his. When we earned a pile of money, change or dollar bills, we would put it in these jars. Douglas and I had discussed what we were saving for; and two things came into mind, either a new Schwinn Bicycle or a motor go-cart. Of course, we never got around to purchasing either of them; and the jars are still buried in the woods behind the soccer field somewhere. The last accounting, each of the jars held over one hundred dollars in change and bills. I wonder now just how much the contents of those treasure jars are worth today, taking in the age of some of the money into account.

During the summer of 1967, I turned 15 and applied for my first job dealing with the public. I lied about my age. Fortunately, the Villa Rica City Hospital didn't require a birth certificate. I hated to lie about my age, but I needed the job in order to help out at home.

Since the hospital was a nonprofit organization, it did not have to meet minimum wage requirements. I was started out at $1.30 an hour and was paid every two weeks. This wasn't too shabby at that time. A meal ticket at the hospital cost $5.00, and a good sized meal cost about 50 cents. Equally important, employees of the hospital didn't have to worry about going to a doctor's office unless they had something seriously wrong because the hospital employees were treated without charge.

When I applied for the job, I was very naïve. The children of Fullerville were very sheltered by their parents. I thought that an orderly mopped floors and did laundry. After I found out what I was really hired to do, I questioned my abilities to learn what was required. Mopping floors, dusting, cleaning, and laundry seemed simple because I did that at home. I didn't realize that I was going to be a part of the nursing team taking care of patients. After giving it a whole lot of thought, I decided to take the challenge of my first real job. I realized that a door had opened for me at an early age. I decided I would buckle down and learn everything because I was determined to keep this job. I only had sixty days in which to learn it all. I must have passed the test because I stayed employed with Villa Rica City Hospital from 1967 until 1969.

My first thirty days of orientation were something else. I had never seen a person actually die before, and that was an experience. Taking care of the dead was more than I had bargained for. I will never forget my first experience with death, and how my co-worker really pulled a good one on me. Remember that I was just fifteen and very naïve. The orderly helping me that night informed me that I had to sit with a dead patient until the funeral home employee arrived. An orderly would help the funeral home employee put the deceased on a gurney for transfer. This was all new to me since I had never even touched a dead person before.

Then my co-worker instructed me to sit by the door and turn out the lights until the funeral home employee arrived. I had a lot of questions come to mind. After saying "Say what?" about four times and "Why?" about five times, my main question was why the lights had to be turned off. My co-worker asked if I had ever been to a funeral home where they had bright lights on the deceased. I answered "No" to him, and he said that dim lights show respect to the dead.

Being naïve to all this hospital and funeral home business, I went along with it, but I didn't like it. I even asked about turning on the lamp in the patient's room, but he said it was too bright. My co-worker left the room, and I turned out the lights and took my post by the door. He returned to check to see if I had done what I was told saying that I was going to make a great employee because I knew how to follow instructions.

After he left, I sat in the dark at my post by the door. I noticed how quiet the room was. You could hear a pin drop. But low and behold, trapped air suddenly left the deceased patient's lungs, making a noise that sounded to me as though he had exhaled in a loud breath. It made me think that the dead gentleman was still alive! I thought I was going to be the one going to the funeral home!

I jumped up from my chair, but I felt as though I were moving in slow motion. In my panic, I ran into things and knocked things over. I stepped into the waste basket and hopped around with it stuck to my foot. I finally managed to open the door losing a button off my orderly's jacket when it caught on the door knob. I made it to the nurse's station and informed them that the patient was still breathing. I looked up to see Mr. J. T. Fuller from Jones Funeral Home coming down the hall. I was shaking, and I remember J. T. telling me that I was as white as a sheet--as though I'd seen a ghost or something. I still couldn't speak. J. T. told me to help him get the gurney into the room and load the deceased patient on to it. All I could say was a weak, "Uh Huh." J. T. said, "Perry, this must be your first encounter with the dead." I was still trying to talk, but I could barely get a "Yes sir" out. When he pulled the sheets back, I could tell the man was truly dead. As we loaded him on the stretcher, J. T. explained things to me. He told me not to fall for some of the jokes that my co-workers might pull on me like hoping that I would hear trapped air leaving a deceased patient. He told me that they had pulled this trick before on new co-workers and nearly scared them to death. So that's how I learned what happens to deceased patients. Needless to say, I never sat in a dark room with a deceased patient again. Now I laugh at myself when I think about that night.

It's amazing how much one can learn just by working in a public place, especially a fifteen year old kid from Fullerville. After five or six months, I was seeing and hearing things that I never thought possible. I could not believe how much information could be obtained that was supposed to be confidential just by looking at a chart. The charge nurse never questioned the orderly's or nurse's aides about their doings when things were slow. At these times, we pulled out the chart of the patient of our choice and started reading. One soon found out those who had influence and power. When certain people came in as patients, the top officials from the hospital board would instruct the administration to tell the employees to "roll out the red carpet for them, to be extra nice, and to go out of the way to satisfy them." And so we did.

It didn't take me long to know who was who and who ran the hospital. We knew those hooked on medications and those who weren't. It was surprising to learn that half of the city was hooked on nerve pills; even morphine. It was even more surprising to learn where we had to take the afterbirth and surgery parts which were to a small incinerator located in the emergency room parking. Before the biohazard laws came into effect, the city sanitation department was in charge of the city hospital's wastes. The needles and expired medicines were carried away to the city dump. Harvey George, who drove a sanitation truck and supervised his crew, started asking the hospital to separate the regular garbage from biohazard waste so that his men would not come in contact with contaminated items. Thanks to him, the housekeeping department started separating the regular trash from the biohazard garbage.

The Villa Rica City Hospital had many wonderful nurses, nurse's aides, and housekeeping employees. The majority of people working there were caring people. Maybe I can talk more about them in another book.

I will never forget an encounter with a female patient who kept asking for an orderly. Remember that I was only fifteen and naïve in so many ways. She was over twice my age and very attractive. I can definitely say that she was not a Carroll County resident. She would ask me to walk her down the hall. Each time I went to her room, she would ask me to help her out of her robe. Her gown was very low cut, but I didn't catch on to what she was leading up to.

About seven o'clock one evening, I walked her back to her room; and she asked me to help her get her robe off. While shedding her robe, she put her hand around my neck and started rubbing it. Every time I watch the movie *The Graduate* with Dustin Hoffman, it reminds me of what took place at the hospital that night. As she was rubbing my neck, she pulled me closer to her. My heart was flip-flopping, and I was scared to death at the thought of her husband walking in. I didn't know what to do. I had never had an encounter with an older woman, especially a married one. She was sexy, attractive, and smelled good. Before I knew it, her lips were on mine. I felt weak, and I knew that I was enjoying what was taking place. However, according to my upbringing, I wasn't supposed to like it or let it happen.

While working in the hospital, I had an opportunity to interact with all types of people from the very wealthy to the very poor. It's amazing how some of them think alike and how some of them think differently. I always enjoyed the ones who thought differently. I listened to their thoughts on everything from religion, politics, and education to their favorite foods. When the census was down, there wasn't much to do. I would find myself talking to patients who asked me to come in and visit with them because they were either lonely or just wanted someone to listen to them. For whatever reason, I'm glad they chose me because I learned so much from them.

I remember talking to one very wealthy gentleman who was terminally ill. I remembered a slogan in my family that was "Work and save to be wealthy." In talking with me, this gentleman said that a man working in a factory will never be rich; and the man he's working for may become rich. He said, "Son, if you think you might work for this hospital until you retire, you will never become rich." He said that the majority of rich people's wealth has been passed down from generation to generation and that rich men get their money from inheritance while some poor men or women may just get lucky and marry into wealth. He certainly drew my interest. I asked many questions wanting to learn more.

I told him that I didn't want to work in a cotton mill all my life and asked what I had going for me, He told me, "Son, you have hope and a dream going for you. If you believe in yourself hard enough, you will accomplish these things. This was from a wealthy gentleman from Villa Rica who was being honest with me. He wouldn't talk to me when his family was visiting, but he would invite me to his room to talk more when things were slow. I even visited him some on my off days when he didn't have company. I shared so much with this gentleman about my hopes and dreams. He even told me that he wished he had gotten to know me a lot sooner because of our newly found friendship.

He shared his life with me telling me how he had never known what real work was because he had always had a silver spoon in his mouth. He wanted me to tell him what it was like to be without. When I shared some of my stories from Fullerville and the rural counties surrounding Carroll County, I saw his heart open up and big tears in his eyes. A nurse's aide walked in one time when we were visiting, saw him crying, and went to the charge nurse. She told the charge nurse that I was upsetting the gentleman. I was asked to leave the room and not to go back. I tried to explain that I had not upset the patient, that I had just shared some stories that got next to him. However, they didn't believe me.

Two days later, his door was open, and he saw me pass by his room. He called out, "Perry, come here a minute." I didn't know what to do because I had been told not to go into his room. So I poked my head in the door just long enough to say, "Yes sir, do you need something?" He asked why I didn't come to visit him anymore. I told him that I had been told not to come to his room anymore because they thought I had intentionally upset him with my stories. He said that he wanted to hear more of my stories because he knew they were true. He told me that I should go on and that he would have things cleared up in a day. And he did.

When I returned to his room, I told him that I couldn't get these people to listen to me and that they even threatened to fire me if I brought it up again. He told me the difference between the two of us was that I was just a below minimum wage teenager while he had power and influence because of his wealth. I asked him how many phone calls it took to clear this up, and he answered, "Two." One was to his doctor, and the other was to the hospital administrator. He told me that he even went a little bit further to help me, but I had to keep it to myself and not discuss it with my co-workers. He informed me that I would have a pay raise on my next paycheck, but I was the only one to know. I promised him that I would keep our little secret. I told him, "Thank God there are nice people like you who have power, money, and influence; and who don't misuse it." That's when he told me, "Son, maybe I'm confessing to you to make things right with God. We all have hearts when we want to have hearts; but my problem has been greed; and it has ruined me. And now I'm on my death bed, and I can't buy salvation. My friends come here to see me at the hospital, but none of them have taken the time that you have taken. Perry, I can honestly say you are my only true friend that I didn't have to purchase."

My experiences at the Villa Rica City Hospital helped me to learn about people and brought me into adulthood. Villa Rica was a small town in those days. I didn't have to read the weekly newspaper to find out what was going on. At the hospital, we already knew. (Perhaps to be continued in another book.)

Andy was in the Marine Corps and Jimmy was married and out on his own. So Douglas and I were the only two boys left at home.

I was truly fortunate that the hardships which come with growing up were softened by my having some very wonderful friends. One was a young lady from the elite side of Villa Rica who believed that I had promise and encouraged me. With friendship and encouragement, dreams can build and come true. Another special young lady also had an impact on my life beginning in the sixth grade. I fell in love with her at an early age. She was never aware of my feelings. After growing up, becoming successful, and returning to Villa Rica, I found that I was too late; she was married. If she reads this book she will know I remember her very kindly.

One of my best friends is to this day, Kenneth Fields. He lived on Old Stone Road in Villa Rica at the time I lived on Rockmart Road. Kenneth was into electronics and music. He enjoyed spending his time playing around on turn tables and other kinds of media equipment. Kenneth and I listened to music recorded on records and on 8 track tapes at first, then cassettes. At that time radio stations had to keep several copies of their single records because all the air play resulted in the loss of the quality of the sound due to a thing called needle burn. Things were a bit fragile back then when compared to now. Then the CD came along.

I was really fascinated by what Kenneth was doing, paid close attention, and learned much from him. I was really glad that Kenneth Fields came into my life because he was so knowledgeable and seemed to be a little bit ahead of his time when it came to electronics. We had so much in common when it came to music. I was only fifteen and did not have a driver's license at the time, so I double dated with Kenneth and his girl. This got me out of the house on weekends; and I looked forward to those weekends because there was always something to do, especially when you had a friend with a car. There was nothing to do in Villa Rica itself unless you were heavily involved in sports. Villa Rica had a swimming pool and Fullerville a ball park. If one could find enough people to play ball, then you could create something to do. But for the younger teenagers, Villa Rica scored zero in activities. The movie theatre had closed down; so if you wanted to see a movie, you had to go to either Lithia Springs or Carrollton to their drive-in theatres. We would usually go to Atlanta on our dates to the nicer theatres. Kenneth was dating Susan Haley, and I was dating Joyce Harry at the time. They were two fine girls who were brought up in good Christian homes.

We really enjoyed going into the big city of Atlanta to shop at the big department stores. I could always buy clothes at a lower price in those department stores than I could in Villa Rica.

Kenneth got me started back in church at the Concord Baptist on Rockmart Road in Villa Rica. We were constantly doing research on music, listening to the music that was coming across the air waves, and we discovered WPLO 103.3, which was playing some serious music.

Things had changed drastically by 1968. Music was changing; fashion was changing; manners were becoming a thing of the past; and even religion was changing. I'm not so sure that people have adjusted to all these changes even today. Even more astounding, we were witnessing history in the making on our very own black and white television sets. The horror of real violence and real killings came right into our living rooms, prompted by the Civil Rights Movement that resulted first in the Civil Rights Act of 1964 and continued on to the Civil Rights Act of 1968.

The 1968 Atlanta Radio Time Warp, describes those chaotic times so close to home.

The Vietnam War was raging and tearing the country apart in 1968. Atlanta was a magnet in the south for hippies and youthful war protesters. The sidewalks in the "Tight Squeeze" area around 10th and Peachtree Streets were packed with so many hippies that pedestrians literally had to walk in the streets. People driving through the area stopped to stare, creating massive traffic jams that snaked for blocks around the area. The alternative newspaper The Great Speckled Bird was hawked by vendors wearing tie-dyed T-shirts from street corners for 15 cents a copy. As a sign of the changes that were to come, Plough's WPLO-FM would soon convert to an automated underground rock format.

Military service was mandatory in 1968. The young men who were drafted that year who were fortunate to make it back to Atlanta would find a big change in the radio scene. When they left, people were listening to AM. When they returned, people were listening to FM...

This was a time of new sounds. The "I Want to Hold Your Hand" style of music was giving over to music like Helter Skelter which was music protesting Vietnam. Some people loved the change and some didn't. The new music was fascinating and known then as progressive psychedelic rock. There was also a goodly dose of folk music thrown in as well, also full of social comment. It was a time of music with a message. Some people paid attention; some didn't. Some people loved it; some hated it. So very much was going on in that time period; the Vietnam War, civil rights, environmental protection, the Ku Klux Klan--still strong and violent, the peace movement verses pro war movement. Indeed, some very interesting times in history were taking place every day.

As 1968 rolled on, more history in the making was to come. It was blowing my mind to see all the events crowding in right before my eyes in black and white. Reverend Martin Luther King shot and killed in Memphis, Tennessee, and Robert F. Kennedy shot and killed while campaigning in California. The world was changing rapidly with all the actual events right there in your ears and before your eyes.

I remember all of us kids from Fullerville and Villa Rica discussing the Vietnam War as well as the Civil Rights Movement. The high school kids were hoping not to receive a draft notice in the mail. You would hear some make statements that they were going to college because they didn't intend to go to Vietnam. The ones with low grades were the ones with the biggest threat of being drafted. Our high school principal often threatened that he would turn us into the Carroll County Draft Board if we didn't buckle down and get our grades up. The protest of the Vietnam War was the biggest ever, even to this day. The reason we no longer have large protests against war anymore is because there is no such thing as a draft, so there's no threat to anyone of having to go into combat. Our military is now all volunteered and contracted. So today's kids, their parents, and grandparents don't have to worry about their kids being called up to serve.

I lost my grandmother, whom we called Granny George, in November of 1968. She was found in her yard on Walker Street in Villa Rica, where she had suffered a heart attack. My mother took her mother's death pretty hard. Christmas was around the corner, and I was trying to think of a way to make her smile again. So, on a Monday morning, I went to my savings account and took out enough to purchase my mother and my dad a leather sofa and chair. It took me some time to save that kind of money because the hospital only paid one dollar and 30 cents an hour. I guess this was because the hospital was a non-profit hospital and did not have to meet the minimum wage, which was one dollar and 60 cents per hour. Not too long after that, I purchased our first television entertainment system, with a color television right in the middle. It had a turn table, AM-FM radio, and an eight track tape player which all set into a finished wood cabinet. Kenneth Fields, Jimmy Causey, myself, and others listened to my stereo as we would sit and talk about music. We would even watch a little color television. My dad enjoyed watching the Braves games and Bonanza in color. I was told that I was probably the first one in Fullerville to have an entertainment system this size, but who knows or cares. It didn't matter to me whether I was the first or not. What mattered to me was the fact that I was able to buy it with my own money.

Chapter 5

Farewell to Fullerville

As the spring of 1969 approached, I sensed that change was coming. I just wasn't sure what kind of change. In 1968, Richard Nixon became president of the United States. This was a big change because everybody had voted for the democratic ticket for years. But something else was about to happen. The last change I ever thought possible was that my mom and dad would move away from Villa Rica. Even stranger yet, I didn't realize that I would be the one to cause that change.

Ruth Bailey   Photo courtesy of the author

It was spring. I was not feeling well. I never dreamed that the change which was about to take place would happen right in the Bailey home. I called the high school that day and let them know that I was going to be out. I also called the hospital to let them know that I would not be coming in. Our mail carrier, Herman Holloway Jr., delivered our mail around half past eleven that morning. Little did I know that there was a letter in our mail box that was going to give a big lift to the Olin and Ruth Bailey Family. I did not go to the mailbox immediately. Instead, I watched the *Andy Griffith Show* that ran until at noon. But something inside me hounded me to go out to the mailbox. So when the commercial break came on, although I didn't feel like it, out I went. It seemed as though it took me forever just to get to there and back. I looked through the mail tossing junk mail to one side and important mail to the other. I noticed a letter from my Uncle Shelton Bailey, my dad's brother, who lived in

Shannon, Georgia. It was addressed to Olin and Ruth, not to me. Now, I did not usually go through my parent's mail. That was a no-no in the family. However, as I sat holding my Uncle Shelton's correspondence in my hand, I couldn't even finish the Andy Griffith Show. I had a powerful urge to open the letter instead. I kept reminding myself that it was not my mail and that I shouldn't open it. I have never had that kind of feeling in whole my life, the urge to open somebody else's mail. My curiosity was getting to me because my Uncle Shelton never wrote long letters and because the envelope was so thick. After all, it took two 13 cent stamps to mail the letter. We had a phone. Why didn't Uncle Shelton just call? I wondered if it could be because calling was long distance from Shannon to Villa Rica. I took my chances. I opened the letter. I'm glad I did!

I read the letter over and over again. I realized that it would be up to me to sell my folks on what Uncle Shelton had to say.

The letter read, "Olin, you and Ruth need to get to Shannon and put in your applications at Klopman Mills, which is owned by Burlington Industries. They are hiring both men and women. I can even get Perry on. All three of you will be making good money; and you will have benefits like health insurance, life insurance, retirement, paid holidays, and paid vacation time. It would also be an upgrade in your social status."

After reading the letter over and over and over again, I knew that it was going to be my job at age 16, soon to be 17, to convince them that they could not afford to turn down this opportunity. But how in the world was I going to do it?

In his younger days, my dad went after change and life improvement and was successful. However, my mother's family always lived in anxiety. They lived in fear of change and hammered this fear into their daughter's head. Perhaps they felt that it was better to suffer the misery of the status quo than to take a risk! Over the years, the folks joined together in this attitude. Maybe they were just older and were just plain tired out. Now I must deal with two people who have been convinced that they should fear change. Two people afraid to take a chance in life! My work was cut out for me! How can a 16 year old give a heart to heart talk with his parents just as though they were his own kids? I was hoping that they would come home in a good mood. Just to be sure, I did some needed things around the house to lift their spirits. I washed the dirty clothes and hung them out on the line. I also swept and mopped the floors. I knew my folks would be home around ten or fifteen minutes after three. At a quarter of three, I called Tastee Freeze and ordered burgers, fries, and shakes. I told them not to have my order ready until three o'clock. This gave me just enough time to pick the order up and have everything ready as they walked through the door. Thank God they were laughing when they came in from work and seemed to be happy! I had done a spectacular job with the house cleaning. Mom was especially happy that she didn't have to cook. After we ate, I asked them if we could just leave the mess on the table and go out on the porch to talk. I promised that I would clean it all up afterward.

They knew immediately that something out of the ordinary was up. Of course, they never thought about a positive up. They sort of took a negative view of most surprises.

So we all sat down on the porch. The folks were together on the glider, and I was in the chair.

My mother said, "Perry, you are scaring me."

Dad had a serious look on his face that plainly said, "What is my son about to tell me?"

I was grinning from ear to ear. I said, "Mom and Dad relax! It's good news; not bad news!"

I didn't bring up Shelton's letter right away. It's amazing how hard work can help one think. While I was scrubbing the floors, my brain was exploring ways to convince my parents that they should take this opportunity.

While sitting on the porch and breaking the ice, I started off by saying, "Dad, how are we doing financially?"

Dad said, "Son, we are paying our bills, meeting our obligations, and we are not doing too badly."

I said, "Dad, that old 1963 Chevrolet you are driving is giving you a little trouble here and there. You are going to have to trade or spend some major money getting it repaired."

Then I looked at my mom and said, "Mom, how would it be if you had a new washer and a dryer too?"

She answered, "It would be great."

"And Dad, what if you could afford to buy a new car?"

He replied, "Son, it would be nice too; but if you are thinking about talking me into trading cars, forget it. If you are trying to talk your mother into buying a brand new washer and a clothes dryer, forget it. I was just informed by Curt Sauls, who is our superintendent at Banning Yarn Mills, that some of us may be getting laid off for a short while because orders have been cut back. Mr. Sauls informed me that I could night watch, but that would put just one of us working because your mother would be laid off."

I was sitting there thinking to myself that my prayers had been answered. A layoff could not have come at a better time. Wow! Is this good or what? Of

173

course, they were sitting there watching me grin like a 'possum from ear to ear. My Dad asked why I was grinning, "This will affect you too because me and your mother will need your paycheck to pick up the slack."

I said, "Dad and Mom, what if I said to you that Someone up above has been looking out for you and has found a way for you to make a better way for all of us?"

Mom replied, "Son, it would be a blessing."

I said, "Thank the good Lord because your prayers have been answered! First thing when you get up in the morning, I want you to call into work and give an excuse to be absent."

"What?" they cried out together.

I said, "Think of this, Mom and Dad. We all three have jobs waiting on us, with higher pay, health insurance, life insurance, paid holidays, paid vacations, and more respect for us to boot. It will mean a better house, one that you can own yourselves, with an inside bathroom, shower, and a bathtub. Mom and Dad! No more outhouses!"

I really couldn't believe the response that I was getting back from them. They were grinning ear to ear as if they were ready to go right then and there. After I explained Shelton's letter to them, they really seemed to be convinced. My dad called my uncle to get more information on the job offers.

I remember my dad saying, "I'm a Mason. I will need to find out how to transfer from the Mason lodge here to the Shannon Mason lodge." My dad was a proud Mason.

My little brother came home from school, and we shared the news with him. He was a bit sad because he didn't want to leave his school friends and the people that he played music with. But we didn't let that stop us. I couldn't believe after all these years that we were finally leaving Fullerville and Villa Rica. Not because we disliked the people of Fullerville and Villa Rica, for we had always loved them. My parents had a lot of friends here as well as many relatives on both sides of the family. The reason for leaving was for opportunity, more money, and a better life. The difference in the pay and benefits was awesome.

The three of us had to have physical examinations in order to go to work with Klopman Mills. This was not my first physical since I had to have one in order to work at the hospital. However, taking a physical to go to work was an unheard of requirement when applying for a job in factories such as the local hosiery or cotton mills. My mom and dad found it hard to believe that they were required to take a physical before getting employment, but take one they did. We all three passed the physical, and we returned home with jobs.

My dad and mom both went to Curt Sauls to turn in their notice. Curt told both of them, "I hate to see both of you leave because both of you are good workers and good people. But I certainly understand, and I am happy for anyone who wants to do better." Curt went on to say, "Olin and Ruth, if things don't work out for you at Klopman Mills, you will always have jobs waiting on you at Banning Yarn Mills." My dad shook hands with Curt Sauls, and my mother gave him a big hug. Curt wished them well.

We proceeded to make the arrangements to move into our new home, purchased and owned by Olin and Ruth Bailey; not one that they had to rent. Mom bought that new washer and a dryer. Dad bought his new car. I stayed on working in cotton mill for a time. I knew I had to stay long enough for the folks to gain confidence in their new life, and then I could gently pull away.

There was a whole new road awaiting me, and the time had finally come to set out toward the new horizons and the accomplishments I had always dreamed of.

"Bill" at Work   Photos courtesy of Rhonda Hovater Bailey

Note: Perry "Bill" started his career as a disc jockey then branched out to more responsible positions. He worked for the St. Jude Children's Research Hospital serving as the regional representative over: Texas, Oklahoma, and New Mexico. In this capacity, he set up fundraising radiothons and traveled widely to obtain public support for St. Jude's. Though he enjoyed working there, he chose to return to his first love, radio broadcasting.

He has functioned as a morning man and production manager. He can look back on a long and productive career in radio broadcasting and management. Today, he is employed in north Alabama.

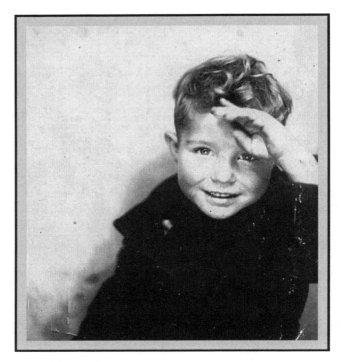

Jimmy Bailey Photo courtesy of the author

I can sum it all up very simply: I have lived the Great American Dream, and I continue to live it today.

Epilogue

The cup of success is sweetened by failures. - Catherine Burns

I have led a varied life; full of joy and sorrow; full of lessons and rewards; full of hardships and achievements.

My wonderful family is my greatest blessing.

I have gained success in my chosen career, and it is a joy to me.

I know that the Great American Dream is not a myth.

Only in the United States of America, the land of freedom and opportunity, could a story like mine be possible.

God bless America!

Perry

Part 4

Update

Photo courtesy of the author

Where Would Villa Rica Be Without Fullerville?

Poem by Rhonda Hovater Bailey

There once was a town called Fullerville,
Home of the hosiery and cotton mill,
With Cannon Caskets and the lumber mill,
It was all right there in Fullerville.

There were stores and even some barber shops,
They even had a couple of restaurants,
A school, churches, and a baseball field,
It was all right there in Fullerville.

Where would Villa Rica be without Fullerville?
Where would Villa Rica be without Fullerville?

Behind each house was a tiny little building,
Made of wood with spiders on the ceiling,
We all dreaded going to the old outhouse,
Afraid we would encounter a snake or a mouse.

Traveling down the road was a mule and a wagon,
And anyone behind it was sure nuff a gagging
Clean out an outhouse, some would have a fit,
It was shoveled into barrels and then to the city pit.

Where would Villa Rica be without Fullerville?
Where would Villa Rica be without Fullerville?

Its first little jail was made of wood,
Was burnt by a prisoner who was up to no good,
The jail was rebuilt with a cement jail,
So that down through the years, it would prevail.

Then there was 'Roger', who kept the kids in fright,
You could find him at Slickems on a dark dreary night,
Half man, half beast, he was known to kill,
And he made his home down in Fullerville.

Where would Villa Rica be without Fullerville?
Where would Villa Rica be without Fullerville?

In 1974, Perry Bailey took a stand,

He called up **WSB** and they came up with a plan,
They showed some of the outhouses and the mayor on TV
For all of **W**est Georgia and Atlanta to see.

After seeing all the coverage on the television news,
The City of Villa Rica finally paid its dues,
Bathrooms were installed along with sewer lines,
Fullerville got it's sewage after such a long time.

Where would Villa Rica be without Fullerville?
Where would Villa Rica be without Fullerville?

The way has not been easy or swift. There have been many hurdles to over come, and Fullervllians may be proud of the progress that has been made.

How Perry Got Sewage to Fullerville

In 1969, my family moved to Shannon, Georgia. I had been living with them and worked in the Klopton Mill. At age 22, I was making good money. When I left, my dad thought I was crazy to give up health insurance, dental insurance, life insurance, and retirement. My reply to him was my health was worth more. The people who worked in that mill had to breathe the lint and dust, and I didn't want to follow my mom and dad's footsteps and work in a cotton mill all my life. I always knew what I wanted to be. I just had to find the way to get the education to get me there.

So, what did I do? I loaded up my car with my clothes, and for some reason I went back to Villa Rica. At the time, I didn't realize that I took the wrong turn by returning to Villa Rica; but then, it might have been the best way to find out what the real world was really like. I was seeking information, and I wanted to do something with my life.

I returned to Villa Rica to find that there were no jobs to be found. I rented a place on Wilson Street, and my rent was $45.00 a month. I paid up three months rent in advance. When my money started running out, I realized I had made a mistake when I quit the cotton mill.

I later returned to the cotton mill for a short while to pay for my schooling. I drove to West Georgia College. They had a radio station on campus, probably about a 10 watt one that could be heard all over the campus and in some parts of the city of Carrollton. I talked to the Program Director of the radio station and pleaded with him, almost to the point of begging, to teach me radio. I told him I had no money for school, but that I had spent a lot of time reading in libraries and improving my reading skills and pronunciation. He called me to the office where I met with another man, and they heard my story. I don't remember who they were, but I wish I could shake their hands today. They were the reason that I learned the basics of radio. But much more work was needed on my part so that I could work even in a small radio station; much less a larger one. My next step was to go to Atlanta and pass the FCC test because at that time you had to have a Third Class License with Broadcast Endorsement

As a teenager in Fullerville, WLBB in Carrollton was the local station in Carroll County that most Carroll County residents listened to and depended on it for news, funeral announcements, and the party line. It was just a small "mom and pop station." I used to call them up and give them news tips because the best news tip of the week could win $25.00 cash and dinner for two at the Pizza Palace in Carrollton.

It is important that I give some highlights from past minutes of the Villa Rica City Council and Mayor. The minutes were provided to me for the book by the City of Villa Rica City Hall earlier in 2009, and I thank them for sharing this information. It will help a little bit to explain how Villa Rica ran the city back in the days before sewage in Fullerville. (See Appendices B and C)

I will begin with highlights from the minutes that made me scratch my head. Who knows, it may make you scratch yours.

Mayor and Council met in regular session Oct. 4, 1958, 7:30 O'clock P. M. at City Hall. Mayor Griffin in Chair and the following council members present: Ray Matthews, John B. Bailey, H. G. Brown, and Herman Newell.

Mayor Griffin dispensed with regular order of business in order to hear complaints of J. D. Gray and H. P. Cooper that too many peddlers were working within the City limits of Villa Rica without paying a business license and that the peddling license were too low.

Mayor and Council met in regular session Oct. 4, 1958.

The city council voted unanimously to raise pay for the mule work in Fullerville to $4.00 per day on motion by Herman Newell and second by John Bailey.

Motion was made by Herman Newell and seconded by John Bailey that heater be installed on garbage truck. Motion carried.

City of Villa Rica Mayor and Council met in regular session on January 4, 1977 at 7:30. Members present Mayor Joyce Connally, Councilman Frank Black, Chester Ergle, L. L. McBride, J. V. Warren and E. D. Ray. City Manager C. H. Woodruff also in attendance.

The City of Villa Rica was advised that public works grant of $410,000.00 for Fullerville sewage and $94,250.00 for the Villa Rica City Hospital had been awarded to this City. This was all prepared under the administration of Chuck Woodruff our City Planner and Manager.

The City of Villa Rica, Mayor and Council met in regular session Tuesday, February 6, 1979. Those present were Mayor Joyce Connally, Councilmen Steve Cleghorn, Doyal McCain, Monroe Spake, Bob Dean, Mac Hembree, City Manager Greg Young, Acting City Clerk J. W. Conner, City Attorney Ted Lee.

Harold Smith asked for a decision concerning his tapping onto City Sewerage on Hwy 78. It was noted in discussion that the city did not have adequate equipment and man-power to complete the job at this time. Mr. Smith presented the council with an estimate of $3500 labor from Pruett Construction Co. to do the work required for his tap. Based on the agreement that Mr. Smith furnish the materials and the city furnish the labor, Steve Cleghorn made a motion directing Greg Young to make arrangements with Pruett Const. Co. for the work on Mr. Smith's sewer line. Doyal McCain seconded. Five (5) yes votes.

Monroe Spake made a motion to allow the residents of Fullerville to tap onto city sewerage without charge for a period of one (1) year beginning February 1, 1979 thru January 31, 1980. Doyal McCain seconded. Five (5) yes votes. (decision based on Grant wording).

Steve Cleghorn made a motion the city would discontinue cleaning the out-houses in Fullerville effective immediately due to the availability of city sewerage and the city would notify the residents by publication, the mandatory fee for sewerage will be charged effective May 1, 1979. Monroe Spake seconded. Five (5) yes votes. (fee of 75% water consumption if sewerage available due to city ordinance)

The City of Villa Rica, Mayor and Council met in regular session on Wednesday, January 2, 1980. Those present were Mayor Joyce Connally, Councilmen Steve Cleghorn, Doyle McCain, Monroe Spake, Bob Dean, Mac Hembree, Acting City Manager J. W. Conner, City Attorney Ted Lee.

Minutes of the December, 1979 meetings were read and approved.

Mayor Connally gave the following recap of the year 1979:

1979 has been a good year for Villa Rica. The dream of almost 17 years work by various Mayor's and Councilmen came to fruition with the completion of the Fullerville Sewage Project. In February of 1979, the residents of Fullerville were having bathrooms built or installing the pipes necessary to tie onto the new sewer lines.

There you have it. These are the highlights of the minutes that should grab your attention. One may read them in their entirety in Appendix B.

The mindset of the time is clearly shown. For example, a supposedly highly respected business man came to a city council meeting asking that the city council raise the business license fee on the peddlers who were just small farmers raising their own crops and trying to make a living. Evidently these small farmers were a threat to his business. The produce in his store was brought in from out of state. I blame the voters of Fullerville just as much as the City of Villa Rica for the neglect of Fullerville. The people of Fullerville failed to stick together and push for something to be done by the city. But what held these people in Fullerville back from making a stand? Could it be fear of losing their jobs in the mills in Fullerville; or could it be that they knew that they would be fighting a lost cause? It's so important that people vote and demand comprehensive coverage from their local news agencies. It's not good to be naïve and not informed or misinformed as to what's going on in your local state and federal government. You blame the politicians but you vote them in. It takes all the people to make things happen.

In the 1979 minutes, Mayor Connally praises "the dream of almost 17 years work by various mayors and councilmen came to fruition with the completion of the Fullerville Sewage Project." I have to kindly disagree with Mayor Connally. In fact, I wrote many letters to the elected officials concerning the lack of sewage in Fullerville. However, my letters were ignored. In fact, a city council member told my dad to have me stop writing letters concerning sewage because it wasn't going to happen anytime soon.

Actually, it was a news story that aired on **WSB** Television, Channel 2 in Atlanta that finally opened the door for sewage in Fullerville.

I introduced two news stories to **WSB** Television, Channel 2, which carried the **NBC** network. I called a news reporter who was well known with **WSB** and suggested that he should do a couple of stories concerning Villa Rica. I suggested that he do a story on Coca Cola and a second story on Fullerville telling him that in 1974 outhouses still existed in the twentieth century in Fullerville, Georgia.

He was shocked and interested saying, "I've got to see this." He came to Villa Rica and met me privately. He felt that the Coca Cola story was a positive one and that the Fullerville story was one of great concern. We drove around, and we talked. It was a good thing that the car he was driving didn't have a **WSB** logo on it. After I finished the story, he told me to duck when we went to Fullerville to film and get interviews keeping me anonymous as to who tipped the media off on the stories.

First we visited Mrs. Ann Anders. She was very knowledgeable about the Candler history and background of Coca Cola. That was why I chose her for the interview. After her interview, we got into the **WSB** car, and off to Fullerville we went. I pointed out the outhouses, and people were caught on camera going to and fro. I wondered if I had made a mistake. My intentions were good. I just wanted to shine light on the problem and wake up the local elected officials so that something would be done. I had tried for years only to find out my letters had ended up in File 13; the garbage can.

The WSB-TV news reporter came to our final stop at the mayor's house to question him about plans for getting sewage lines into Fullerville. While on camera, the mayor was asked about the number of outhouses operating in Fullerville. Perhaps he really didn't know. However, he told the news reporter that one or two outhouses were in operation in Fullerville. When the story aired on WSB, one outhouse after another was shown in a small frame behind the mayor disproving his estimate.

The story ran nonstop for a whole week. It was obvious that the Carroll County Heath Department and the State of Georgia either ignored the problem, or they did not know it existed. The TV revelation pushed the local officials into doing something about Fullerville's sewage problem.

I was informed by a city council member who asked not to be named that my news story laid the foundation for many changes; not only in Fullerville, but Villa Rica as well. Action had to be taken on the city dump and the little pit at the hospital that sat on the curb. There surgical and child birth wastes were burned in the incinerator that looked like a barbeque pit.

A prominent businessman, a well known Villa Rican at the time the Fullerville story aired, was furious. He sent word for me to see him, telling the person contacting me not to say why he wanted to see me. It didn't dawn on me that he would be upset over a story that should have come out a long time ago. This prominent businessman praised my Coca Cola news story, but he cussed me out and called me every name in the book for tipping off WSB on the Fullerville story. I was scared to death. It seemed that he raged at me forever. I just stood there and listened to him. He then said "Perry, you embarrassed the town with that story airing on WSB." My reply was, "Sir, how could I embarrass a town that was allowing it to be embarrassed on its own? People had to tolerate the honey wagon with two barrels of human waste covered with flies traveling down Montgomery Avenue and through the town of Villa Rica going all the way to the city dump?" He didn't answer the question, and just stood there with a stunned look on his face. I walked out the door.

My thinking, as I walked out the door, was that the City of Villa Rica was installing sewage lines in the new subdivisions; and here it was, 1974, and Fullerville still had no sewage lines. The city applied for a grant and received $410,000.00 for Fullerville improvements. They paved a few streets and finally got the sewage lines installed. Yet the mayors and city council of 17 years have been given credit for something they made no effort to achieve.

185

Fullerville: The Outhouse Capitol of the World

A year or two after my story broke on **WSB TV** in Atlanta; another attempt was made to draw the attention of the elected officials to installing sewage lines in Fullerville. This time it was not from me. A group of teenagers from Villa Rica decided to go to Fullerville, load up an outhouse, and carry it to the Villa Rica High School. They set it inside the front entrance of the school. It did get attention! Some of the school teachers and the principal looked as though they had no idea what it was until they opened the door and took a sniff. I was told that the whole thing started out as a joke, but the teenagers really did it on behalf of Fullerville to get sewage lines installed in that community. This was in the mid seventies, and the youngsters of Fullerville and Villa Rica could not understand why any community should have outhouses in the twentieth century. They made up a little title for Fullerville, and it was, **"FULLERVILLE, THE OUTHOUSE CAPITOL OF THE WORLD."**

A Tragedy in Temple
By Joyce Massey Fain

Note: This incident occurred in 1994 at the Citizens Bank & Trust of West Georgia of Temple, Georgia which is now known as the Bank of North Georgia Citizens Bank & Trust of West Georgia

I am proud that I came from Fullerville because the obstacles we had to overcome made me a much stronger person in my adult life and helped me to deal with the worst of all obstacles in my life so far.

As with any job, there are good days and bad days, and I would be remiss if I did not tell you in detail an incident that happened at the bank that changed my life forever. I will not name names in order to protect the families that were hurt by this. My best friend and secretary to me had separated over a money issue and she had filed for divorce. Her husband always acted liked she walked on water and that he loved her very much. But he had some mental problems that you would never know about just to meet him. Myself and my girls at the bank never thought he would hurt her after she filed for divorce, but he did try to beg her to come back to him. That was not going to happen and that is what caused the incident.

On March 7, 1994 at 9:58 a.m., he walked into the bank and came to my office which had windows all the way around, and said "hello Joyce, how are you today" in the most pleasant normal voice and I said I was doing okay, how was he? He answered me fine but I was immediately on alert watching his every move. He left my office and went to the teller window and made a deposit and then to my secretary's desk. When they were married he had given her a marble name plate that she kept on her desk. Her desk faced me and she was no further than 6 feet from me. She had not said a word during all of this, she just kept on working. As he got to her desk, I saw him throw a folder down on her desk and heard him speaking loudly to her but I do not have any remembrance of what he said because I was so focused on his every move. After he threw the folder down, he reached over to get the marble name plate and I thought he was going to hit her because with everything he did, I could tell he was changing. I immediately left my desk approx. 6 feet away and started running to grab his hands so he could not hit her. I got within two to three inches of his arms and he pulled out a gun from his jacket pocket and shot her in the throat. She fell back in her chair and I could here her gurgling so I thought she was still alive and that I had to get to her to help her but he kept the gun between he and I the whole time and would not let me help her. I started begging him to let me call for help- He had hurt her and she needed help. I finally convinced him that she needed help and he said he would call 911. At every stage you could see the change in his eyes that he was completely losing it. He went around in front of her in the chair and pushed the chair back and called 911 and told them who he was and that he had just killed his wife. I didn't know until later what they asked him, but it was 'How did you kill your wife?" and at that point he shot the gun at me. Fortunately God had an angel on my shoulder and protected me because the bullet lodged in some books on her desk; At that point I realized that if I wanted to help her, I had to go outside and call 911 not realizing that he had just notified them. I did not know this at the time but my girls had hidden behind the teller line and at the point of the second shot, they thought he had killed me.

The girls later told me what happened after I ran out for help. They said that he picked her up and placed her in the floor making a comment about her having gained weight. He positioned her just so in the floor and called her father who had never liked him and told him that he had just killed his daughter and then shot her in the heart while her father was on the line. He then positioned himself where he would fall on her and said "Lord, I am coming too" and shot himself in the head. He was dead instantly.

This all took place in 6 minutes from start to finish but it seemed like a life time. Within minutes we were covered by the police, state patrol, sheriff deputies and news helicopters appeared almost instantly. I had to get back in that office because I did not know if she was alive or not and I knew I had to try and help her. I thought of every excuse possible to get back in and finally realized that the vault and all the teller windows with money in them were not locked, so they surrounded me with the sheriff's deputies to escort me back in the building and to protect me from seeing her. When we got inside the door, I could see the bottom of his feet and I broke free but I was stopped by an old friend who was a state patrolman guarding the desk because he knew what I would do.

He got me in a bear hug and just started talking to me. From that point on I was encircled completely by sheriff deputies. It wasn't long until the bank had a whole crew up there to take over the bank and the girls and I were led to the back room to get our statements. Amazing as it is, I was not afraid during all of this time, but when I saw my family and my girls in the bank, I realized just how much danger we were in and that he had brought enough ammunition to kill us all if necessary to carry out his plan.

Each of us dealt with this in our own way! I had the hardest time because I heard her gurgling and thought she was alive and I felt so guilty that I had not saved her life. I have been treated for Post Traumatic Stress Syndrome since that day over 15 years ago. I still feel the guilt a lot but I have had to learn to deal with this. I went to the deepest hole of depression I think is possible and many people including the doctors thought that I might not come out of it. When I looked around at my beautiful family, my husband who was so good to me, my children, and all of my family, I knew I had to fight and I have been fighting that battle and winning ever since. I know that it will always be in my mind and sometimes I have to pull it out and shed some tears over that day, but then I just put it back in its place and keep on fighting and loving my life.

I remained in banking until 2006 when I retired and am now just staying home and enjoying my family. If there is one thing that I would like my story to do, it is to show people that if you are having bad times and you want to do better, you can if you set your goals and always work towards them.

Most of all, I want people to know that even though bad things happen to good people, you can survive and have a good life.

A stronger and better person, the friends I made along the way will always be my friends.

Progress

In 2009, the city demolished the old Villa Rica Electric and Light building and the E. L. Esterwood Mill (later known as the golden City Hosiery Mill), which contributed to the country's Eastern National Register in order to install a green space, amphitheatre and a future city hall.

Former Mayor Monroe Spake of Villa Rica, who served from 1991 through 2003, recalls that during his time as mayor, he and his city council were able to bring higher paying jobs into Villa Rica.

Former Mayor Spake and the city council set up an industrial development authority to attract industry that was high paying.

The authority gave the land to Flowers Bakery to get them to come in. Flowers Bakery's starting salary was about $15/hr but that was 15 years ago.

Mayor Spake also said the city was also able to get bonds to help bring Lowe's to Villa Rica.

All the manufacturing in Villa Rica now is more high tech, like the Diamond Tool Company on the bypass road, the plastic injection mold company in the industrial park, and Print Pack in Villa Rica. - Monroe Spake

Current Mayor J. Collins has been responsive to the requests of the Fullerville people. Working with the city councilmen and the city managers, Larry Wood and Jeff Reese, improvements have been made such as the construction of side walks, the recognition of two deserving Fullerville citizens, Sarah Sauls and Reverend Wayne Shelton, and the designation of Fullerville as a historic area.

STATE OF GEORGIA COUNTY OF CARROLL RESOLUTION

to signify the Historic and Industrious nature of the Fullerville area of Villa Rica

WHEREAS, from the late 1800's, the Fuller family played an important role in the growth of Villa Rica, starting with Judson H Fuller who owned the Villa Rica Cotton Mill and continuing with the establishment of the Villa Rica Hosiery Mills in 1911 along with his sons Hardy, Tom and DeWitt; and,

WHEREAS, the Fuller brothers built eight homes for their original employees in the area of the City which was to become known as Fullerville; and,

WHEREAS, those employees of the Villa Rica Hosiery Mills assisted in the success of the Mills by increasing, in less than eight years, the daily production of men's hose from seventy dozen pairs to five hundred dozen pairs; and,

WHEREAS, from the 1930's and beyond the Mills' heyday in the 1950's, these men and women were the backbone of the City and lived, worked and raised families, many of whom still call Villa Rica home; and,

WHEREAS, the City wishes to honor the hard work and dedicated spirit of the Fullers, those early employees, and their successors at the Hosiery and Cotton Mills;

NOW, THEREFORE, be it hereby resolved by the Mayor and Council of the City of Villa Rica that signage be placed on Rockmart Road on both ends of the area known as Fullerville, and that the signage indicate the historic nature of the area for all who pass through to see.

So resolved this 7th day of November, 2006

This document was signed by:
J Allen Collins-Mayor
Perry Amidon-Council member

Woody Holland-Council member
Verland Best-Council member
Danny Carter-Council member
Joseph Kelley-Council member
Attest was signed by Danny Mabry-City Manager

The Past Meets the Present

Sarah Sauls, Perry, and Street Sign   Photo courtesy of the author

Sidewalks for Fullerville   Photo courtesy of Joyce Massey Fain

Today Fullerville, as a part of the city of Villa Rica, is moving into the 21st Century. Its citizens are being recognized and improvements are going in. Work is being done on a Comprehensive Plan for the Villa Rica area which takes the valued attributes of the past into consideration and looks toward the future. http://www.villarica.org/comprehensive-plan-docs.html

The West Georgia Mills and Their People by Perry "Bill" Bailey

Appendices

Appendix A

Textile Mill Songs

Robert Burke Warren, a music historian and contributor to FIQL, has compiled the Playlist, *Textile Mill Songs*, with comments.

Reprinted by permission of Mike Wu, FIQL.com 03/03/10)

http://www.fiql.com/forum/thread.php?id=143

Textile Mills have a long and varied history in America. Some of that history is not pleasant. Today, as textile mill employees are laid off due to cheap overseas labor we take a look at some of the music that speaks to the plight of the textile worker. From the days when working conditions were sub-human and unions waged war against mill owners to the plight of today's unemployed. - Robert Burke Warren

1. Si Kahn – "The Aragon Mill" *from the album "New Wood"*
The Aragon Mill was written by Si Kahn in 1979 and refers to the closing one of the main employers in Aragon, Georgia; The Aragon Textile Mill.

2. Pete Seeger – "Winnsboro Cotton Mill Blues" *from the Smithsonian Folkways compilation "American Industrial Ballads"*
Winnsboro, SC is about 75 miles south of Gastonia, NC. This track comes from the Smithsonian Folkways compilation *"American Industrial Ballads"*, which documents the unprecedented industrialization of the 19th century. The album contains songs of struggle, which emerged from the coalmines, textile mills and farmland of America.

3. Dave McCarn - "Cotton Mill Colic" *from the compilation "Hard Times Come Again No More Vol. 2 CD"*
In 1905 Dave McCarn was born in Gaston County, NC. Like many in the area, he became a textile industry worker. He took up guitar and harmonica and began writing songs, which became a vehicle to express the hardships of a mill-working life. In 1926 Dave McCarn wrote *"Cotton Mill Colic"* and released it in August 1930. The song was soon adopted by striking Carolina Piedmont mill workers. In 1939 Alan Lomax found the song and published it on the compilations *"Folksongs of North America"* and *"Our Singing Country"*.

4. Almanac Singers - "The Weaver's Song" *from the compilation "Songs For Political Action"*
Members of the the Almanac singers included such names as Woody Guthrie, Lee Hays and Pete Seeger. The group's music remained closely tied with the members political beliefs, which were far-left and at times controversial. *"The Weaver's Song"* is a traditional folk song from the late 1800's, which speaks about the hard life of the weaver.

5. Fisher Hindley – "Weave Room Blues" *from the compilation "Hard Times Come Again No More Vol. 2 CD"*
The *"Weave Room Blues,"* was written by Dorsey Dixon in 1932 and is perhaps his most significant industrial composition, he called it his "first blues". In *"Weave Room Blues"* the author expresses his dissatisfaction with farmers who traded their vocation for the life of a mill worker.

6. Pete Seeger, Jane Sapp and Si Khan – "Bread and Roses" *from the compilation "Carry it On: Songs of American Working People"*
On a bitterly cold New Year's Day, 1912, textile workers in Lawrence, Massachusetts, began a 9-week strike. The strike would have national repercussions. During one of the striker's parades, a group of young girls carried a banner with the words: "We want bread and roses too." This sign

sparked James Oppenheim to write the poem, "*Bread and Roses*," later it was put to music by Caroline Kohlsaat, and is performed here by Pete Seeger.

7. Lee Brothers – "*Cotton Mill Blues*" *from the compilation "Work Don't Bother Me: Old Time Songs from North Georgia" on Rounder Records*
The Lee Brothers were an obscure folk trio that made their living in the industrial South. "*Cotton Mill Blues*" tells the dispiriting story of life in the cotton mill straight from the horse's mouth.

8. Pete Seeger – "*Mill Mother's Lament*" *from the Smithsonian Folkways compilation "American Industrial Ballads"*
Gastonia, NC resident and union leader Ella May Wiggins wrote "*Mill Mother's Lament*". Pete Seeger performs it here. Ella May Wiggins was shot dead by anti-unionists on September 14, 1929 during the Gastonia Loray Mill Strike.

9. Natalie Merchant – "*Owensboro*" *from the 2003 album "The House Carpenter's Daughter"*
One of only a few modern songs in this collection, "*Owensboro*" by Natalie Merchant is a poignant and updated spin on the textile mill hardship song.

Well, our children
Grow up unlearned
With no time to go to school
Almost before they learn to walk
They learn to spin and spoon

10. The Star Room Boys – "Gastonia" *from the 2005 album Why Do Lonely Men And Women Want To Break Each Other's Hearts?*
The Athens, Ga country band The Star Room Boys released this track in 2005. Although it is a traditional country song about lost love, the antagonist lives in Gastonia, NC, which happens to have one of the nation's richest textile histories, including the Loray Mill Strike in 1929.

11. Charlie Poole – "White House Blues" *from the album "You Ain't Talkin' To Me: Charlie Poole And The Roots Of Country"*
Charlie Poole is not necessarily known for textile mill protest songs like many others included here, but he is from Randolph County, NC and is credited with being a founding father of Country and Bluegrass music. Charlie Poole was also a textile mill worker who traveled and worked in many mills throughout the region. Charlie Poole died in 1931 of alcoholism.

12. The Chieftains with Sinead O'Connor – "Factory Girl" *from the album "Tears of Stone"*
Sinead O'Connor sings with the Chieftains on this traditional and melancholy song. In the 1800s, many young women worked in American textile mills. Working conditions and pay were deplorable, but Mill owners ran dormitories with strict rules, which helped the recruitment effort since parents were not apt to let their daughters leave home without such oversight.

13. Pete Seeger – "Hard Times In The Mill" *from the Smithsonian Folkways compilation "American Industrial Ballads"*
Living legend Pete Seeger is now 86 years old; both of his parents were faculty members of the famous Julliard music school. He was an assistant in the Archive of American Folk Song at the Library of Congress and has penned or revived many great songs that speak to the plight of the American worker. "*Hard Times in the Mill*" is specific to the Textile worker.

14. Doc Watson and Clarence Ashley – "The Old Man at the Mill" *from the album Original Folkways Recordings of Doc Watson and Clarence Ashley, 1960-1962*
North Carolina's own Doc Watson is considered a living American Folk Music legend. On this track Watson, who is blind since birth, teams up with banjo picker Clarence Ashley who worked with a traveling medicine show in the south from 1911 to 1943.

15. Malvina Reynolds – "Carolina Cotton Mill Song" *from the Smithsonian Folkways album "Ear To The Ground"*
Born into a socialist family in 1905, Malvina Reynolds was an activist singer-songwriter up until her death at age 75 in 1980. "*Carolina Cotton Mill Song*" is a scathing rebuke that points the finger at textile companies for the brown lung (*Byssinosis*), which is a disease caused by inhaling cotton, flax, hemp, or jute fibers.

16. Pete Seeger - "We Shall Not Be Moved" *from the album "Carry It On: Songs Of American Working People"*
"*We Shall Not Be Moved*" is most closely associated with the civil rights struggle of the 1960s. What most people don't know is that the song was originally penned in the 1920s by striking African-American textile workers in North Carolina. The song has since been tweaked to fit a variety of causes.

17. Peter, Paul and Mary – "Weave Me The Sunshine" *from the album "Around The Campfire"*
I thought this track would be the perfect ending for the playlist since it uses a "weaving" metaphor, fits in with the folk-heavy theme and has an optimistic tone for the future.

Out of the falling rain.
Weave me the hope of a new tomorrow,
And fill my cup again.
Weave, weave, weave me the sunshine
Out of the falling rain.
Weave me the hope of a new tomorrow,
And fill my cup again.

Appendix B
Villa Rica Mayor and Councilmen Minutes
Part 1

The Villa Rica Mayor and City Council Minutes were submitted to Perry Bailey for the Fullerville Book by the City of Villa Rica City Administration in the year 2009.

The minutes contributed by the city of Villa Rica, Georgia, in the year 2009 are presented without editing, additions or deletions.

Villa Rica Mayor and City Council Minutes

City of Villa Rica, Georgia

Regular Sessions

Wednesday, January 2, 1980

City of Villa Rica,Ga Mayor and Councilmen Minutes

Oct. 4,1958

Mayor & Council met in regular session Oct. 4, 1958, 7:30 O'clock P. M. at city Hall. Mayor Griffin in Chair and the following council members present: Ray Matthews, John B. Bailey, H. G. Brown, and Herman Newell.

Mayor Griffin dispensed with regular order of business in order to hear complaints of J. D. Gray and H. P. Cooper that too many peddlers were working within the City limits of Villa Rica without paying a business license and that the peddling license were too low.

After discussion, the Mayor appointed H. G. Brown, Dr. J. E. Powell, Jr. and John B. Bailey as a committee to investigate the problem and report back to the Council.

Minutes of previous meeting read and approved.

Financial statements of various departments read and approved.

On motion by J. B. Bailey and second by H. G. Brown the Council voted unanimously to exempt all churches from the garbage collection fee after November 1958.

The City was asked by Justice of Peace that city accept garnishment against City employee, James Bailey (no relationship to James Olin Bailey of Fullerville), in favor of Herman Smith. Motion was made by H. G. Brown that city accept the garnishment and seconded by Herman Newell. Vote was three in favor and one against, with John B. Bailey voting no.

The council voted unanimously to raise pay for the mule work in Fullerville to $4.00 per day on motion by Herman Newell and second by John Bailey.

H. G. Brown made a motion that the outstanding bills be paid as money is available. Motion was seconded by Herman Newell. Motion carried.

Motion was made by Ray Matthews and second by H. G. Brown that City buy rebuilt motor for Police car at a cost of $356.95 from Richards Motor Co. Motion carried.

Motion was made by Herman Newell and seconded by John Bailey that Heater be installed on garabage truck. Motion carried.

Motion was made by John Bailey and Seconded by H. G. Brown that new fire station be remodeled to take care of both fire trucks at once. Motion carried.

Motion was made by H. G. Brown and seconded by Herman Newell that all oil be stored in supply room and issued by City Clerk as used. Motion carried.

Clerk was told by council to notify Mr. Hixon of the City's intention of moving Patrol barracks.

Meeting was adjourned at 9:30 P. M. on motion by Ray Matthews and seconded by John Bailey.

This document was signed by Ray Dodson, Clerk, and C. W. Griffin, Mayor

City of Villa Rica,Ga Mayor and Councilmen Minutes

The Building application of Fruman Ellis on West View Drive was approved on motion by Chester Ergle and 2nd by H. G. Brown.

On Motion by H. G. Brown and 2nd by Chester Ergle, the Council voted that the salary of the Council be $50 a year and the Mayor salary be set at $200 a year.

On motion by Chester Ergle, the Meeting was adjourned at 8:00 P.M.

This document was signed by Ray Dodson, Clerk, and W. Paul Camp, Mayor.

Colonel Cole Gave oath of office to the Mayor and to Councilman H. G. Brown and Herman Newell.

Mayor and Council met in regular session Jan. 5, 1960, 8:25 P. at the City Hall. Mayor Camp in chair and full Council present.

Ray Dodson was appointed temporary Clerk on motion by Herman Newell and 2nd by H. G. Brown until clerk for 1960 was appointed.

The Mayor decided that the old committees would stand until the regular meeting in Feb. at which time there would be a full Council,

Letter was read from the Villa Rica Hospital Authority stating that Mr. James Voughn was elected by the Authority on Dec. 15 to serve as a trustee to fill the vacancy left by the resignation of Mr. C. A. Reeves, and that Mr. Herman Holloway, Mr. W. D. Tyson and Mr. Jack Lassitter were unanimously reappointed for a three year term and asking for the Council's approval. On motion by H. G. Brown and 2nd by Chester Ergle, the Council unanimously accepted the Hospital Authority's recommendations.

The Following committees were appointed by the Mayor, W. Paul Camp.

City of Villa Rica,Ga Mayor and Councilmen Minutes

January 5th, 1960, 7:30 pm at City Hall

Mayor and Council met in regular session on Jan 5, 1960, 7:30 P. M. at the City Hall. Mayor Camp in chair and the following Council members present: Herman Newell, Ray Matthews, Chester Ergle, and H. G. Brown.

Mayor Camp introduced the following resolution:

RESOLUTION I

The death of Mayor Charles M. Griffin on November 20, 1959 has brought sorrow to the Council and Officials of the City of Villa Rica, all of whom were privileged to serve with him as Councilman and Mayor for the past several years.

As a former member of the Council and later as Mayor, his loyal service through the years was most outstanding, and those who worked with him accepted his judgement as good and sound. He stood for progress in our town, and always had a keen interest in the schools, church activities, civic projects, and youth development programs. His great love for the High School and College athletic sports was outstanding.

The fact that he served so long and in so many capacities in the community was proof in itself of the high esteem in which the citizens of Villa Rica held him.

At the time of his death Mr. Griffin was 56 years of age, having been born in Villa Rica, where he lived ail of his life.

The Council and Officials of Villa Rica extend their deepest sympathy to his family and we shall always cherish the fine friendship that was our privilege to have with him.

This resolution shall be spread upon the minutes of the City

by the City Clerk, a copy shall be given to the family of

Mr. Griffin, and it shall be published in the local newspaper.

W. Paul Camp, Mayor Protem H. G. Brown Herman Newell Chester Ergle Ray Matthews

Councilmen

Op motion of Herman Newell and 2nd by H. G. Brown, the resolution was unanimously adopted.

Minutes of previous meeting were read and approved.

Financial statements of various departments were read and approved.

The Mayor appointed H. G. Brown and Herman Newell as committee to see about repairing rent house.

On motion by Chester Ergle and 2nd bssee about repairing rent house.

On motion by Chester Ergle and 2nd by Herman Newell, the council voted unanimously to cancel the rent the tenant now owes for past months.

On motion by H. G. Brown and 2nd by Chester Ergle the council voted to pay outstanding bills as money is available.

Tax Assessors:

Ralph Smith   3 Years

H. G. Roberds   2 years

Bill Berry   I year Recreation:

Herman Newell, Chairman

Mrs. M. D. Henslee

H. G. Brown

Ray Matthews

Mrs. H. C. Adams City Welfare:

Mr. C. L, Roberds

Mr. J. A. Ariail

Mrs. E. P. Candler

On motion by H. G. Brown and 2nd by Chester, the following City

employees were hired for 1960:

Ray Dodson   **City Clerk**

H. 0. Luther   **City Engineer**

Ralph Smith Assist   City   Clerk

Street Supt

Sanitary Supt

Chief of Police-

Policeman

Policeman

Policeman

Policeman

Supt. Gas

225.00

D. W. Wren

Ralph Thornton

Wm. Posey

Bryce Cole

Roscoe Slate

Cleve Turner

Otis Newman

Gus Cobb

Fireman:

Jr. Loyd

H. 0. Luther

Wheeler **Brown**

Harris Wilson

Robert Samples

Harold Smith

Cap Carnes

M. D. Henslee Fireman to receive $100 On motion by Ray Matthews and 2nd by H. G. Brown, the Council voted to give all fireman and City officials and all of their wives one meal a year.

On motion by Herman Newell and 2nd by H. G. Brown, Chester Ergle was made Mayor Protem 1960.

On motion by Ray Matthews and 2nd by H. G. Brown, $400.00 for the Villa Rica Cemetery and $50.00 for the New Hope Cemetery was appropriated for 1960.

On motion by Ray Matthews and 2nd by H. G. Brown, the Council voted to pay $5.00 to Ed Harper for work he did on street in front of his home.

On motion by H. G. Brown, and 2nd by Ray Matthews, the Council voted to install pipe in ditch in front of Fullerville Baptist Church and for the City to bear the Cost.

On motion by H. G. Brown and 2nd by Chester Ergle, the Council voted that the 1960 Business License would be the same as 1959.

On motion by Ray Matthews and 2nd by H. G. Brown, the Council Voted

To use City gasoline for Civil Defense purposes.

On motion by H. G. Brown, the meeting was adjourned at 9:45 P. M.

These documents were signed by Ray Dodson, Clerk and W. Paul Camp, Mayor

Mayor and Council met in called session Jan. 11, 1960, 4:45 P. M, in the City Hall to purge voters list and to open sealed bids on new truck for City Engineer. Mayor Camp in chair and the following council members present: Ray Matthews, H. G. Brown, and Herman Newell.

The Voter's list was purged and put into order.

Bids on New truck were opened by clerk and found to be as Follows;

(Upchurch Chev. Co.   1195.00.) (Richards Motor Co.   1230.00)

On motion by H. G. Brown and 2nd by Ray Matthews, the Council voted unanimously to buy truck from Upchurch Chev. Co. and for it to be paid for 1/2 out of Gas department and 1/2 out of water department.

On motion by Ray Matthews and 2nd by Herman Newell, the Council voted to build another cell to the Jail and add a commode and laboratory to the woman's cell.

On motion by Ray Matthews, the Meeting was adjourned at 5:35 P.M.

These documents were signed by Ray Dodson, Clerk and W. Paul Camp, Mayor

City of Villa Rica,Ga Mayor and Councilmen Minutes February 6,1979

The City of Villa Rica, Mayor and Council met in regular session Tuesday, February 6, 1979. Those present were Mayor Joyce Connally, Councilmen Steve Cleghorn, Doyal McCain, Monroe Spake, Bob Dean, Mac Hembree, City Manager Greg Young, Acting City Clerk J.W. Conner, City Attorney Ted Lee.

Mayor Connally called the meeting to order at 7:38 p.m. After welcoming all in attendance, Mayor Connally opened the floor to the public.

Harold Smith asked for a decision concerning his tapping onto City Sewerage on Hwy 78. It was noted in discussion that the city did not have adequate equipment and man-power to complete the job at this time. Mr. Smith presented the council with an estimate of $3500 labor from Pruett Construction Co. to do the work required for his tap. Based on the agreement that Mr. Smith furnish the materials and the city furnish the labor, Steve Cleghorn made a motion directing Greg Young to make arrangements with Pruett Const. Co. for the work on Smith's sewer line. Doyal McCain seconded Mr....

Five (5) yes votes.

February 6, 1979 Page 2 Minutes of the January Council Meeting were read and approved.

The Mayor and Council presented plaques in appreciation of

service on the Gas Board to Mr. J.V. Warren and Mr. Wheeler

Brown. Mr. Boyd Perry also had a plaque to be presented at a later date.

Greg Young requested the council table for further study the tie in and acceptance of Phases I & II in Carroll Vista Subdivision.

Mr. Charles Cole requested the council consider making sewerage lines available in the Liberty Road-I-20 area. It was noted the cost of running sewer lines with one lift station would be approximately $50,000.00. The council directed Mr. Greg Young to look into the matter.

Mrs. Boyd Perry requested the city pay $60.00 of the $120.00 plumbing bill concerning the sewer problem among the Perry, Tarpley, and Dyer property. It was noted all three sewer lines tie into one main line due to an unexplained reason in past years.

Steve Cleghorn made a motion the City pay the $60.00 under the condition an easement be granted the city in order to maintain the lines properly. Monroe Spake seconded. Five (5) yes votes.

Leyman Williams informed the Council he had located property that seemed to be favorable for the new recreation site. The property is owned by Bill Berry on Herrell Road.

Monroe Spake make a motion directing Mr. Williams to obtain permission from Mr. Berry to bore for the rock content on the property then negotiate a price for the purchase of the property. Doyal McCain seconded. Five (5) yes votes.

Monroe Spake made a motion to accept the appointment of Rusty Dean, LeRoy Miller, and John Brown to the Recreation Committee and to pay the $45.00 membership fee for the group of nine members to join the GRSP. Steve Cleghorn seconded. Five (5) yes votes.

Steve Cleghorn made a motion authorizing Leyman Williams to contract with Hulsey Pool in Marietta at a cost not to exceed $6400 and payable after April 1 to repair the swimming pool and other work needed on the pool. Monroe Spake seconded. Five (5) yes votes.

Monroe Spake made a motion to allow the residents of Fullerville to tap onto city sewerage without charge for a period of one (1) year beginning February 1, 1979 thru January 31, 1980. Doyal McCain seconded. Five (5) yes votes. (decision based on Grant wording)

Steve Cleghorn made a motion the city would discontinue cleaning the out-houses in Fullerville effective immediately due to the availability of city sewerage and the city would notify the residents by publication, the mandatory fee for sewerage will be charged effective May 1, 1979. Monroe Spake seconded. Five (5) yes votes. (fee of 75% water consumption if sewerage available due to city ordinance)

February 6, 1979 Page 3

Doyal McCain made a motion authorizing Greg Young to make the final payment to Duncan & Associates contingent to the completion of several minute details on the job in connection with Round I of the EDA Grant. Steve Cleghorn seconded. Five (5) yes votes.

The discussion on the adoption of the Fair Housing Ordinance was tabled for a later date.

The council was advised the American Legion Building has been offered for sale. The council advised they would consider the offer.

The council was advised there is a party interested in purchasing the Dixie Hardware Property. Bob Dean was directed to gather the necessary information needed to negotiate a price.

Mr. Robert D. Tisinger requested the city destroy the old Simms property on Highway 78 by controlled burning. The council advised Mr. Young to check into the matter.

Mac Hembree made a motion to appoint Joseph Lowery, a member of the Business Association, to sit as a non-voting member on the Industrial Development Authority. Doyal McCain seconded. Five (5) yes votes.

The Council asked Lisa Miller of the Villa Rican to publish the fact that there is a vacancy on the Zoning Board of Appeals. The appointment was tabled pending recommendations.

Mac Hembree made a motion to allow a road block for the Heart Fund on Sunday, February 25, 1979. Doyal McCain seconded. Five (5) yes votes.

Steve Cleghorn made a motion to extend the limits of the Fireman's Reimbursement pay thru March 31, 1979. Mac Hembree seconded. Five (5) yes votes.

The meeting was adjourned to executive session at 11:22 p.m.

These documents were signed by J. W. Conner, Acting City Clerk and Joyce O. Connally, Mayor.

City of Villa Rica, Ga Mayor and Councilmen Minutes

From the city of Villa Rica 2009

Molly Dobbs asked the Council to reconsider her charge of $200 for a fire call on November 2. 1978. Mrs. Dobbs stated the fire was not on her property and the Fire Department could not extinguish the fire due to an inadequate amount of water available. Mrs. Dobbs was advised the Council would check into the matter and contact her at a later date.

Ken Young, representing the Villa Rica Area Business Association,

requested the Council reconsider the new Business License Schedule

based on three points 1. The Advolorem taxes to be collected.

2. Water and Sewerage income. 3. Schedules from other towns of

comparable size. The Council advised Mr. Young they would be happy

to work with his group to improve the present Business License

Schedule.

David Schoerner requested the council consider extending the water and sewer lines in the new Industrial Park under the right of way for the new by-pass before the road is completed. The Council directed Greg Young to check into this possibility.

Mr. Lawrence Garrett of Richard's Homes in Carrollton requested the council to allow his company to do business in the City of Villa Rica. Council advised Mr. Lawrence they would discuss the matter.

Mr. Bob Matthews of Ross, Saarinen, Bolton & Wilder informed the Council the EPD had determined the current Plan of Study for the 201 Facilities Plan was not grant eligible. A Plan of Re-study of the plan was revised at an estimated cost not to exceed $2000. Mr. Matthews requested the council authorize him to go ahead with the Plan of Re-study and stated it would be ready for the March Council Meeting.

Bob Dean made a motion authorizing Ross, Saarinen, Bolton & Wilder to go ahead with the Plan of Re-study of the 201 Facilities Plan at a cost not to exceed $2000. Monroe Spake seconded. Five (5) yes votes.

Villa Rica Mayor and Councilmen Minutes   Part 2

The Villa Rica Mayor and City Council Minutes were submitted to Perry Bailey for the Fullerville Book by the City of Villa Rica City Administration, in the year 2009.

Note: The minutes contributed by the city of Villa Rica, Georgia, in the year 2009 are presented without editing, additions, or deletions.

Villa Rica Mayor and City Council Minutes

City of Villa Rica, Georgia

Regular Sessions

Wednesday, January 2, 1980

The City of Villa Rica, Mayor and Council met in regular session on Wednesday, January 2, 1980. Those present were Mayor Joyce Connally, Councilmen Steve Cleghorn, Doyle McCain, Monroe Spake, Bob Dean, Mac Hembree, Acting City Manager J.W. Conner, City Attorney Ted Lee.

Everyone repeated the Lord's Prayer.

Minutes of the December, 1979 meetings were read and approved.

Mayor Connally gave the following recap of the year 1979:

1979 has been a good year for Villa Rica. The dream of almost 17 years work by various Mayor's and Councilmen came to fruition with the completion of the Fullerville Sewage Project. In February of 1979, the residents of Fullerville were having bathrooms built or installing the pipes necessary to tie onto the new sewer lines. The first industrial building was completed in our industrial park on the West side of Villa Rica. This building was constructed by the W. Linton Howard Company and it's president Mrs. Sarah Burnett has moved her office staff here and they await arrival of their machinery from Europe to open full-time scale. The City spent $12,000 relocating water and sewer lines in order that the DOT could build a road into that park and an additional $2,000 was spent placing highway signs and markers on this road according to DOT specifications.

In order to continuing meeting the standards required by the Senior Citizens Nutrition Program, improvements amounting to approximately $2,000 were made at the recreation center. The Nutrition Program, which offers a noon time meal to those over 60, with a special emphasis on the extra-curricular program of sharing hobbies, crafts, classes of instruction is one of our outstanding achievements in getting this in our City. Improvements and repairs to the swimming pool at the recreation center amounting to about $6,000 were made prior to it's opening last summer. The council recently adopted a resolution re-naming this park the John E. Powell Park to be known as Powell Park.

During the year 1979, 6" water mains were installed along S. Carroll Road, Old Tanyard Road, Old Stone Road, Sylvan Road, Darden, Hayes, Myrtle Street and Russell Street. The Sewer System Evaluation Survey Phase I was completed at a cost of $10,000 and the cost of Phase II is already allocated out of the water bond money. Improvements inside City Hall were numerous this year. We've acquired a new council-conference table and chairs, new desks, chairs, filing cabinets, and electric typewriter for the front office, all of which were badly needed. We recently purchased a new truck for the street department and a new police car was delivered last week to the chief. Our Street department did a vast amount of work in the assisting in the construction of a track around the football field at the Villa Rica High School. Our Police Department served weekly in offering police protection and traffic control at all the football functions.

We purchased, new to us but really second hand, Christmas decorations for the street light poles. And we have completed the wiring of those poles according to the specifications required by Southern Bell Telephone and Georgia Power. The Villa Rica Merchants Association shared the expenses of acquiring the lights for out city. The Department of Transportation, under the LARP Program, resurfaced the following roads in Villa Rica: Memorial Drive, Northside Place, Anderson Road, Elm Drive, E. Montgomery, Glanton Street and a portion of Old Bankhead Highway up to Old Punkintown Road. We paved the following dirt streets: Myrtle, Russell Darden, Ruby, McCauley, First, Second, and Third Streets and Pate Drive. We've spent $30,000 paving the road and running the water lines into the new Federal Housing Authority Project off Bankhead Highway. The target date for families to move in is now sometime in May. I cannot close this message without a word of thanks to the departments of this city and to the loyal, hard working employees that we have. Our police department under the leadership of Chief Ray Cole will continue to improve it's services. Our street department with Mr. Don McGill will work diligently to keep our city trimmed and clean. Our sanitation department with Mr. Ralph Thornton and his small group of men will continue to try and keep our city healthy and help the other departments whenever necessary. Our Water and Sewer Department headed by Mr. Horace Luther and Mr. James White will continue that quiet operation that we take so much for granted little realizing the long hours that are spent by these men in serving our needs. Our volunteer Fire Department led by Chief Jimmy Wilson is ready to go 24 hours a day, and these brave men should be thanked by the citizens of Villa Rica everyday of the year at least once a day.

The members of the Recreation Department have something for everyone going on at all times. Our twelve months program has been a huge success and to these employees for you and myself I say thank you. We have numerous citizens serving on the Hospital Board, the Housing Authority, the Zoning and Planning Commission, the Industrial Board, the Library Board, the Villa Rica Relief Board. All of them work without pay and they serve long and diligently for us and deserve a very special thanks. The last group to be thanked would be those in the office. J.W. Conner, our Acting City Manager who stepped in to guide us through the confusion that must of necessity arise when a city manager resigns and leaves. It's not an easy task to pick up another man's work, but he has done so and since I've worked with him for 22 months, I know he will continue to do so. The front office staff consisting of three ladies, Mrs. Crisp, Mrs. Carden, and Mrs. Spiva have a very bad task at times. Unless you walk in the woman's shoe, you can't know the troubles they might encounter. Working the window, taking your money for taxes, a large water bill, all of these things irritate us when we come into City Hall and I think we tend to vent our feelings on these girls, but they keep a smile on their face at least 99% of the time and if they fail that one percent, forgive them and remember what I told you. Don't forget people like Mr. Tom Hall, Henry Fraser, W.O. Smith who read our meters and who go back out after 5 O'clock to cut our water back on should it be cut off. They have the unpleasant task of cutting it off too and sometimes get up-rated for that. But they're very loyal servants.

Our City at present is operating within the boundaries of it's 1979 budget. We are in the black and unless there comes another problem arising about the 1% local option sales tax, we will continue to be a stable and progressive town. There are some fine councilmen sitting at this table and a new Mayor will sit here whom I'm sure wants Villa Rica to continue to grow as much as I do.

My four years at City Hall has brought me many friends. I shall always think of all of you and I wish the happiest of new years for the City of Villa Rica, it's elected officials, it's employees, and the town people. Thank you everyone.

Mayor Pro-Tem Mac Hembree presented Mayor Connally and Councilman Bob Dean with plaques from the City, Mayor and Council in appreciation of their devotion and service during their terms of office.

Mayor Connally asked for a motion to adjourn the meeting. Steve Cleghorn so moved. Bob Dean seconded. Meeting adjourned.

Mayor Pro-Tem Mac Hembree called the meeting to order. J.W. Conner, City Clerk was directed to swear in Mayor-elect Bill Warren, Council-elect Chester Ergle and Mac Hembree. Mayor Warren, Councilmen Ergle and Hembree accepted their chairs.

Mayor Warren asked for a recommendation for position of Mayor Pro-Tem.

Doyle McCain recommended Mac Hembree be appointed Mayor Pro Tem. Monroe Spake seconded. Five yes votes.

Recreation Director Leyman Williams asked for council approval of J.A. Arail and Mary Frances Mitchell to serve as Recreation Committee Volunteers. Mac Hembree made a motion to approve the recommendation of Mr. Williams. Steve Cleghorn seconded. Five yes votes.

Mr. Williams advised the Mayor and Council the State Department had expressed concern over the failure of the bond issue and had asked for a tentative letter of commitment of $50,000 matching funds for Phase II of the Park Grant.

Monroe Spake made a motion directing J.W. Conner to prepare a letter of intent guaranteeing the $50,000 matching funds for Phase II of the Park Grant. Mac Hembree seconded. Four yes votes, one abstain. Chester Ergle- due to lack of knowledge of the program.

Monroe Spake apologized to the Recreation Commission for not following the proper protocol with his motion to re-name the Recreation Center the John E. Powell Jr. Park.

Mayor and Council heard the first reading of the Cable T.V. Ordinance.

Steve Cleghorn made a motion to offer the surplus equipment for sale at public auction with the money from the fire car to go for the balance due on the beepers purchased last year.

Council agreed to direct J.W. Conner to prepare a list of equipment to be sold at auction and place an advertisement for said auction.

Monroe Spake made a motion to authorize mayor Warren to sign the resolution approving the execution of the proposed Fullerville Grant contract. Doyle McCain seconded. Five yes votes.

Steve Cleghorn made a motion to authorize Ross, Saarinen, Bolton & Wilder to proceed with the design work on the Fullerville Water project at a cost not to exceed $12,000 for design and engineering fees. Monroe Spake seconded. Five yes votes.

Monroe Spake made a motion to accept the appointments to the following committees:

Public Safety- Chester Ergle, Doyle McCain

Street- Mac Hembree, Monroe Spake

Sanitation- Monroe Spake, Doyle McCain

Water-Sewer- Mac Hembree, Chester Ergle

Recreation- Doyle McCain, Steve Cleghorn

Finance- Mac Hembree, Chester Ergle

Hospital- Monroe Spake, Chester Ergle, Mac Hembree

Housing- Doyle McCain, Steve Cleghorn

Fire- Steve Cleghorn, Chester Ergle

Charity- J.A. Arail, Kathleen Candler to serve in a voluntary capacity.

Mac Hembree seconded. Five yes votes.

Chester Ergle expressed concern over the procedure used in the past for the reduction of the cost of tapping onto the City's water and sewer lines. Council agreed they should look into the matter.

Mac Hembree made a motion to adjourn. Doyle McCain seconded. Five yes votes. Meeting adjourned at 9:10 p.m.

J.W. Conner, City Clerk   Bill Warren, Mayor

City of Villa Rica, Georgia

The City of Villa Rica, Mayor and Council met in regular session Tuesday, February 6, 1979.

Those present were Mayor Joyce Connally Councilmen Steve Cleghorn, Doyal McCain, Monroe Spake, Bob Dean, Mac Hembree, City Manager Greg Young, Acting City Clerk J.W. Conner, City Attorney Ted Lee.

Mayor Connally called the meeting to order at 7:38 p.m. After welcoming all in attendance, Mayor Connally opened the floor to the public.

Harold Smith asked for a decision concerning his tapping onto City Sewerage on Hwy. 78. It was noted in discussion that the city did not have adequate equipment and man-power to complete the job at this time. Mr. Smith presented the council with an estimate of $3500 labor from Pruett Construction Co. to do the work required for his tap. Based on the agreement that Mr. Smith furnish the materials and the city furnish the labor, Steve Cleghorn made a motion directing Greg Young to make arrangements with Pruett Const. Co. for the work on Mr. Smith's sewer line. Doyal McCain seconded. Five (5) yes votes.

Molly Dobbs asked the Council to reconsider her charge of $200 for a fire call on November 2, 1978. Mrs. Dobbs stated the fire was not on her property and the Fire Department could not extinguish the fire due to an inadequate amount of water available. Mrs. Dobbs was advised the council would check into the matter and contact her at a later date.

Ken Young, representing the Villa Rica Area Business Association, requested the council reconsider the new Business License Schedule based on three points. 1. The Advolorem taxes to be collected. 2. Water and Sewerage income. 3. Schedules from other towns of comparable size. The Council advised Mr. Young they would be happy to work with his group to improve the present Business License Schedule.

David Schoerner requested the council consider extending the water and sewer lines in the new Industrial Park under the right of way for the new by-pass before the road is completed. The Council directed Greg Young to check into his possibility.

Mr. Lawrence Garrett of Richard's Homes in Carrollton requested the council to allow his company to do business in the city of Villa Rica. Council advised Mr. Lawrence they would discuss the matter.

Mr. Bob Matthews of Ross, Saarinen, Bolton & Wilder informed the Council the EPD had determined the current Plan of Study for the 201 Facilities Plan was not grant eligible. A plan of Re-study of the plan was revised at an estimated cost not to exceed $2000. Mr. Matthews requested the council authorize him to go ahead with the Plan of Re-study and stated it would be ready for the March Council Meeting.

Bob Dean made a motion authorizing Ross, Saarinen, Bolten & Wilder to go ahead with the Plan of Re-study of the 201 Facilities Plan at a cost not to exceed $2000. Monroe Spake seconded. Five (5) yes votes.

Minutes of the January Council Meeting were read and approved.

The Mayor and council presented plaques in appreciation of service on the Gas Board to Mr. J.V. Warren and Mr. Wheeler Brown. Mr. Boyd Perry also had a plaque to be presented at a later date.

Greg Young requested the council table for further study the tie in and acceptance of Phases I &II in Carroll Visa Subdivision.

Mr. Charles Cole requested the council consider making sewerage lines available in the Liberty Road-I-20 area. It was noted the cost of running sewer lines with one lift station would be approximately $50,000.00. The council directed Mr. Greg Young to look into the matter.

Mrs. Boyd Perry requested the city pay $60.00 of the $120.00 plumbing bill concerning the sewer problem among the Perry, Tarpley, and Dyer property. It was noted all three sewer lines tie into one main line due to an unexplained reason in past years.

Steve Cleghorn made a motion the city pay the $60.00 under the condition an easement be granted the city in order to maintain the lines properly. Monroe Spake seconded. Five (5) yes votes.

Leyman Williams informed the council he had located property that seemed to be favorable for the new recreation site. The property is owned by Bill Perry on Herrell Road.

Monroe Spake made a motion directing Mr. Williams to obtain permission from Mr. Berry to bore for the rock content on the property then negotiate a price for the purchase of the property. Doyal McCain seconded. Five (5) yes votes.

Monroe Spake made a motion to accept the appointment of Rusty Dean, LeRoy Miller, and John Brown to the Recreation Committee and to pay the $45.00 membership fee for the group of nine members to join the GRSP. Steve Cleghorn seconded. Five (5) yes votes.

Steve Cleghorn made a motion authorizing Leyman Williams to contract with Hulsey Pool in Marietta at a cost not to exceed $6400 and payable after April 1 to repair the swimming pool and other work needed on the pool. Monroe Spake seconded. Five (5) yes votes.

Monroe Spake made a motion to allow the residents of Fullerville to tap onto city sewerage without charge for a period of one (1) year beginning February 1, 1979 thru January 31, 1980. Doyal McCain seconded. Five (5) yes votes. (decision based on Grant wording).

Steve Cleghorn made a motion the city would discontinue cleaning the out-houses in Fullerville effective immediately due to the availability of city sewerage and the city would notify the residents by publication, the mandatory fee for sewerage will be charged effective may 1,

1979. Monroe Spake seconded. Five (5) yes votes. (fee of 75% water consumption if sewerage available due to city ordinance).

On motion by H. G. Brown and second by Herman Newell the meeting was adjourned at 10:00 P. M.

__Ray Dodson____   ____C. M. Griffin_____

City Clerk   Mayor

Mayor and Council met in regular session Oct. 4, 1958, 7:30 O'clock P. M. at City Hall.

Mayor Griffin in chair and the following council members present: Ray Matthews, John B. Bailey, H. G. Brown, and Herman Newell.

Mayor Griffin dispensed with regular order of business in order to hear complaints of J. D. Gray and H. P. Cooper that too many peddlers were working within the city limits of Villa Rica without paying a business license and that the peddling license were too low.

After discussion, the Mayor appointed H. G. Brown, Dr. J. E. Powell, Jr. and John B. Bailey as a committee to investigate the problem and report back to the Council

Minutes of previous meeting read and approved.

Financial statements of various departments read and approved.

On motion by J. B. Bailey and second by H. G. Brown the Council voted unanimously to exempt all churches from the garbage collection fee after November 1958.

The City was asked by Justice of Peace that city accept garnishment against city employee, James Bailey, in favor of Herman Smith. Motion was made by H. G. Brown that city accept the garnishment and seconded by Herman Newell. Vote was three in favor and one against, with John B. Bailey voting no.

The council voted unanimously to raise pay for the mule work in Fullerville to $4.00 per day on motion by Herman Newell and second by John Bailey.

H. G. Brown made a motion that the outstanding bills be paid as money is available. Motion was seconded by Herman Newell. Motion carried.

Motion was made by Ray Matthews and second by H. G. Brown that City buy rebuilt motor for Police car at a cost of $356.95 from Richards Motor co.. Motion carried.

Motion was made by Herman Newell and seconded by John Bailey that Heater be installed on garbage truck. Motion carried.

Motion was made by John Bailey and seconded by H. G. Brown that new fire station be remodeled to take care of both fire trucks at once. Motion carried.

Motion was made by H. G. Brown and seconded by Herman Newell that all oil be stored in supply room and issued by city Clerk as used. Motion carried.

Clerk was told by council to notify Mr. Hixon of the city's intention of moving Patrol barracks.

Meeting was adjourned at 9:30 P. M. on motion by Ray Matthews and seconded by John Bailey.

Ray Dodson, Clerk   C. M. Griffin, Mayor

Mayor and Council met in regular session Jan. 5, 1960, 7:30 P. M. at the City Hall.

Mayor Camp in chair and the following Council members present: Herman Newell, Ray Matthews, Chester Ergle, and H. G. Brown.

Mayor Camp introduced the following resolution:

RESOLUTION

The death of Mayor Charles M. Griffin on November 20, 1959 has brought sorrow to the Council and Officials of the City of Villa Rica, all of whom were priviledged to serve with him as Councilman and Mayor for the past several years.

As a former member of the Council and later as Mayor, his loyal service through the years was most outstanding, and those who worked with him accepted his judgment as good and sound. He stood for progress in our town, and always had a keen interest in the schools, church activities, civic projects, and youth development programs. His great love for the High School and College athletic sports was outstanding.

The fact that he served so long and in so many capacities in the community was proof in itself of the high esteem in which the citizens of Villa Rica held him.

At the time of his death Mr. Griffin was 56 years of age, having been born in Villa Rica, where he lived all of his life.

The Council and Officials of Villa Rica extend their deepest sympathy to his family and we shall always cherish the fine friendship that was our privilege to have with him.

This resolution shall be spread upon the minutes of the City by the City Clerk, a copy shall be given to the family of Mr. Griffin, and it shall be published in the local newspaper.

W. Paul Camp, Mayor Protem

H. G. Brown

Herman Newell

Chester Ergle

Ray Matthews

Councilmen

On motion of Herman Newell and 2nd by H. G. Brown, the resolution was unanimously adopted.

Minutes of previous meeting were read and approved.

Financial statements of various departments were read and approved.

The Mayor appointed H. G. Brown and Herman Newell as committee to see about repairing rent house.

On motion by Chester Ergle and 2nd by Herman Newell, the council voted unanimously to cancel the rent the tenant now owes for past months.

On motion by H. G. Brown and 2nd by Chester Ergle the council voted to pay outstanding bills as money is available.

The Building application of Fruman Ellis on West View Drive was approved on motion by Chester Ergle and 2nd by H. G. Brown.

On motion by H. G. Brown and 2nd by Chester Ergle, the council voted that the salary of the council be $50 a year and the Mayor salary be set at $200 a year.

On motion by Chester Ergle, the meeting was adjourned at 8:00 P. M.

Ray Dodson, Clerk   W. Paul Camp, Mayor

Colonel Cole gave oath of office to the Mayor and to Councilmen H. G. Brown and Herman Newell.

Mayor and council met in regular session Jan. 5, 1960, 8:25 P. M. at the City Hall.

Mayor Camp in chair and full Council present.

Ray Dodson was appointed temporary Clerk on motion by Herman Newell and 2nd by H. G. Brown until clerk for 1960 was appointed.

The Mayor decided that the old committees would stand until the regular meeting in Feb. at which time there would be a full Council.

Letter was read from the Villa Rica Hospital Authority stating that Mr. James Voughn was elected by the Authority on Dec. 15 to serve as a trustee to fill the vacancy left by the resignation of Mr. C. A. Reeves, and that Mr. Herman Holloway, Mr. W. D. Tyson and Mr. Jack Lassitter were unanimously reappointed for a three year term and asking for the Council's approval. On motion by H. G. Brown and 2nd by Chester Ergle, the Council unanimously accepted the Hospital Authority's recommendations.

The Following committees were appointed by the Mayor:, Clerk   W. Paul Camp, Mayor

Mayor and Council met in called session Jan. 11, 1960, 4:45 P. M. in the City Hall

to purge voters list and to open sealed bids on new truck for city Engineer. Mayor Camp in chair and the following council members present: Ray Matthews, H. G. Brown, and Herman Newell.

The Voter's list was purged and put into order.

Bids on new truck were opened by clerk and found to be as follows:

Upchurch Chev. Co.	1195.00
Richards Motor Co.	1230.0

On motion by H. G. Brown and 2nd by Ray Matthews, the Council voted unanimously to buy truck from Upchurch Chev. Co. and for it to be paid for ½ out of Gas department and ½ out of water department.

On motion by Ray Matthews and 2nd by Herman Newell, the Council voted to build another cell to the Jail and add a commode and laboratory to the woman's cell.

On motion by Ray Matthews, the Meeting was adjourned at 5:35 P. M.

Ray Dodson, Clerk   W. Paul Camp, Mayor

City of Villa Rica Mayor and Council met in regular session on January 4, 1977 at 7:30.

Members present Mayor Joyce Connally, Councilman Frank Black, Chester Ergle, L. L. McBride, J. V. Warren and E. D. Ray City Manager C. H. Woodruff also in attendance.

The City Mileage renewal was brought up for motion, a motion was made by Mr. Warren for the mileage to stay at .13, seconded by Chester Ergle, 5 affirmative votes.

Mayor Connally said farewell to the old Councilmen and the meeting was closed, a ten minute recess was called.

Mayor Connally called the Council meeting to order on January 4, 1977 to swear in new members, Mayor Connally sware in the new Councilmen and welcomed them into their new positions. New Council in Chair as follows: E. D. Ray, Bryce Cole, Jean Williams, Chester Ergle and Frank Black.

Mayor Connally read a report from Mrs. Kathleen Candler, Treasurer of the Villa Rica, Georgia Charity Fund. Amount on hand as of Jan. 1, 1976- $355.17 amount paid out $85.07, balance $270.10, balance on hand in the Bank of Villa Rica-$270.10.

Mayor Connally heard appointments for Mayor of Pro Tem. Frank Black nominated Chester Ergle, no second. Mr. Bryce Cole nominated Mr. E. D. Ray, seconded by Jean Williams, 3 votes yes. Mr. E. D. Ray is the Mayor Pro tem.

Mayor read appointments to Commissions: Public Safety. Chester Ergle and Frank Black, Streets: Frank Black and E. D. Ray, Sanitation: Bryce Cole and Jean Williams, Gas Board: E. D. Ray and Jean Williams, Water and Sewage: Chester Ergle and Bryce Cole, Finance: Chester Ergle and Frank Black, Housing: Bryce Cole and Jean Williams, Recreation: Jean Williams and E. D. Ray, Hospital Board: Frank Black and Chester Ergle and E. D. Ray, Welfare: Mrs. Kathleen Candler and J. A. Ariail Jr.

J. B. Warren is to take the place of Travis Goss who is tetiring from the Gas Board. The Mayor asked for the approval of these appointments. Motion was made by E. D. Ray, seconded by Frank Black, 4 votes Affirmative.

Mayor Connally brought up various complaints about the dirt roads of the city. It seems that Mayor and Council have been hearing numerous complaints from residents in this area. It was made motion by E. D. Ray and seconded by Frank Black to do what we could to call in some Gravel and have these roads patched up to the best of our ability. This move was voted by all 5 council members in the affirmative.

GMA Mayors day was then discussed. This is to transpire on Monday 17th which includes a lunch reception and a dinner party and dance. It was decided by motion by E. D. Ray and seconded by Chester Ergle that Mayor Connally and Mr. Woodruff attend the occasion, 4 votes in the affirmative.

A motion was made by Mr. Ray, seconded by Frank Black and approved by 5 votes in the affirmative, by the council that an ordinance be drawn on to prevent Fund drives by the City or any City related activity unless this has been approved by at least 2/3rds majority of the Council.

The Mayor gave an accounting for Mayor and Council Activities in 1976.

January the Mayor was sent to the GMA Convention in Atlanta. In January the Mayor acted as Hostess for Ralph Parkman State Rep. as a personal guest of Villa Rica, and met the dignataries through the courtesy of Mr. Parkman.

In March the Mayor attended a meeting of the office of DOT Director Tom Moreland, to discuss the possibility obtaining an access road to the Industrial Park as well as to discuss alternatives to getting Hwy 61 paved, since the money allocated to us fell $15,000.00 short of the sealed bids received by the former Mayor and Council. I further discussed with Mr. Moreland the needed assistance from the state highway Dept. to put back the parking line so that parking on the main street would be done at the uniform level that it had been done previously, before resurfacing. I also pointed out to him the extreme hazardous corner at the Gulf Service Station and asked that an engineer be sent out to discuss with the Mayor and Council, any recommendations we thought we possibly make or hear his alternatives to the solution of that bad pie-shaped corner.

In April, a DOT man came out and did not feel that cutting the end of the pie-shaped corner off would do the job, he wanted to circle through it, however after another series of phone calls and a letter with Mr. Moreland and the man down in Thomaston as you can see, they are now cutting the pie-shaped end off the road. On that same date two councilmen and the Mayor asked that the one way street for the Georgia Power Company be resended it had never been a one way street and was causing a great deal of difficulties among the drivers who for more that 40 to 60 years had gone up and down the street, and he graciously told us to take an ax and go and knock the sign down and we had achieved our first positive thing the street became two way.

Permission as obtained from Southern Railway to build steps from Bankhead Hwy across the Railroad tracks to unite both sides of town this work was supervised by Mr. Ergle and Mr. Frank Black in conjunction with assistance from the City Crew. They completed this work in April and the town was re-united.

We allocated $1,000.00 to match the Lions Club contribution for the building of a new restroom at the recreation center this work was completed in late May and Mr. Ergle and Mr. Black and several other members of the City did the physical work.

We allocated $500.00 in kind to the Bi-Centennial committee to use in building a park in the City in money or time, our money was matched by a $500.00 grant which came from the Bi-Centennial Committee of Georgia. This Park located on Hwy 78 and Leslie Drive in front of Dr. J. E. Powell's home was completed in December of 1976 thru the diligent work of Mrs. Dyer Chairperson of the Bi-Centennial Committee and Mrs. Jean Williams.

The Mayor serving on the Bi-Centennial Committee acted as Co-Hostess along with Mrs. Dyer and the Bi-Centennial Committee to John J. Flint, Congressman who delivered the Key Note Speech on our July 4th Holiday Celebration City Wide. Other dignitaries attending were Mrs. Helen Robinson Ordinary of Carroll County, Sen. Eb Duncan, Mr. and Mrs. Harvey Duncan Commissioner of Carroll County Roads.

The parking lines were painted back on the street in July of 1976 as promised to the Mayor by Mr. Moreland.

Jones Street was resurfaced in September of 1976 as was Clearview, Meadowlark, and South Street.

City Planner Chuck Woodruff was hired on August 1976 on a Cedar Grant. A Police car and a Detective car was purchased by Council and the Mayor and City Planner in September.

Step 1 of the 201 facilities plan was begun by William Schweizer and Barnum in August 1976. This study will take 9 to 12 months to completely survey present sewage and show our prospective needs over the next 20 years in late October City Planner Woodruff was named City manager by the Council and Mayor.

The Mayor Represented the City on speakers stand when notable John Connally of Texas came to Carrollton to make a political speech in early October.

Mike Harper was hired as full time Director of Recreation in October.

In December the Mayor and City Manager had a presentation of the Four Star City Program presented to them and we voted to participate in the year 1977.

In late December a new City Fire Truck was purchased the first since 1969.

The City of Villa Rica was advised that public works grant of $410,000.00 for Fullerville sewage and $94,250.00 for the Villa Rica City Hospital had been awarded to this City. This was all prepared under the administration of Chuck Woodruff our City planner and Manager.

In late December the DOT men came out and began to remove the hazardous corner from the corner of the Gulf Station and they plan to complete it early in January.

The city voters list has been purged letters were mailed out as of December 31st and by January 21st we will have an up to date City voters list the first time in 10 years. I think we have had a profitable year.

The Mayor then gave a report on the activities for the Police Department.

It was determined by the council to place $25,000.00 worth of liability on the new GMC Fire Engine and reduce the existing insurance to 10,000.00 on the American LaFrance.

The meeting was adjourned at 9:30 P. M.

Joyce Connally, Mayor   C. H. Woodruff, City Clerk

The Council of the City of Villa Rica met in a regular scheduled meeting on Tuesday, February 5, 2002 at Villa Rica City Hall.

Those present were Mayor Pro-Tem, Shirley Marchman, Council members Perry Amidon, Verland Best, Woody Holland and Jeane Williams; City manager Steve Russell; and City Attorney David Mecklin. Mayor Spake absent with notification. Approximately 35 people were in attendance.

The meeting was called to order at 7:30 p.m. by Mayor Pro-Tem Marchman, invocation by Councilmember Holland, all recited the pledge of allegiance.

Motion to accept the January 8, 2002 minutes as presented by Amidon, seconded by Williams. Carried 5/0.

Soudi presented RA-2-02 an Annexation and Rezoning request to annex 126 acres from Douglas County into the City and rezone 96 acres of the property from R-D to P-D. He informed council that the applicant Bob Greer of Gateway Equities originally planned to develop for 163 single family residential lots and 60 owner occupied condominiums but at the request of the public and Gale Hale of the Douglas County Commission had changed that to 223 single family residences with no condominiums or apartments. Soudi then noted that the Planning Commission had reviewed this Monday night and recommended approval to Council. Bob Greer of Gateway Equities said the community would consist of one to two story homes with the master bedroom downstairs and from 1850 square feet to 3200 square feet homes. Williams asked if the majority of the trees would be left, Greer said as many as possible. Holland asked if it would be on sewer, Greer said yes. Amidon asked if it would have convenants, Greer said yes, a Property Owners Association. Marchman opened the Public Hearing for comments both for and against the application. Gale Hale, Douglas County Commissioner spoke in favor of the project saying it is reasonable due to the water and sewer needs, She said she had met with the developer and he had agreed to build 223 single-family homes instead of condominiums. John Camp, 8578 Brewer Road said he was opposed last night at the Commission meeting but is in favor with the change to all single-family homes. Doug Camp, 8441 Brewer Road spoke in favor of the project for the same reasons as John Camp. Stewart Camp, 8509 Brewer Road spoke in favor of the project for the same reasons as John and Doug Camp. Jody Wagner, 8888 Brewer Road spoke against the project due to the small lots and increased traffic. With no further comments, Marchman closed the public hearing and asked for a vote. After discussion between council members, Holland said he was concerned that the presentation tonight does not agree with the original application. Best agreed but noted that we are "swapping one for one" by changing the condo's to single family homes. Best also noted that the Planning Commission would be metting on the Thursday before the first Tuesday of the month from now on and Council would be receiving an updated memo from Soudi, amending his staff report, as well as the minutes from the Planning Commission meeting. Holland made the motion to approve the annexation request as presented, seconded by Williams, carried 5/0. Holland motioned to approve the rezoning request to Planned Unit Development with a maximum of 223 single-family units and a minimum of 1850 square feet homes. Seconded by Williams, carried 5/0.

Russell presented the Minimum Standards Clarification Density Revision saying this was for discussion only and did not require a vote tonight; he noted that we need to decide if we want to regulate the amenities with an ordinance revision or administratively. He said the amendment could be prepared to quantify the minimum amount of amenities in multi-family residential projects. Best questioned the legality of using as a guideline rather than an amendment to the ordinance. Russell spoke of his concern about regulating the depth of pools in an amendment since we would be unable to police; as a guideline it could be "pools should meet the standards of the industry". Council agreed to handle the clarification process administratively rather than through an amendment.

Russell explained the presiding officer vote; when the mayor is present he votes only when there is a tie but when the mayor pro-tem or another council member conducts the meeting their ward is left without representation if their council member does not vote. Williams said the presiding officer should be allowed to vote, Holland agreed. Williams motioned that whoever presides over the meeting in the absence of the mayor should be allowed to vote, seconded by Best. Carried 5/0.

CITY UPDATE: Russell said the Department of Transportation would be issuing the permit within the week for the entrance to Industrial Park. The budget for the year 2002-03 will be advertised and presented to Council at the March meeting for review and adoption at the April meeting. Liberty Road, south of the interstate improvements will start soon. We have acquired the properties on Anderson Road for a passive park, the Recreation Director showed me plans today and it will contain a basketball goal and several picnic tables. Russell asked Council to go by Fullerville to check on the progress being made there. Marchman asked about the repairs on Wilson Street where the construction for the townhouses took place. Russell to look into.

PUBLIC COMMENTS: Frances Languirand of the New Hope Primitive Baptist Church Cemetery Foundation presented a check for $750.00 for the clean up of their cemetery. She thanked the City and Hugh Bone for all the hard work this past year. With no further business, Williams motioned to adjourn, seconded by Best. Motion carried 5/0. Adjourned at 8:20 p.m.

Shirley Marchman-Mayor Pro-Tem

ATTEST: Steve Russell- City Manager

Appendix C

City Financial Statement

CITY OF VILLA RICA, GA.
FINANCIAL STATEMENT
DECEMBER 31, 1963

ASSETS

CASH	$17,403.47
Accounts Receivable	51,861.80
Receivables – Ad Valorem Taxes	9,959.04
Deposit Required for Social Security	2,579.52
Prepaid Interest	88.16
Due From Other Funds	2,305.16
Gas System Consolidated Fund	46.70
	$84,243.85

LIABILITIES

Accounts Payable	$26,171.88
Accrued Expenses	1,099.46
Due Other Funds	14,728.78
Notes Payable	1,754.88
Customer's Water Deposits	2,532.50
	Prior Years' Uncollected Tax
Proration	1,860.72
Customer's Gas Deposits	6,285.00
Surplus	29,810.63
	$84,243.85

The Sons and Daughters of Fullerville and Villa Rica

CITY OF VILLA RICA, GEORGIA

PROPOSED BUDGET 1964

ESTIMATED REVENUES:

Taxes	$26,500
Fines, Forfeits, Penalties	24,000
Business Licenses	10,000
Sales and Service Charges	5,510
Special Assessments	1,775
Sanitary Fees	10,500
Gas System	159,430
Water and Sewer	64,535
Police Account	2,500
Total Current Revenue	$304,750
Surplus – Prior Year	13,900
Total Revenue	$318,650

EXPENDITURES

General Government	$13,000
Police and Fire Dept.	24,500
Streets Dept.	15,000
Sanitary Dept.	10,500
Water and Sewer	56,965
Gas System	156,320
Contingency Fund	42,365
Total Expenditures	$318,650

Source: From The Villa Rican Newspaper, April 15th, 1964 issue
Submitted by the author

219

Appendix D

Places

The Old Orphanage at Tallapoosa

**Photos are from the time the building was owned by Olin Bailey.
Sadly the building burned shortly after the Bailey family moved away.**

Top left: Olin Bailey and Perry   Top right: Ruth George Bailey and Perry
Bottom middle: Olin Bailey, Perry, and Douglas
Bottom left: Olin Bailey   Bottom right:

Photos courtesy of Perry "Bill" Bailey

Note: the photos have been donated to the Tallapoosa Museum.

Credits

Note: This book uses in text citations

The Stewards of the Past
Those graciously contributing their knowledge and memories

Their Stories

Nancy McPhearson Bailey

Perry "Bill" Bailey

Katie Marvene Bice

Gertrude Swafford Blair

Morris Brooks

Ann Morris Broom

Bob Broom

Edwin Busbin

Jimmy Causey

Paulette Farr Crutchfield

Alan Dobbins

Kate Elliott

Gerald Fields

Kenneth Fields

Joyce Massey Fain

Margret Washington Henry

Kenneth Johns

Jimmy Matthews

Doug Mabry, historian

Fran Leathers Newton

Evelyn Y. Padgett

Patricia Kinney Pope Robinson

Sarah Sauls

Dorothy Seals

Danny Skinner

Sandra Matthews Smith

Alton Washington

The Reverend Charles Williams

Diane deVault Wilson

M. F. Word

Those graciously contributing the glimpses of the past:

The Photographs

Marykate Allen

Darling Allenthrop

Nancy McPhearson Bailey

Perry Bill Bailey

Rhonda Hovater Bailey

Ernie Blevins, historian

Ann Broom

Charles Broom

Kay Cashin

Kate Elliott

Joyce Massey Fain

Melvin Fain

Paul Free

Joe Garofalo

The George family

Ruth Holder

Paul Mararmol

Frances Leathers Newton

Paulding Roots

John Wayne Sauls

Dorothy Seals

Sandra Matthews Smith

Monroe Spake

Helen Waldrop

Charles Williams

Vicki Mattox Williams

Diane deVault Wilson

Bibliography

Books

Anderson, Mary Talley, *History of Villa Rica City of Gold,* Villa Rica: 1935, Georgia Bicentennial Committee, 1976, 2000

Documents

City of Villa Rica (Georgia), Mayor and City Council Meeting, Jan. 2, 1980

City of Villa Rica (Georgia), Mayor and City Council Meeting, Oct. 4, 1958

The Fullerville, Georgia Charter, Jan. 5, 1916

Newspapers

The Villa Rica News

The Villa Rican

Periodicals

Grit and Steel

The Carroll County Historical Quarterly, Spring and Summer issue, Vol I no 2 1968

Web Sites

FIQL. "Textile Mill Songs" FIQL, http://www.fiql.com/forum/thread.php?id=143

http://healthmad.com/conditions-and-diseases/byssinosis-the-brown-lung-disease-on-textile-workers

1968 Atlanta Time Warp http://users.ece.gatech.edu/mleach/radio/warp/1968.html

The University of West Georgia Public History Center Textile History. "Carroll County's Textile and Apparel Industries" University of West Georgia http://www.westga.edu/cph/index_6834.php

Villa Rica Compresive Plan Documents.

http://www.villarica.org/comprehensive-plan-docs.html

West Georgia Archives. "Hogue" West Georgia Archives, www.usgwarchives,org

Wikipedia. "Villa Rica Georgia" Wikipedia, http://en.wikipedia.org/wiki/Villa_Rica,_Georgia

Made in the USA
Charleston, SC
27 March 2011